More Than 100
Furniture
Repairs

You Can Do Yourself

A
**Practical Handbook
for Anyone
Who Buys, Sells, or Owns Furniture**

Donna S. Morris

Phoenix Press, Ltd.
La Verne, California

Library of Congress Cataloging in Publication Data

Morris, Donna S.,
More than 100 Furniture Repairs You Can Do Yourself A Practical Handbook for Anyone
Who Buys, Sells, or Owns Furniture/ by / Donna S. Morris
First Printing 1998

      Includes index.
      1.   Furniture- Repairing.   2. Furniture finishing

Library of Congress Catalog Card Number: 98-91678

ISBN 0-9665673-3-1 : $24.95 Softcover

Photography and illustrations by Donna S. Morris
additional illustrations by Lawrence A. Morris

Phoenix Press, Ltd.
1407 Foothill Boulevard Suite 141
La Verne, California   91750

Manufactured and printed in the United States of America

The instructions in this book are not intended to be used for the restoration or repair of costly, "museum-quality" pieces. Rare or valuable furniture belongs in the hands of a qualified professional. Even a minor repair, improperly done, can have a major effect on the appraised value.

The contents of this book are intended as a guide, to be intelligently used. The restoration and repair methods have been described in detail, and precautions in handling the various chemicals that are potentially hazardous if improperly used have been explicitly pointed out. Every effort has been made to make this book as complete and accurate as possible. All instructions and precautions should be carefully followed. Because the actual use of the methods and materials described in this book are entirely in the hands of the reader, neither the author, nor the publisher, can guarantee the results of any instructions or formulas, and therefore each of them expressly disclaims any responsibility for injury to persons or property through their use.

If you do not wish to be bound by the above, you may return this book to the publisher for a full refund.

Dedicated
to the craftsmen of yesterday for their efforts,
the people of today who preserve them,
and the generations of tomorrow who will appreciate both.

Acknowledgements

I would like to extend my gratitude to the hundreds of students, clients and friends who have over the years contributed to this book with their questions, problems and furniture.

Special thanks to my parents, Hazel and Don for the challenge, to Carmen and Larry for their love and support, to Susy, Jason, Richard, John, Heléne and Sharon for believing, to Kevin for his unlimited patience and computer knowledge, to David Long and the College for Appraisers for the reunion, to Paul and Deborah and the strange quirk of fate that brought us together, and belated thanks to the Captain who was instrumental in starting this book, but set sail before its completion.

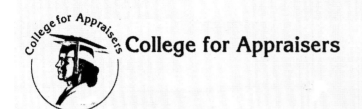

College for Appraisers

120 S. Bradford Avenue
Placentia, CA 92870
(714) 579-1124

FOREWORD

Sixteen years ago I met Donna Morris in an Antique Mall. Talking to her I was impressed by her depth of knowledge in furniture repair and refinishing.

I immediately invited her to do a seminar for the College for Appraisers, and it was a smashing success! Many of our students missed the first seminar and they pleaded for a repeat.

Over the next few years Donna gave us additional seminars and they were always well received. We are pleased to announce that we have invited her to resume the seminars at the College for Appraisers in the Fall of 1998.

Congratulations Donna on your book. It is very well done and will provide an education in this field for many in the future. It's so good... it's almost like sitting in a seminar.

David Long, Ph.D.
President
College for Appraisers

Table of Contents

A sign of the times in L.A. – "new antiques".

A Few Basics Before You Begin

This book was written for all of those people who have always wanted to repair or restore furniture, but have been overwhelmed by the vast array of products and intimidated by the lack of clear, concise and practical instructions. In this book you will find what you need to know, presented in simple, nontechnical terms. You will learn how to do the right things in the right way, so you can begin those repairs right now. Along the way, you will pick up little facts and helpful hints that will give you additional information on both the problems and the solutions.

There are as many reasons why people want to repair or restore furniture as there are potential projects for them to do. One of the most obvious is simple economics. Furniture is the fourth largest investment most families make in their lifetime, and routine maintenance and prompt repairs can prolong the life of this investment. But, with the price of professional restoration or repair becoming more expensive with each passing year, furniture repairs may appear to be out of the question for most budgets. Fortunately, the "do-it-yourselfer" can accomplish many repair jobs safely and correctly with a minimum investment of time and money.

If your prospective project is a family heirloom, sentiment may be the motivation for the repair. By repairing the piece yourself, you can control how much (or how little) work will be done. You will also have a well-earned sense of accomplishment when your finished project becomes a useful addition to your home.

Many furniture repairs require only a moderate amount of skill, and can be successfully completed with common tools and easily accessible supplies. When properly done, repairs can make furniture more attractive and serviceable, and prolong its life. But the value of the furniture and its antique status, may be jeopardized by extensive repairs, or repairs which are poorly done. Valuable antiques require expert knowhow, special supplies and advanced techniques and should not be undertaken by a novice. An improperly restored, repaired, or refinished antique can lose up to 75% of its value.

Familiarize yourself with these eight basic rules before starting any repair or restoration project:

Rule 1: Remember the old Boy Scout motto "Be prepared" and think of safety first.

All woodworking products and chemicals have some inherent danger associated with them. It is very important to take proper precautions before starting any project. Provide proper ventilation at floor level and in the upper portion of the room when using solvent based products. Check labels for information concerning the flammability or combustibility of products used. Open flames, or spark causing equipment should be removed from the work area. Smoking should not be permitted in or around the area. If you have handled chemicals, and are a smoker, remember to thoroughly wash your hands prior to smoking to avoid chemical contamination. Many liquid solvents can cause skin irritations, spontaneous combustion, poisoning (if taken internally or absorbed), and eye or respiratory irritations. Wear proper gloves, eye protection, etc. when working with these products. Persons pregnant, or thought to have heart or respiratory problems should seek medical advice before using solvents of any kind. Drinking alcohol before, during or after exposure to solvents may cause undesirable effects.

Rule 2: Thoroughly clean furniture before you begin repairs.

Sometimes a good cleaning is all that is needed and you may find repairs are unnecessary. Cleaning will give you an unobstructed view of the furniture and allow you to see the full extent of any damage. A good cleaning will also prevent contamination of the repair area and prevent further damage.

Rule 3: Always try the product or the repair technique in an inconspicuous area before attempting any repair.

Products should be spot tested prior to every application. Their appearance and performance can be affected by many variables (including age, humidity, and heat) and results may vary accordingly. Experiment in an inconspicuous area with a new technique until you are satisfied with the results.

Rule 4: Fix a minor repair before it becomes a major break.

Loose joints, furniture splinters, loose veneer, etc. will only become worse with use and age. Minor repairs are relatively inexpensive, are considerably easier to do than major ones, and prevent further deterioration and subsequent loss of value.

Rule 5: Nails, screws, or metal plates should not be used for furniture repair unless they were used in the original construction.

Wood glue or hide glue are the proper materials for joining wooden furniture parts. Remove as much old glue as possible prior to the repair, and use a clamp or other method of applying pressure while the glue sets, to ensure a good bond. A large collection of expensive furniture clamps is not necessary for most repairs. In many cases, weights, books, elastic "tie-downs", or rubber bands can be used. It is not important how the pressure is applied, but it must be sufficient to bring the two pieces of wood completely together with no gaps, as most glues do not have the strength to bridge gaps.

Wood glue or white glue are the proper adhesives for most furniture repairs.

Hide glue is available in pellet form or in liquid form. The pellets are melted in an electric glue pot before use. Hide glue is the traditional glue of choice.

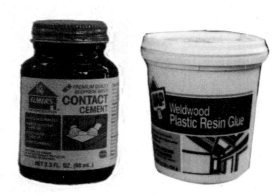

Contact cement can be used for veneer repairs, but is not recommended for most furniture repairs. Plastic resin glue can be used for veneer repairs, edge repairs or where extra resistance to water, solvents or decay is needed.

19

Rule 6: Do not use too much glue.

Excessive glue will create a big oozing mess. If allowed to dry, it will become a thick, ugly glue line that will not bond well and will break easily. Glue does all of its work on the butted surfaces within the joint. There is absolutely no holding value in glue on the outside of a joint. Excess glue can seal wood pores limiting the penetration of stain or finish applied over it. Remove glue before it dries by wiping with damp cloths or paper towels. In some cases, if the wood is to be stained after it is glued, you may be better off not wiping excess glue off the wood surface. Damp cloths or paper towels may force glue deeper into the wood pores. Allow excess glue to dry, then carefully chip off with a sharp chisel or razor blade. Test in an inconspicuous area to see which method will work best for your project.

Rule 7: Do not overtighten clamps.

Excessive pressure can compress wood fibers and damage wood, or squeeze out glue so there is an insufficient amount for a proper bond. Clamps only need to be tightened until the glued surfaces are held firmly together and can not move around. When more than one clamp is being used to hold a joint together, place clamps so pressure is evenly distributed all along the glue line. Remember to match the size of the clamp to the job at hand. A clamp that is too large or too small will be unable to supply proper pressure for a good glue bond and may damage the wood.

A large assortment of clamps is not necessary for most minor furniture repairs. Rubber bands, clothes pins, elastic "tie-downs", and clothesline are some of the many common household items that can be used. Also shown are a band clamp, steel bar clamp with sliding head, C clamps, wooden hand screw, and spring clamps.

Rule 8: *Only white paper towels or soft cotton rags should be used on furniture.*

Colored paper towels or patterned paper towels may transfer their color to lighter colored wood or wood finishes. All rags used on furniture should be soft, lintless cotton. Do not use synthetic fabrics such as nylon or rayon for any refinishing job. Synthetic fabrics may be adversely affected by chemicals, have limited absorption qualities and can scratch some finishes.

• • •

Examine furniture carefully before beginning any restoration or repair job, and determine the minimum amount of work needing to be done. The less done to the piece, the more value it will retain. It is especially important not to damage the *patina* on an old, or potentially valuable piece of furniture.

Patina is a mellowed, aged look that is acquired over time. Almost everything acquires a patina: metal, wood, wood finishes, cloth, paper. Everyone has seen yellowed pages in an old book, or the softened off-white color of an old wedding gown. Wood and wood finishes mellow in the same way.

Wooden furniture with a protective finish will acquire a patina at two different levels: in the finish and in the wood itself. The finish will begin to lose its gloss from dusting, polishing and normal use. Its color will quite often darken with age.

At the same time, the wood is also changing. Heat and humidity expand and contract wood fibers causing the grain to become more apparent. Wear marks may appear on arms, legs, and corners of often used furniture. Sunlight and fluorescent fixtures may bleach color from wood. Or, as wood matures, the natural colors may deepen: dark walnut may mellow to a reddish hue, oak will soften to a rich, golden brown, and maple will evolve from white to an aged tan.

Chemical removers will destroy the patina of a finish on contact, but most will not destroy the patina of the wood. However, sand paper, coarse steel wool, metal scrapers, or electric heat guns will remove 100 years of patina in a matter of seconds.

It is possible to duplicate the patina of a finish if it's damaged or removed, but there is no way to duplicate the patina in the wood. Antique counterfeiters have tried to duplicate the process with a variety of methods: exposing furniture to weather, applying various chemicals, even going to the extreme of burying furniture under piles of horse manure. Painted pieces can be aged by dousing the surface with lighter fluid, then lighting it. The fluid will flash and burn off, leaving behind a honey-colored, crackled finish. While this may accelerate the mellowing process and give the furniture an aged look, the results are never the same as those acquired naturally, over a period of time.

A Clean Start

All furniture needs some preparation before repairing, restoring, finishing, or refinishing. At the very least, a thorough cleaning will be in order as it is virtually impossible to successfully repair or restore a dirty piece of furniture. Removal of accumulated dirt, wax or polish allows you to analyze the condition of the piece, and helps determine what additional work is required. Cleaning may reveal a beautiful finish that is still intact and requires no further work, or it may expose flaws and problems you didn't know existed.

Furniture finishes can be safely cleaned by wiping with a soft rag or white paper towels moistened with mineral spirits. (Mineral spirits is also commonly called "paint thinner".) Use a damp, **not wet**, rag to rub the dirty surface. Wipe off loosened dirt and grime with a clean rag. Do a small area at a time, being careful not to let the furniture become wet. This should dissolve any accumulated wax, oil, polish, or grime.

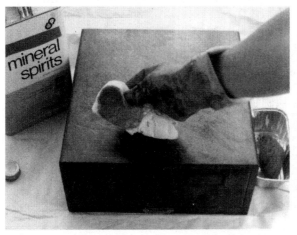

Mineral spirits and a soft cloth or white paper towels will remove dirt and accumuulated wax and polish.

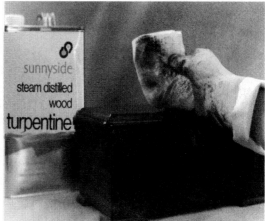

Turpentine will remove dirt, grime and silicones.

When the furniture is finally clean, the finish may appear to have deteriorated. Be assured mineral spirits did not damage the finish, but rather removed wax, polish, and dirt from small cracks and imperfections in the finish. Mineral spirits acts as a lubricant and dirt carrier rather than a stripper or solvent when used to clean furniture. It will not harm any common finish in good condition, but may damage or remove old "homemade concoctions" or very badly damaged finishes. It is a good idea to always test the cleaning solution on an inconspicuous area prior to cleaning, to make sure you are not dealing with one of these problem finishes.

If paint thinner doesn't remove the dirt and grime, a solution of 20% household ammonia and 80% water may be necessary. Use this solution carefully and sparingly. Water can dissolve old glues and loosen joints or veneers, and ammonia can darken some light colored woods. Moisten a rag or sponge with solution so it is damp, **but not wet**. Work on a small area at a time, rubbing gently to soften dirt, then follow up with a clean rag to dry. Work as quickly as possible, on small areas, and dry thoroughly.

Many commercial furniture polishes contain silicones and are formulated to repel water and resist staining. Unfortunately, silicone polishes also resist traditional cleaning and removal methods. The best way to remove silicone polish is with turpentine. Moisten a clean cloth or white paper towels with turpentine, and rub a small area of the surface. Dry thoroughly with a clean cloth. Continue in this manner, changing to a clean cloth when necessary, until the whole piece of furniture has been done. Then, using clean cloths, repeat the procedure to make sure the surface is no longer contaminated with silicones. Decontamination is especially important if you are preparing to apply a new finish or repair an existing finish, as no finish can be successfully applied over a silicone contaminated surface.

Use mineral spirits (also known as paint thinner) or turpentine to remove accumulated grease, dirt or wax from furniture. Turpentine will also remove silicones.

FINISH	CHARACTERISTICS	ADVANTAGES	DISADVANTAGES
Varnish	Clear finish made from natural or synthetic resins. Available in flat, satin or glossy. Does not accentuate the grain as much as other clear finishes. Does not penetrate wood.	Extremely hard and durable. Prices vary.	Extremely long drying time. Can not be successfully applied over an oil-based stain.
Shellac	White shellac will slightly darken wood while accentuating the grain. Orange shellac will add a darker tone. Made from natural resins. Does not penetrate wood.	Inexpensive and easy to apply. Quick drying. Easy clean up.	Very low resistance to water and alcohol. Limited shelf life.
Lacquer	Very hard, very durable clear finish. Available in flat, satin or glossy. Does not penetrate the wood.	Very fast drying. Very clear finish.	Requires thinning and special spraying equipment for application. Can not be applied over silicones.
Penetrating Finishes	Penetrates into the wood pores to provide protection. Available in clear or wood tones. Shows the grain and feel of the wood.	Easy to apply. Provides good protection. Can be easily re-coated to rejuvenate.	Expensive. Extremely difficult to remove. Can only be applied over water-based stains. Can not be used with other fillers, sealers or finishes.
Oil Finishes	Penetrates into the wood pores. Provides protection from water and staining while leaving the wood exposed.	Easy application. Inexpensive. Can be re-coated to rejuvenate.	Multiple applications are necessary to build up the protective qualities. Can not be applied over sealers, fillers or wax.
Paint and Enamel	Available in a variety of colors and in flat, satin and glossy finish. Does not penetrate wood.	Easy application. Prices can vary. Can be re-coated with similar product to rejuvenate.	Difficult to remove from wood with defined grain. Hides wood and grain.

Chapter 1

Repairs to the Finish

There are six types of clear finish commonly applied to furniture: **varnish, synthetic varnish, shellac, lacquer, penetrating finishes**, and **oil finishes**. **Paint** and **enamel** are the most popular non-clear finishes.

There is a large variety of finishes available for the "do-it-yourselfer". From left to right, (top) Antique Oil Finish, (back row) boiled linseed oil, Danish Oil, Wipe-On Polyurethane Varnish, spray paint, spray shellac, spray lacquer. (Front row, from left to right), acrylic varnish, enamel, tung oil varnish, shellac, varnish.

These products are available at most hardware stores, warehouse stores and variety stores. Each type of finish has distinct qualities and characteristics which are detailed on the chart on the previous page. Determine the type of finish on the furniture before attempting to repair or refinish it. Use of the proper finish will help to ensure a successful repair. Most finishes can be used to recoat themselves, but can not be applied over a different type of finish. This will result in cracking, peeling, blistering, or possible removal of the original finish.

Furniture finishes generally fall into two categories: **penetrating finishes** or **surface coatings**. Penetrating finishes, as the name implies, soak into the wood pores giving furniture a natural look and feel. Synthetic oils and resins, and natural oils and resins are the most popular penetrating finishes. Natural oils such as linseed oil, tung oil, or teak oil, are often used on older furniture and are considered a classic, traditional finish. Modern penetrating resins, "Danish Oil" and other synthetic "plastic type" finishes are more commonly used today because they are equal in beauty to a natural oil finish, but easier to apply.

Surface coatings lie on the surface of the wood forming a skin- they do *not* penetrate the wood. Varnish, shellac, lacquer, synthetic varnishes and paint are examples of surface coatings. Surface coatings can help protect wood from heat chemicals, scratches, stains, and other damage. The amount of protection will depend on the type of finish, and how well it is maintained.

You will need two solvents to determine the finish: **denatured alcohol** (also known as **shellac thinner**) and **lacquer thinner**. Do not use rubbing alcohol as a substitute for denatured alcohol; it is a diluted solution and will not give the correct results. It is important to remember to *always* use denatured alcohol <u>first</u> and lacquer thinner <u>last</u>. Denatured alcohol will not affect lacquer, but lacquer thinner will soften shellac, giving a false reading on the test.

Find an inconspicuous spot on the furniture and clean off all accumulated wax, polish and dirt with mineral spirits. Rub a clean cloth or white paper towels moistened with mineral spirits over the area until it wipes clean. Change cloths or towels as necessary to avoid recontaminating the area. Dry the area thoroughly.

Moisten a cotton swab or soft cloth with denatured alcohol and rub the cleaned area. Rub for a few minutes, remoistening the swab when necessary. If the finish is shellac, denatured alcohol will soften it, and begin to remove the finish. You will see softened finish on the swab, and it will tend to spread around in the area you are rubbing. If the finish does not soften, you are probably dealing with a lacquer or varnish finish.

Apply lacquer thinner to a cotton swab or soft cloth and rub the cleaned area. Rub for a few minutes, remoistening the swab as necessary. If the finish is lacquer, lacquer thinner will soften it and begin to remove the finish. A varnish finish will not be affected by either denatured alcohol or lacquer thinner.

Oil finishes are usually very easy to identify by sight and feel, and therefore require no testing. They give wood an unfinished but slightly polished look, and allow the natural beauty to show through. The wood will not be coated, and you will be able to feel the grain and see it clearly. An oil finish is easy to apply, and any type of finishing oil can be applied over the original coat for an easy repair. One disadvantage of an oil finish is that they offer virtually nothing in the way of protection from heat and other abuse.

Synthetic varnishes and synthetic penetrating resins can be identified by the plastic look and feel they give wood. Seventy-five percent of all varnishes sold today contain synthetic resins. The label will list the type of resin: acrylic, vinyl, alkyd, or phenolic. The hardness of the varnish is determined by the type of resin used and the ratio of resins to oil; the higher the resin content, the more durable the finish will be. There is a wide variety of synthetic varnishes for the home refinisher to choose from: polyurethanes, urethanes, and alkyds, just to name a few. These synthetic finishes can not be repaired like other finishes, but their durable qualities make most repairs unnecessary.

FINISHING MATERIAL	SOLVENT
Shellac	Denatured alcohol
Lacquer	Lacquer thinner
Lacquer enamel	Lacquer thinner
Latex paint	Water
Milk paint	Ammonia
Linseed oil	Turpentine
Oil-based varnish	Turpentine *
Synthetic varnish	Turpentine *
	* while finish is in a liquid state.

Reviving a Dull Finish

Some old finishes can be revived and made to look "new" again without going to all the trouble of refinishing. This is especially important if the furniture is an antique, as the old finish will add to the value. Furniture should be thoroughly cleaned with mineral spirits and soft rags or white paper towels to remove any accumulation of wax, polish, or dirt before attempting to revive the finish. In some cases, this thorough cleaning is enough to remove the cloudy look.

Shellac finish- Shellac may be revived with a mixture of 2 parts paraffin oil and 1 part white shellac. (If you can not find paraffin oil olive oil may be substituted.) Or use a mixture of 2 parts mineral oil and 1 part clear shellac. For mild cases, apply the oil mixture to a soft cloth and lightly rub the shellac surface, making sure your strokes are with the grain. Use a 3/0 steel wool pad instead of the soft cloth for severe cases, and rub with the grain using gentle pressure. Wipe dry with a clean cloth.

Varnish finish- Varnish finishes can generally be revived with a mixture of 50% raw (not boiled) linseed oil and 50% turpentine. Apply the mixture to a soft cloth or 3/0 steel wool and rub the varnish surface briskly, keeping your strokes with the grain. Wipe dry with a clean cloth and buff until dry and shiny.

Some varnishes may develop a foggy appearance. This should be treated with a mixture of 1 quart water to which you have added 1 to 2 tablespoons of vinegar. Dampen a clean cloth with the vinegar mixture and wring out any excess moisture. Rub the cloth on the varnish surface, keeping your strokes with the grain. Buff dry with a clean, soft cloth.

A milky appearance on a varnish finish is usually an indication that an inferior grade of varnish was used. This problem becomes most apparent in damp climates. A good rubbing with a mixture of 50% turpentine and 50% raw linseed oil will sometimes improve or completely remove the defect. Use a soft cloth, dampened with the turpentine/oil mixture and rub the varnish finish with the grain. Buff with a clean dry cloth. If this technique does not revive the finish, the varnish will have to be removed and replaced.

Lacquer finish- Lacquer finishes can be revived with a mixture of 2 parts turpentine, 2 parts boiled linseed oil and 4 parts lacquer thinner. Combine the ingredients and apply to the lacquer surface with 4/0 steel wool or a soft cloth. Buff dry with a clean cloth.

Removing a Cloudy Finish ("Blushing")

"Blushing" is similar to an alcohol stain. It is a white cloudy-looking surface generally found on old finishes that were continuously exposed to high humidity or low temperatures. If the blushing isn't too bad, try rubbing the area with a piece of fine steel wool and oil. Any kind of oil will do. Rub with the grain of the wood using gentle pressure. Clean the surface with a soft cloth, and apply a coat of furniture wax or lemon oil. If the blushing is quite bad, the surface may need to be refinished to remove the white area.

Reviving an Oil Finish

Oil finishes lubricate dry wood, enrich grain patterns, and darken wood. Any type of finishing oil can be used to replenish an oil finish. Moisten a soft cloth with water and wring out excess moisture. Apply a small amount of oil to the dampened cloth and lightly rub the wood, working on a small area at a time. **Never pour oil directly on the wood!** Wait for a couple of hours for the oil to be absorbed, then wipe off any excess with a soft dry cloth.

Oil finishes can be revived with a mixture of 1 part turpentine and 1 part boiled linseed oil (or mineral oil). Combine ingredients and apply to surface with 4/0 steel wool or a cotton cloth. Buff with a clean cotton cloth.

> ⚠ **Safety tip:**
> *Rags coated with linseed oil should always be spread out for a few days after use to prevent them from spontaneously causing a fire. Linseed oil will oxidize in the presence of air, generating heat. If the used rags are wadded up, the heat will be retained and the rags may ignite.*

Most antiques with an oil finish were originally treated with linseed oil, as it was the traditional oil of choice. But, linseed oil can be temperamental and has some disadvantages. It will become hard and difficult to remove if allowed to set. To prevent this, wipe all excess oil off the surface after it has had sufficient time to penetrate the wood. An oil finish should be considered a permanent finish. After application, normal solvents will not be able to penetrate into wood pores to remove the oil.

Unless oil-finished furniture receives hard or very abusive wear, dusting should be the only regular care it needs. Scratches, rings and stains can usually be removed by gently rubbing the surface with fine steel wool, lightly moistened with lemon oil or boiled linseed oil. Follow-up by buffing with a soft cloth. Never use wax on furniture with an oil finish.

Repairing Crazed, Cracked or "Alligatored" Finishes

The two greatest enemies of wood are extreme temperatures and humidity. Wood will expand when exposed to moisture and heat, and shrink when exposed to cold temperatures or dry environments. Modern furnaces may be efficient heaters but can act as dehumidifiers and unintentionally remove moisture from the air. In colder months the humidity level in overheated buildings can be reduced to 8-10% drier than the Sahara Desert. Seasonal changes can raise the indoor humidity level to 75% or higher. The optimum humidity level for furniture is around 50%. Lowering the temperature by as little as 10°F will raise the humidity approximately 5% and put furniture in a much safer environment. Older finishes lose their ability to keep up with the expansion and contraction of the wood and this results in crazing, cracking, and "alligatoring".

"Cracking" is self explanatory, "crazing" is defined as a small network of lines in the finish, and "alligatoring" is a rough, bumpy finish resembling the back of an alligator. These problems can usually be solved by a process called *reamalgamation*. Reamalgamation involves softening the existing finish with its solvent, then spreading the now liquid finish smoothly over the wood surface. Shellac finishes are reamalgamated with denatured alcohol. Lacquer finishes are reamalgamated with lacquer thinner. Some early 20th century finishes, known as "tough shellac" can be reamalgamated by a mixture of 3 parts denatured alcohol and 1 part lacquer thinner.

FINISH	SOLVENT
shellac	denatured alcohol
"tough shellac"	3 parts denatured alcohol and 1 part lacquer thinner
lacquer	lacquer thinner
lacquer-based enamel	lacquer thinner
milk paint	ammonia
latex paint	water

Varnish finishes are generally not considered good candidates for reamalgamation. "Varnish" has become a catchall term for a variety of finishes of various chemical composition and there is no one solvent that will work on all of them. Turpentine is a good solvent for most varnishes while in their liquid state but can not soften varnish enough to be re-worked once it has completely cured. Commercial "amalgamators" are available at specialized hardware stores or woodworking supply stores and can be effective on some types of varnishes but the results may be unpredictable. These amalgamators consist of acetone, ether, or other harsh chemicals potentially damaging to wood and finishes. For best results damaged varnish finishes should be removed not repaired.

Thoroughly clean furniture with mineral spirits and clean rags or white paper towels (see page 22). Determine the type of finish prior to reamalgamation (see page 26). Concentrate on one small area at a time. Completely remove any wax, polish, or dirt, changing towels or cloths if necessary to avoid recontamination. Allow sufficient time for the mineral spirits to work. Dry furniture with a clean cloth.

If old wax has accumulated on the finish, warm the mineral spirits before use. Warm solvent will soften the wax build-up and removal will be easier.

Loosen the lid on the mineral spirits container to prevent pressure build-up and place the container in warm water or in the sun for a few minutes. **Do not warm over direct heat! Mineral spirits are flammable!** Turpentine should be used to pre-clean furniture if you know or suspect that silicone wax or polish has been applied to the finish. Silicones can contaminate wood or finishes and jeopardize any repair efforts. Turpentine is the only solvent capable of removing silicones. Wipe turpentine on the furniture with a clean rag or white paper towels, concentrating on one small area at a time. Change towels or cloths often to avoid recontamination. Follow the turpentine cleaning with a final cleaning with mineral spirits.

To begin reamalgamating, make sure the surface is horizontal and level. Use a new paint brush and liberally baste the surface with lacquer thinner if reamalgamating a lacquer finish or denatured alcohol if it is a shellac finish Stroke over the wet surface with the brush, in the direction of the grain. Brush the softened finish for about a minute, then use light strokes to smooth off the surface. Allow the finish to set for 30 minutes. When dry, the surface should look like a freshly applied coat of finish. Remove any surface roughness by lightly rubbing with 4/0 steel wool, then apply a coat of furniture polish.

Repairing a Crazed Shellac Finish

Heavily crazed shellac can also be revived with a mixture of 2 parts turpentine, 2 parts boiled linseed oil and 4 parts denatured alcohol. Combine the ingredients and apply to surface with 4/0 steel wool or a soft, lint-free cloth. Buff dry with a clean cloth.

Repairing a Crazed Varnish Finish

Some crazed varnish finishes can be repaired by filling the small surface cracks with a thin varnish mixture: Mix together 2 oz. of varnish, 2 oz. boiled linseed oil, and 1 oz. of turpentine. Use a soft lint-free pad and gently rub the mixture into the crazed area with a circular motion. Continue to rub, using light pressure, until the finish starts to set up. Wipe any remaining varnish mixture from the surface. Allow sufficient time for the surface to dry thoroughly. If necessary, repeat the process after the first coat has completely dried.

Repairing a Blistered Finish

Blistering or peeling finishes are usually a result of improper finish application or an inferior finish product. Finishes applied over moist wood tend to blister or peel because they can not form a proper bond with the wood. The use of two or more incompatible finishing or refinishing chemicals can also result in a blistered or peeling finish. In most cases, the finish will have to removed and any contaminates neutralized, before the wood can be successfully refinished.

Very small blister-like bubbles can be repaired by reamalgamating. Thoroughly clean the area with mineral spirits and clean cloths or white paper towels (see page 22). Determine the type of finish (see page 26). Allow to dry. Check the chart on page 30 to determine the solvent for the finish. Use the solvent to reamalgamate the finish following the instructions on page 31. If reamalgamating does not give satisfactory results the finish will have to removed and reapplied.

Repairing a Chipped Finish

If the finish has chipped off in a small area the repair can usually be successfully completed. If the area is extensive, it is usually more practical to remove the entire finish and apply a new one.

Thoroughly clean the surface with mineral spirits to remove any dirt, wax, or grime prior to making any repairs (see page 22). With a fine artist's brush, carefully fill each chipped area with lacquer or shellac. (Clear nail polish can often be used as a substitute for the lacquer or shellac.) Allow to dry, then repeat. Multiple coats will need to be applied until the height of the repair is the same as the surrounding finish. When the repair is complete, lightly buff the area with 4/0 steel wool to blend the edges.

Repairing a Chipped Painted Finish

Painted surfaces can be difficult to repair, and in many cases need to be completely stripped or left alone. Badly deteriorated finishes that flake-off when touched can't be saved, and will have to be removed. Small chipped areas can be repaired, but the degree of success often varies with the type of paint.

The finish will need to be thoroughly cleaned prior to repair to ensure the best results. Spot tests should be done to determine the effect cleaning solutions will have on the finish. Try a simple soap and water solution first, then proceed with mineral spirits or turpentine. Use a clean soft cloth for the test, and use a new cloth for each solution.

After the tests are complete, determine which solution cleaned best without removing the paint. This will be apparent by the amount of pigment left on the cloth after each test. Use the selected solution to thoroughly, but carefully, clean the entire piece of furniture. Work on a small area at a time. Do not over-wet the finish, and dry thoroughly.

After cleaning, begin the touch-up. Some old paints can be *stretched,* a process similar to reamalgamation. Paint stripper is used to soften the old paint, which is then brushed into the cracks and chips. Properly done, the repairs are almost imperceptible, and the color match is as close as you can get to the original paint, because it is the original paint.

Painted surfaces can also be touched-up with artist oil paints. Match the color as closely as possible. Mix more than one color together if necessary to achieve the correct color. Apply a thin coat of paint with a fine artist's brush. Feather the edges to blend the repair and make it less noticeable. More than one coat may be necessary. Allow sufficient drying time between coats.

If the paint has chipped away leaving a depression, it may need to be filled with spackle compound before applying paint. Build up thin applications of spackle, feathering the edges to blend the repair. Allow sufficient drying time between applications. Touch up patched area with paint as described above.

Repairing Chipped Milk Paint

Some antique furniture (predominately country furniture) was finished with a special type of finish called *milk paint.* Milk paint has a very distinctive, characteristic look. It is more transparent than conventional paints and has a tendency to vary in hue across the painted surface. Its flat finish, and muted colors, are also easy to distinguish from modern paints.

Early milk paint was a homemade concoction consisting of rancid milk or buttermilk, with clay, blood, berries or other natural ingredients added for coloring. Buttermilk, skim milk or the whey from cheese-making was preferred over whole milk because the fat in whole milk interferes with the curing process of the paint. Lime was often added to increase the paint's durability. Lime produces a chemical reaction when combined with the lactic acid in the milk and thickens the paint to make it more durable. Milk paint dries to a very flat, lustreless sheen. If a higher sheen was desired egg whites were added to give the paint a semi-gloss sheen.

It is no longer necessary to make milk paint "from scratch". Powdered milk paint is available from woodworker's supply stores and other specialty stores, and is sold in a variety of colors. Add water to the mix, stir until well blended, and the paint is ready to use.

If you would like to try your hand at making milk paint "from scratch", mix hot water and non-fat dry milk together until you get a thick syrup consistency. Natural pigments can be added for color or use acrylic paints or universal colorants.

A cup of milk paint will usually be more than enough to repaint the average chair or small table. If you are unsure how much paint you'll need, mix up a little extra. Milk paint does not keep well, so all necessary painting should be done at the same time. Color matching from batch to batch can be difficult, if not impossible, and the application of a second coat can often dissolve the first coat. If you want to protect the paint and provide a light sheen, a coat of furniture paste wax can be applied after the paint has completely dried and cured. Milk paint will dry to the touch in about an hour, but will need two to three days to fully cure.

Milk paint becomes a very durable, long-lasting finish once it has dried and completely cured. Primitive furniture finished with milk paint often withstood generations of use. The natural stains and deep penetration of milk-base paint, often stain wood beneath the paint layer and wood can retain color long after the surface coating has powdered away.

Homemade or commercial milk paint can be used to repair small chips in the finish. Carefully match the color of the paint. Apply paint with a fine artist's brush. Feather the edges to blend the repair.

Deeper chips in the finish, and colors that are difficult to match can often be repaired by "stretching" the damaged paint. The only known solvent for milk paint is undiluted full strength ammonia used straight from the bottle. Modern strippers are for the most part ineffective on milk paint. Follow the instructions for stretching paint (see page 33) using ammonia as the solvent.

Repairing Scratches in the Finish

Scratches on furniture generally fall into one of two categories: scratches only in the finish and scratches penetrating the finish and the wood. Light finish scratches will be covered here. Deeper scratches penetrating the finish and the wood can be repaired in the same manner as dents. (See "Removing Dents" page 49.)

Small scratches in lacquer or shellac finishes can be removed by performing a small-scale reamalgamation. Determine whether the finish is shellac or lacquer (see page 26). Use a fine artist's brush and lightly brush solvent over the scratch, then across the scratch. The solvent will soften the finish and fill the scratch. Work on one scratch at a time and try to avoid undamaged parts of the finish.

Minor scratches on a varnish surface can sometimes be removed by lightly rubbing with a soft, lint-free cloth moistened with turpentine. The surface should be thoroughly cleaned before attempting a repair as dirt in the scratch may make the scratch appear darker.

Scratches can also be made less noticeable by a variety of less permanent methods. Rub broken pieces of Brazil nuts, walnuts, or pecans over the scratched area. The oil from the nutmeat will penetrate the scratch and darken it. This works especially well on walnut finishes. Raw linseed oil rubbed over the scratch can also replace natural oils and re-darken the wood.

Paste shoe polish will hide scratches on some wood finishes. Apply shoe polish to the scratch with a cotton swab, then buff dry. If the polish is too dark, wipe it off with naphtha (a liquid solvent used to remove spots from clothing and available at most hardware stores) and try again with a lighter shade. Test polish in an inconspicuous area before making the repair. Shoe polish will develop a shine when buffed, and the resulting shiny area may not blend with the finish on the rest of the piece. The repair may become more noticeable than the scratch.

Iodine, nut meats, paste shoe polish, eye brow pencil, crayons and oil paints are some of the common household items you can use to repair scratches in the finish.

Scratches on red mahogany are easy to hide with iodine. Carefully apply iodine to the scratch with a very fine brush. Avoid getting iodine anywhere except on the scratch. Keep a cloth handy and promptly wipe off any excess. Old iodine turns dark brown with age and works well for repairing scratches on brown mahogany.

Scratches on maple can be touched up with a solution of 50% iodine and 50% denatured alcohol. Allow sufficient drying time after any iodine repair, then wax the surface and buff it well to protect your repair. Scratches in ebony wood can be touched up by rubbing over the scratch with black eyebrow pencil. Small scratches in teak wood can be repaired by brushing with a solution of 50% linseed oil and 50% turpentine.

Repairing Worn Edges and Worn Spots

The finish on the edges of tables, desks, and drawers can wear off from normal use. Small wear spots may also appear on the top of furniture that receives excessive use. In most cases the worn area can be successfully repaired to blend with the surrounding finish. In severe cases, the finish may have to removed and the furniture refinished.

Wear is a matter of degree, and can be divided into two categories: *simple wear* and *deep wear*. Simple wear is indicated by a dull, or possibly nonexistent finish and stain (or other wood colorant) that remains the same color as the rest of the surface. Deep wear is indicated by a nonexistent finish and lighter areas in the wood where the stain (or other colorant) has been removed as a result of damage or use.

Simple wear is easy to repair. Clean the area thoroughly with a clean cloth or white paper towels moistened with mineral spirits or turpentine (see page 22). Determine the type of finish (see page 26). Apply one or more coats of finish with a fine artist's brush. Feather the edges to blend the repair. Remember to allow sufficient drying time between coats.

Deep wear requires a bit more effort. Thoroughly clean the area to be repaired (see page 22). Use a fine artist's brush to apply wood stain, oil paint, acrylic paint, or other colorant to restore color to the wood. This may take some experimenting to find a good color match. Allow stain to penetrate, then wipe off any excess. Allow sufficient time for stain to dry. Do a spot test in an inconspicuous area to determine the type of finish previously applied to the piece of furniture. Apply one or more coats of finish with a fine artist's brush, feathering the edges so they blend with the existing finish. Allow sufficient drying time between coats.

Removing White Spots

White spots develop when hot or wet containers are left in contact with shellac or lacquer finishes. Water from the container penetrates the finish surface and becomes trapped underneath. Varnish finishes do not develop white spots because they can not be penetrated by water. If you are lucky enough to catch a white ring in the making, use a hair dryer on the low setting to dry the moisture from the finish before the spot has a chance to set. To prevent a heat mark from developing on the finish use only low heat and keep the blow dryer moving. Do not attempt to remove white spots with furniture oil, wax or polish. Polishes or waxes will inhibit moisture evaporation and seal in the water mark. They will not remove white spots.

White spots do not usually penetrate deep into the finish and can be easily removed a number of ways. For minor cases, gently rub the white spot with one of the following combinations:

- cigarette or cigar ashes moistened with a light oil
  (i.e.: baby oil or sewing machine oil)
- regular toothpaste and a small dab of water
- salad oil and table salt
- oil and rottenstone or pumice
- water and mild metal polish

Many common household items can be used to remove white marks from a finish. Shown above are baby oil, salt, Vaseline, pumice, alcohol, ammonia, silver polish, Spitits of Camphor, toothpaste and cigarette ashes.

The idea is to use a mild abrasive and a liquid to help lubricate the finish. Rub only with the grain when applying the abrasive, do not use excessive pressure and check frequently on your progress. Wipe off excess abrasive when the white spot has been removed. Apply a coat of wax to cover any dullness that might occur, and blend the repair with the rest of the finish.

A liberal coat of Vaseline petroleum jelly can be an effective, nonabrasive method of spot removal. Spread Vaseline over the damaged area, let it stand for a 24 to 48 hours, then wipe off the excess. Vaseline is very effective on certain finishes, and is good for large white areas. This treatment is especially effective on mahogany furniture.

White spots can be removed from some lacquer surfaces without using abrasion. Moisten a cloth with a few drops of ammonia, spirits of camphor, or essence of peppermint and flick it *over* the spot. Do not rub the cloth *on* the spot. The fumes from the ammonia (or other fuming agent), not the ammonia itself, is what does the trick. Some lacquer finishes might be helped by lightly wiping with alcohol. Alcohol softens the finish around the spot causing it to flow over the damaged area.

If the white spot has penetrated all the way through the finish, you will need to use a process other than abrasion to remove it. Try wiping the spot with a small cloth pad dampened with lacquer thinner. Brush with quick, light strokes. Gradually add a few more drops of lacquer thinner if necessary. This process may create a shiny area that may need to be dulled to match the remaining finish. Allow the finish to dry 3 or 4 hours after the white ring has been removed, then dull the shiny spot by lightly rubbing with 3/0 or 4/0 steel wool. Apply a coat of wax or polish when the repair is complete.

White water marks in a finish before repair.

The same finish with white water marks removed.

Removing Black Water Marks

Black water marks develop when water penetrates the finish and soaks into wood fibers. The finish is usually cracked or missing altogether when black marks appear, but this is not always the case. Moisture can penetrate through pinhole size imperfections in the finish and leave black water damage under a visibly undamaged finish. The only successful method of removing black water marks is to bleach them out. Regular household bleach can be used to remove some black water marks. Brush undiluted bleach over the darkened area with a new natural bristle paint brush, and allow it to penetrate.

After the stain has been removed (or if you determine that household bleach is not going to remove the discoloration) wipe off excess bleach with white paper towels or clean white rags. Neutralize the area by wiping with white vinegar, then wipe with water. Dry the finish to prevent further water damage. Stubborn spots may require repeating the process with additional applications of bleach and neutralizer.

Hydrogen peroxide, laundry bleach and oxalic acid can each be used to remove black water marks and some other stains from furniture. Always use white vinegar after bleaching to neutralize the area.

For more serious black marks, a concentrated solution of oxalic acid may be necessary. This solution will work almost instantaneously on even the most difficult water marks, so be prepared to remove it and neutralize the area as soon as the job is done. It usually has no effect on the existing finish and can be applied on the finish to remove the black marks under the finish.

Special note:
Oxalic acid is very poisonous! Care should be taken during use, storage, and disposal. Do not breathe fumes or dry dust particles. Do not get in eyes. Do not allow mixture or dry particles to come in contact with skin. Read warning label carefully and follow all instructions.

Oxalic acid is available from chemical supply stores and some wood-working supply stores. A concentrated solution of oxalic acid can be made by mixing 1 cup of hot water with approximately 3 tablespoons of oxalic acid crystals in a nonmetal container. Pour the crystals into the water while stirring, and stir until completely dissolved. Wear gloves to protect hands, goggles or other eye protection, and a respirator or other mask to prevent inhalation of fumes.

Brush oxalic acid solution over black marks with a small disposable natural bristle brush. Wipe off the solution with white paper towels or clean white rags when the marks have lightened or disappeared. Use a new, natural bristle brush to apply the vinegar to the area to neutralize it after bleaching. Allow to remain on the surface for a few minutes, then wipe off with white paper towels or white rags. Wipe the neutralized area with water, then dry thoroughly to prevent further water damage.

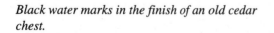

Black water marks in the finish of an old cedar chest.

The same cedar chest after treating the black water marks with oxalic acid solution, then refinishing.

Removing Ink Stains

Removing ink from wooden furniture is really a matter of trial and error. If the ink has been freshly spilled, take a clean cloth and blot the stain. You will have to blot it several times; use a clean part of the cloth each time to avoid spreading the stain.

Blot off all the ink you can, then wipe the stain with white paper towels or white rags moistened with water. Next, use a small paint brush or pieces of cotton to apply lemon juice to bleach out the ink stain. Use a cloth dampened with water to wipe off any excess lemon juice. Dry the surface thoroughly.

Pro Tip:
This process will remove ink immediately from some finishes, but may create a water mark on others. Test solutions in an inconspicuous area prior to repair.

Most stationery stores and office supply stores still carry Ink Eradicator. It can be used to remove ink stains from some types of wood with moderate success, but usually requires multiple applications, and will not penetrate deep enough to remove stains imbedded in the wood. Follow the directions on the bottle carefully, and take care to keep the liquid only on the stained area.

Hydrogen peroxide (the hair bleaching strength available at beauty supply stores, not the 3% solution found in your medicine cabinet) can also be used to remove ink, blood, and some other difficult stains from wood. Apply hydrogen peroxide to the stained area with a small paint brush. Reapply if necessary. Wipe excess hydrogen peroxide from the surface with white paper towels or white rags after the stain is removed. Moisten a clean cloth or paper towel with water and wipe off any remaining hydrogen peroxide. Dry the surface thoroughly.

Some ink stains can be removed by rubbing the area with pumice and oil. Be careful not to apply too much pressure, or you will rub through the finish, down to bare wood, and create a new problem. Apply a coat of paste wax or lemon oil polish to the area after the stain is removed, to eliminate any dullness that may occur.

If the ink stain is old, sand the area lightly to expose the wood. Brush ammonia or a concentrated solution of oxalic acid (see directions for mixing solution and neutralizing under "Removing Black Water Marks" page 39) onto the ink stain with a new, natural bristle brush. Follow the bleaching process with an application of white vinegar to neutralize. Dab the area with damp paper towels to remove vinegar, then dry thoroughly.

 Pro Tip:
The oxalic acid solution works particularly well for removing red ink stains.

Old-fashioned ink formulas were quite different from the ones used today. The tannin-based liquids were strong enough to rot the nibs of pens, and easily penetrated through the old finishes. Old ink stains that were not properly treated or removed, and were sealed in by multiple applications of paste wax, eventually developed a greenish-purple cast. These old stains are difficult, if not impossible to remove. In most cases it is advisable to consider old ink stains permanent "character marks" of the furniture and leave them alone.

Removing Milk Stains
Anything with a milk base (i.e.: milk, ice cream, custard, etc.) contains lactic acid, which can act as a mild but very efficient paint remover and potentially damage finishes or remove paint from furniture. For this reason, it is very important to wipe up spilled milk products as soon as possible. If the spot is dry, clean off any remaining foodstuff with a damp cloth. Make a paste of pumice and oil or use paste silver polish. Apply the paste to the spot with a damp cloth or with your finger. Go over the spot until it has disappeared. Wipe off any surface grit, then apply a coat of furniture wax or lemon oil.

Removing Alcohol Stains
Alcohol stains leave a noticeable white mark on wood finishes, and can be caused by any liquid that has an alcohol base (i.e.: liquor, medicine, perfume, etc.). Spilled alcohol can have a solvent effect on almost all finishes and should be wiped up as soon as possible. After the spill is cleaned off, wipe the area with the palm of your hand. Oil from your hand will help restore some of the oil removed by the alcohol.

If the damage has already been done, try rubbing the spot with a finger dipped in furniture polish or linseed oil. If this doesn't work, lightly moisten a clean cloth with ammonia and rub the spot. If the spot comes off, apply a coat of wax or lemon oil immediately.

Paste silver polish is quite effective for removing alcohol stains from some finishes. Apply a small amount of the silver polish to your finger and gently rub over the white mark. When the stain is removed, wipe off any surface grit, and apply a coat of wax or lemon oil. For really stubborn alcohol stains, make a paste of pumice or rottenstone and oil; use a soft cloth to apply the mixture. When the spot is removed, wipe off any surface grit.

No matter which spot removal method you use, wax or lemon oil the area when the repair is complete.

Removing Candle Wax

Candle wax should be removed as soon as possible *after* the wax has had a chance to cool. **Do not** use a knife to scrape hardened wax off the furniture surface. Instead, wrap several ice cubes in a clean piece of cloth and place on the wax. Allow the ice to harden the wax, then take your thumbnail or a plastic credit card and flick the wax off of the surface. Push along the surface in the direction of the grain. **Do not push down into the wood** as this could bruise the wood fibers! In most cases the whole piece of wax will come off at once. If it doesn't, repeat the ice treatment and scratch again.

Any wax residue can be easily removed by placing blotting paper or tissue paper over the waxy area and applying a warm hot water bottle. The wax will be drawn up from the finish and into the paper. Take care not to spill water from the water bottle on the finish or you may create a water mark.

When the wax is gone, coat the area with furniture wax or lemon oil and rub in well. Buff with a clean cloth.

Removing Paper Stuck to the Finish

Never use a scraper of any type to remove paper stuck to furniture. Scraping can permanently damage the finish. Instead, cover the area with a thin coating of olive oil or baby oil. Let the oil soak into the paper. Then rub the paper off with a soft cloth.

Pro Tip:
Paper labels glued to the backs or undersides of furniture by the manufacturer should not be removed from old or antique furniture, even if they are partially destroyed. Even a partial label will aid in identification of the piece of furniture, and removal may decrease the furniture's potential value. See "Preserving and Protecting Furniture Labels" page 234.

Removing Adhesives from the Finish

Adhesives can be removed, without damaging most finishes, by rubbing the mark with cold cream, creamy peanut butter, or salad oil. Allow to sit for a few minutes, then wipe off with a soft cloth. Polish or wax the furniture after the adhesive is removed.

Removing Decals from Furniture

Cover the decal with white vinegar. Apply pieces of cloth or white paper towels if necessary to keep the decal moist. Allow the vinegar to soak into the decal, then rub with a soft cloth to remove. Dry the area thoroughly after the decal has been removed.

This method works very well on painted furniture. It may also be used to remove decals from some clear finishes. Do a spot test in an inconspicuous area first to make sure the vinegar will not damage the finish. Apply a coat of wax or polish to clear finishes after the decal has been removed and the area has been thoroughly dried.

Removing Spilled Nail Polish

Do not attempt to wipe up spilled nail polish before it has had a chance to dry! The solvents in nail polish will soften most furniture finishes, and you may end up wiping off the polish and the finish! Let the polish dry completely, then gently scrape it off with a plastic credit card. If the finish underneath has dulled, use paste wax and 4/0 steel wool to help bring back the shine.

Removing Paint Spots

If fresh oil based paint spills are discovered on the finish, wipe off immediately with a cloth dampened with turpentine. For latex paint, wipe with a cloth dampened with water. Wipe the finish until the paint is completely removed. Turn and fold the cloth frequently to expose clean areas, or change cloths if necessary, to avoid recontamination. Dry the finish carefully and apply lemon oil polish or wax.

Dried paint spots can usually be softened and removed by moistening a soft cloth with linseed oil and wiping over the paint spots. Allow the linseed oil to penetrate, then wipe dry. Difficult spots that do not wipe off, can usually be removed by scraping with a plastic credit card in the direction of the grain. Or add a small amount of rottenstone to some linseed oil. Moisten a soft cloth with the mixture and lightly rub the cloth over the paint spots. Do not use excessive pressure, and make sure to keep your strokes with the grain. Dry the finish carefully and apply lemon oil polish or wax.

 Pro Tip:
To prevent accidental paint spots, furniture should be polished or waxed on a regular basis. Paint will not adhere as easily to a waxed or polished surface.

Cleaning Smoke Discoloration

Smoke and heat can cause simple surface staining, or can result in serious deterioration of the finish. Start by cleaning the furniture. Rip a 3/0 or 4/0 steel wool pad into 3 or 4 pieces. Dip a piece of the pad into mineral spirits and lightly rub the finish surface. The pad should be dipped frequently into fresh solvent to rinse off what you have removed from the surface. Wipe the furniture with clean rags or white paper towels to remove excess soot.

In severe cases, use non-sudsing ammonia to remove the smoke glaze. Test on an inconspicuous spot, then wait a few days to see what affect, if any, it will have on the finish and wood. If no problems appear, try the ammonia on small areas at a time, and proceed with caution.

If the cleaning efforts reveal the heat or smoke have charred the wood, all of the charred particles will have to be scraped off, or sandpapered away before any finish repairs can be done. Stain or finish applied over the damaged area will accentuate the black discoloration and the charring will prevent proper adhesion of a finish coat.

Removing Scuff Marks and Vacuum Cleaner "Deposits"

Scuff marks on the finish are generally caused by normal wear and tear – kids, pets, shoes and other furniture are just a few of the culprits. The dirt and minor scratches they leave behind can be removed by lightly rubbing the area with a small piece of fine steel wool dipped in turpentine or mineral spirits. Dry thoroughly with a clean dry cloth or white paper towels. When all of the scuff marks have been removed, apply a coat of wax or lemon oil for protection from future scuff marks.

Look at the legs of your furniture or the bottom of chests, desks and other furniture, and you may notice black marks, or small streaks of what appear to be paint. These are deposits left on your furniture from your vacuum cleaner. Most vacuum cleaners have a protective rubber or plastic bumper surrounding the suction area to prevent damaging furniture while the vacuum is in use. Unfortunately, the bumper can pick up paint when it comes in contact with walls, baseboards and other painted trim and then leaves it behind after contact with your furniture. These deposits can be removed in the same manner as scuff marks. Lightly rub the area with a small piece of fine steel wool dipped in either mineral spirits or turpentine. Use very light pressure to avoid rubbing through the finish. When the marks have been removed, dry the area thoroughly with a clean dry cloth or white paper towels. Apply a coat of wax or lemon oil. This will provide the finish with protection from future deposits.

Removing the "Stickies" and the "Gummies"

If you live in an area where the weather tends to get hot or humid, you have probably discovered a piece of often-used furniture with a sticky or gummy finish. The usual culprit is either a build up of oil or wax on the furniture, or linseed oil rising to the surface. The oil and wax are softened by the heat and swollen out by the humidity, and lay on the finish surface where they collect dirt, body oils, acids from skin, etc. Left unattended the trapped dirt, oils, and acids can deteriorate a delicate finish. This problem is easy to correct, if you catch it before the deterioration starts to occur.

Moisten a clean soft rag or white paper towels with either mineral spirits or turpentine. Lightly rub the gummy or sticky area. If the buildup is really thick, moisten a small piece of rag with either mineral spirits or turpentine and lay it over the area. Allow it to cover the area for about 20 minutes. Remove the cloth and wipe with a clean dry cloth. Repeat if necessary, changing cloths often to avoid recontamination.

If the finish is thin or missing after the gumminess has been removed see "Repairing Worn Edges and Worn Spots" page 36.

Pro Tip:
Wet varnish and enamel tend to attract dust and lint, and usually the problem is not discovered until after the job is finished. Follow these simple instructions to make a "pick stick" (a cotton swab dipped in some specially prepared varnish) to use to remove the dust and lint on the surface before the finish has dried. This eliminates the need to rebrush the surface and prevents brush marks and pull marks in the finish. Place a small amount of varnish into a small can set into a larger pan of hot water. Buy some crushed rosin from a music store and add 7 or 8 parts rosin to 1 part varnish. Stir until the rosin is completely dissolved. Allow the mixture to cool. Dip a cotton swab into the mixture, then moisten your fingers with water and roll the mixture on the end of the swab into a pear shape. Roll and tap it in the palm of your hand until it is sticky but firm. Your pick stick is now ready to use. Lightly touch the point of the pick stick to the lint (avoid touching the finish). The lint will adhere to the pick stick leaving the surface clean. Place a bright light between you and the work so you can see the dust more easily.

Chapter 2

Repairs in the Wood

Removing Dents

Dents are one of the most common problems you will encounter when repairing furniture. Many smaller dents can, and should, be left alone. However, if you are determined to try and raise the dent, keep a few things in mind. The dent was caused in the first place by some sort of blow to the wood that compressed the wood fibers. The best way to remove a dent from wood is to apply water. The application of moisture will cause the wood fibers to swell up again, usually to their original shape. The water swells the wood fibers, which makes the dent rise.

But, the water that is so good for swelling wood fibers is also very bad for most finishes and may create more damage than the offending dent. Oil and varnish finishes will not suffer too many ill effects, but shellac and lacquer will turn white and may suffer other damage from water contact. If you know the finish is either shellac or lacquer, you may want to surround the dented area with a coat of paste wax before attempting to repair the dent.

The following technique is very good for removing small dents from table tops or other flat surfaces. If the dent is not on the top of the piece, the furniture must be positioned so that the dented area is horizontal. On smaller pieces this is not difficult. Larger pieces of furniture may have to be disassembled. Apply water to the depression with an eye dropper or fingertip until the water level is above the surrounding surface. A fine sewing needle may be used to poke small holes into the grain of the wood to speed up the absorption of the water. These holes will close and become invisible when the wood swells. Allow water to sit in the dent until it is absorbed into the wood. Some woods are more porous than others and the process may have to be repeated numerous times to achieve satisfactory results. Boiling water or hot water can also be used for harder, more stubborn woods.

After removing the dent, assess the damage to the finish. In most cases an application of lemon oil polish or a coat of wax should be all that is needed. If the finish is cracked or missing, it can be repaired with a quick touch-up of clear nail polish or shellac.

Larger more obstinate dents that are away from glued joints, may require steam swelling to raise the depression. Steam will usually do a better job of raising a dent than just water alone. To speed up the water absorption, prick a few holes with a fine needle into the grain of the wood in the dented area. Then fill the dent with water until it is level with the surface. Place a very moist cloth over the dent and touch it with the tip of a clothing iron set to the "cotton" setting. Hold the iron in place a few seconds to allow the steam to penetrate through the cloth and down into the wood beneath. Remove the cloth quickly to prevent scorching then check for swelling. You may have to do this several times before you see results. The problem with this method of dent removal is that a non-waterproof finish will turn white, and you will then have to remove the water spot.

A heavy soldering iron can also be used as a heat source for dent removal. Allow the soldering iron to reach full heat, then unplug it and test it on a damp cloth until it produces steam without burning or scorching. Keep wetting the cloth and applying heat until the dent disappears.

Wax touch-up sticks can offer another repair solution for dented furniture. They can be bought in almost any lumber or hardware store and can be used to repair small dents. Children's crayons can be used in place of touch-up sticks. Buy the biggest box you can find and pick out all the reds, browns, and tans. The white ones and black ones come in handy for lightening or darkening colors. Beeswax or paraffin can be mixed with analine dyes (an alcohol soluble powder used for furniture touch-ups and repairs) or artist's dry colors if you need more variety to create a perfect color match.

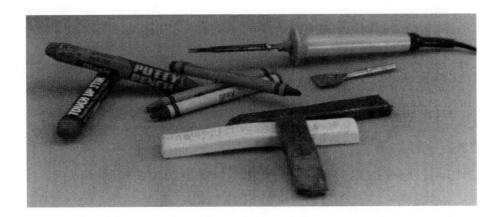

Wax touch-up sticks, crayons, and lacquer sticks or shellac sticks can be used to repair dents in furniture. An electric burn-in knife and an extra wide tip are shown at the top right of the picture.

No matter which wax product you choose for your repair, best results will be obtained by making sure the wood does not have a distinct grain pattern, and the repaired area will not be in contact with body heat when the furniture is in use. Wax products can be used to repair cracks, scars, and holes in furniture They are readily available, affordably priced, and easy to use, but the repairs are not permanent. Remember also that most finishes will not adhere to the wax repair, so any finish repairs should be done first.

Pick a color or mix a color to closely match the wood color. Rub the crayon or wax stick over the dent, or melt the wax with a smokeless heat source (i.e. Sterno or an alcohol lamp) and dribble it into the dent. Allow the melted wax to cool, then scrape excess wax from the surface with a dull knife blade, spatula, or plastic scraper.

The best part of wax stick touch-ups is if you are not satisfied with your repair efforts the first time, they can easily be melted or scraped out so you can try again. If you wish to apply a finish over the repair it is essential that you first apply a sealer coat of shellac regardless of the type of finish on the piece of furniture. Varnish or lacquer applied over wax will either resist the wax and pull away or turn gummy and never dry. Shellac is the only finish that will dry when applied over wax. When the shellac has dried, you may then apply any other finish over your patch.

Lacquer sticks or *shellac sticks* are the professional method of choice for repairing dents, cracks, small holes, and gouges in either solid wood or veneered surfaces. The process of performing these repairs is called "*burning-in*". The sticks are made from resins and either shellac or lacquer. They are sold in a wide variety of colors for repairing all types of wood and finishes, and can be purchased in both opaque and transparent. See the Appendix for a list of mail-order woodworking suppliers that carry lacquer sticks, shellac sticks, and other burn-in equipment. When properly applied, the patch will not lift out, will accept any type of finish, and will be practically unnoticeable.

Before making the repair, clean the area with mineral spirits to be sure the area is free of dirt and oil. If the bottom of the dent is smooth, rough it up a bit with a single edge razor or knife blade to give the melted stick better adhesion. Professionals call this giving the area "tooth". Select the stick color that most closely matches the area to be patched. Light a can of Sterno, or an alcohol lamp, and heat a knife blade or spatula in the flame. (Do not use a candle flame as this will leave carbon deposits on the blade which will discolor the melted stick.) Be careful not to overheat the tool. If it gets too hot the patch will bubble, burn and discolor.

Hold the stick over the area to be repaired and touch it with the hot blade allowing it to melt into the dent. The blade will have to be periodically reheated in the flame to maintain the proper temperature. Use this time to allow the patch to cool before applying more melted resin. When the area has been filled, use the hot blade to smooth out the patch and blend it to the surrounding areas. Allow the patch to cool, then use a single edge razor blade to carefully trim off any rough edges or to round corners. Finish off by buffing with a small piece of 4/0 steel wool.

An electric *burn-in knife* can be used in place of the Sterno or alcohol lamp to melt the resin stick, and can be very useful if you find that you are going to be doing a lot of this type of repair. It will heat to exactly 300° F, the proper temperature for melting the sticks, and maintain a constant temperature during use. A *Rheostat* can also be purchased to give added control over the temperature while working. Check the woodworking supply stores for these items.

Shallow dents can also be filled by brushing multiple coats of shellac or other clear finish into the dented area with a small artists brush. Allow each coat to dry thoroughly before applying the next one. This is a very slow process, and you may have to apply several dozen layers, but it can provide excellent results and is well worth the effort.

Removing Cigarette Burns

Cigarette burns are eyesores, but not all of them are serious repair problems. A lot depends on the type of wood that has been burned, the type of finish on the wood and the depth of the burn. A finish burn can usually be repaired quite successfully. However, if the burn goes through the finish and down into the wood resulting in what looks like a charred trench, it can present a real challenge.

For surface burns, begin by cleaning the area with mineral spirits to remove any dirt, wax or furniture polish that might interfere with the repair. Scrape away any damaged finish with a single edge razor blade or knife blade. If the wood underneath has not been damaged or discolored, you can refinish the spot successfully. Touch-up the wood with wood stain or non-acrylic oil paint to blend the color with the surrounding wood. Then, when the colorant is thoroughly dry, apply a new finish coat to seal.

A deep burn extends beneath the finish and into the wood, and the wood near the surface will usually be charred black. All of the charred wood will have to be removed before a successful repair can be made. Clean the damaged area with mineral spirits to remove any accumulated dirt, wax, or furniture polish. Carefully remove the charred wood by scraping with a single edge razor blade or knife blade, and keep scraping until undamaged wood appears.

This is very important. Any charred wood left behind will leave a dark spot in your repair and will be sealed in under the finish coat. When all the charrred wood has been removed there will be an indentation, sometimes a fairly deep one. The indentation will have to be filled and then the surface will have to be refinished. If the indentation is shallow, you may be able to use varnish, shellac or lacquer as the filler. If it is deep, you should treat the damaged area as a dent or a gouge and use lacquer stick or shellac stick.

To fill a shallow dent:
Paint coat after coat of shellac, lacquer, or varnish (whatever the piece of furniture is currently finished with) into the dent with a small artist's brush. Allow each coat to dry thoroughly before applying the next. After raising the dent to surface level, blend the repair to the existing finish coat.

To fill a deep dent:
Thoroughly scrape the charred wood until undamaged wood appears. Fill the dent with lacquer stick or stick shellac. Then blend the repair to the existing finish coat.

Repairing Wood Rot and Dry Rot
Before you can repair the damage, you will have to determine whether the problem is *wood rot* or *dry rot*. Technically wood rot is caused by water and dry rot is caused by either insects or fungi, but the terms are often interchanged. In either case, you will have to remove the cause of the problem before repairing the weakened wood.

Wood rot is most frequently found in the feet and legs of furniture. It is common in older furniture exposed to dirt floors or water during use or storage. Infected wood has a musty smell, is powdery to the touch, and can structurally weaken a piece of furniture.

Furniture damaged by wood rot will have to be removed from any source of humidity and completely dried before any repairs can be made. Hair dryers and fans can help speed up the drying process. Resist the urge to put the furniture out in direct sunlight as this could create more problems.

Dry rot is incorrectly named as it appears most frequently in furniture exposed to a damp, dirty environment. Moisture, stagnant air, and dirt create the perfect growing condition for either fungi, or wood-boring insects that cause dry rot.

Fungi are spongy, white parasitic growths that live on organic matter in the wood. The fungi seeds, or spores, float in the air and settle on wood surfaces, but usually will not attack wood unless damp conditions exist. If the environment is favorable, the spores will send out roots which spread through the natural cavities of the wood. The roots take away cellulose from the wood, and cause a complete breakdown of the character of the wood. It will change color, soften, lose weight and develop a musty smell. The spores feed on the wood and produce more spores, which in turn spread to other parts of the same wood. They may also be carried to other wood by air, hands, dusting cloths or tools. All live spores will have to be treated with fungicide and killed to prevent the spread of the fungus.

The furniture condition known commonly as *woodworm* is actually a type of dry rot caused by a wood-boring beetle, not a worm. The four most common types of wood-boring insects that attack woodwork are: the common furniture beetle, the death-watch beetle, the powder-post beetle, and the house longhorn beetle. It is the larvae or grubs, not the beetle itself that causes damage to the wood. The female beetle lays her eggs in cracks and old joints in the wood. After approximately four weeks, the eggs hatch and the larvae start to eat their way out of the wood. Depending on the type of beetle, this larvae state may last up to two years. When full grown, the larvae change to pupae and remain dormant for a few weeks, then develop into adult beetles. The mature beetle, who is usually no more than 1/8" long, then gnaws its way out of the wood. The female lays her eggs in the wood, and the cycle begins again.

Spring and early summer are usually when the first signs of insect infestation will appear. Tiny, light-colored piles of powder will appear on the floor underneath the infested furniture. This is *frass*, a combination of fine wood particles from the furniture and deposits from the larvae. Thoroughly inspect your furniture several times a year if you have any reason to suspect dry rot. Wood-boring insects can travel from one piece of furniture to another, and damage a whole roomful of furniture if left undetected. Check all wooden areas, top and bottom, to make sure no small holes appear. Dark holes are evidence that wood borers have been there, but are presently inactive in that spot. Light colored holes that contrast with the surrounding wood, or holes with fine powder in or around them, indicate a current infestation.

The pinhead size surface holes, usually about 1 mm in diameter, are only the tip of the iceberg as far as wood damage is concerned. There can be a maze of tunnels under the surface weakening the wood to the point where the furniture becomes unusable. Wood-boring insects seem to prefer walnut, chestnut, maple, oak, and fruitwoods, but will also attack softwoods like pine and poplar. They are also fond of wickerwork, and because of the small diameter of the spokes, can do substantial damage in very little time. Some woods such as mahogany, cedar and teak wood are rarely attacked.

Dry rot can be treated in one of two ways: fumigation, or the use of liquid insecticide such as Cuprinol or Stop-Rot (available at boatyards or hardware stores selling marine supplies) or liquid fungicide. Fumigation exposes the whole piece of furniture to toxic gases, not just the infested areas, and is a very effective treatment. But, because fumigating gases are extremely hazardous and require the use of a fumigation chamber, fumigation must be done by a professional.

Liquid insecticide or fungicide can be used by the nonprofessional but to be most effective, will need to be dropped into each and every hole in sufficient quantities to penetrate the entire depth of the hole. A small oil can works well for applying the liquid insecticide. Aerosol insecticide for wood-borers is also available in some areas. Common fluids such as kerosene, benzene, and turpentine can also be used to kill wood-boring insects and work quite well in some cases.

Care should be taken to protect your eyes and skin when applying insecticide as the liquid will sometimes come back out from another hole. Wear rubber gloves and goggles and work in a well-ventilated room. Insecticides and fungicides may contain solvents of varnish, so care should be taken to protect the floor and any nearby furniture with plastic drop cloths. If any fluid gets on the finish wipe it off immediately. Use a paint brush to apply the solution to all unfinished areas (i.e.: insides, backs and undersides).

Once the insects or fungus have been killed it is extremely important to eliminate all possible grounds for future egg-laying or spore growth. All cracks in the woodwork should be filled with wax and the furniture should be thoroughly cleaned. Relocate the furniture to an area that is free from moisture or dampness, provide adequate ventilation, and keep it clean.

Woodworm infestations can be very persistent and are rarely completely eradicated. If possible, treat the furniture several times during the first few months after the infestation is discovered. Repeat the treatment for at least two years. Thoroughly inspect the furniture at least twice a year to check the progress of the treatment.

If you are working on an antique, every effort should be made to save the wood. If it has been structurally damaged, wooden braces may have to be applied to the inside of the furniture to provide additional support, or if the woodworms have honeycombed the interior of the wood, it may be impregnated with synthetic resins and bonding agents to help hold it together. The repair of structural damage is a job best left to a professional furniture restoration expert.

To repair dry rot damage, carefully scrape away the rotten wood and remove any dirt or loose particles. Fill the damaged area with wood putty, wood dough, or a homemade putty consisting of sawdust and wood glue. When this is dry, sand the repair to smooth it, and then stain to match the surrounding wood. Finish with a clear top coat of varnish or shellac.

The feet of furniture legs that have been weakened by wood rot can be reinforced by drilling holes through the rotted area and up into the unaffected area. Apply glue to the inside of the hole and insert wooden dowels. If glue is applied to the inside of the hole instead of coating the outside of the dowel, you will have less of a problem with excess glue oozing out onto the surface.

Repairing Furniture Splinters

Wood splinters are an easy repair if you fix them when you first discover them. Left unrepaired, they will catch on a dust cloth or piece of clothing, and that one inch splinter can turn into a three or four inch problem before you can say "I should have fixed that!". Use a toothpick or sewing needle to remove any dirt, dust or threads from the splinter, being careful not to lift or bend the wood. Inject a few drops of glue behind the splinter or apply the glue with a toothpick. Carefully press the splinter back into place and wipe off any excess glue that squeezes out. Apply pressure on the splinter with your thumb and secure it in place with a piece of masking tape. Allow to dry for approximately 12 hours, then carefully remove the tape.

Removing Oily, Greasy Stains from Wood

If the finish has been stripped or the finish is missing, you may encounter oil, grease or other grimy stains in the wood. Clean the area thoroughly with mineral spirits and wipe with clean cloths or white paper towels. Allow to dry completely. Apply a thick coating of rug cleaner containing a base of wood flour and trichlorethylene (check the label for the list of ingredients). Allow the cleaner to dry thoroughly. Trichlorethylene is a grease solvent and the wood flour will absorb the grease from the wood as the solvent evaporates. When dry, the powder can be brushed away with the grease in it.

Chapter 3

Repairing Damaged Veneer

A *veneer* is a very thin layer of wood, usually cut from the more expensive hardwood species, and chosen for the beauty of its pattern or grain. Because veneers are so thin (usually averaging between 1/28" and 1/40" thick) and can become quite brittle with age, great care should be taken when undertaking any veneer repair.

Veneered furniture is more apt to be damaged by hard usage, age and dampness than solid wood furniture. This abuse can loosen the glue bonding veneer to the base wood, resulting in raised edges, cracks, blisters or waves. Most veneer damage appears on the top of a piece of furniture. Fortunately, this makes it easier to repair. Minor veneer repairs can be tackled by an amateur refinisher with satisfactory results. All that is needed are a few tools, sufficient time and patience. Major repairs or veneer replacement can be time consuming and difficult, and involve the use of special tools. These jobs are best left to a professional.

In most cases, surface damage and finish damage can be repaired on veneered furniture in the same manner as solid wood furniture. See "Chapter 1 – Repairs to the Finish" and "Chapter 2 – Repairs to the Wood" for these repairs.

Repairing Dents in Veneer
Dents can usually be lifted from veneers in much the same manner as from solid wood. Prick several small holes into the grain of the wood in the dented area. Place a small piece of damp lint-free fabric over the dent. Apply a clothes iron (set to the "nylon/silk" setting) to the material to produce steam. Remove the iron after a few seconds to check your progress. Do not keep the iron on the wood too long as the heat and steam may damage the finish or soften the old glue. Allow the repair area to dry thoroughly, then apply a coat of wax or lemon oil.

Repairing Lifting Edges
If the veneer is lifting at the edges of the furniture, carefully lift the veneer with a thin knife blade and scrape the old glue from the veneer and base wood. Be careful not to punch the knife blade through the veneer surface. Take your

time and remove as much of the old glue as possible. Take care to brush the crumbled glue forward and out to remove it from the pocket so it will not get trapped under the veneer when it is reglued.

When the glue is completely removed, apply a plastic resin glue or wood glue to both the veneer and the base wood with a palette knife or small pen-knife blade. Do not use ordinary household glue for this repair as it will eventually lose its grip and cause the veneer to buckle and break. Apply clamps to the edge and tighten to apply pressure. **Do not over tighten the clamps!** If the clamps are too tight they will bruise the wood, and may force glue out from under the veneer.

Repairing Veneer Blisters

Veneer blisters are generally caused from moisture penetrating between veneer and the base wood. Moisture causes glue to soften and deteriorate. If the old glue is animal-based, it is often possible to repair the blister by applying heat. If the glue is a synthetic glue or contact cement, it will be necessary to cut the veneer to make the repair.

To repair the blister by applying heat: cover the blister with a piece of wax paper, then apply several layers of lint free cloth. Heat a clothes iron to the "nylon/silk" setting and touch the tip of the iron on the cloth. Remove the iron every couple of seconds to check on your progress. Some old glues are softened by heat and will once again be able to grip the wood. If the glue appears to bond, apply pressure to the repaired area until the glue has completely set.

If the heat method does not work, cut the blister with a new single edge razor blade or X-acto knife, down the full length of the blister. Cut along the grain lines whenever possible to make the repair less noticeable. Apply white vinegar to the inside of the blister with an artist's brush to help remove the old glue. Try to remove as much dirt and dried glue as possible. Allow sufficient time for the veneer and base wood to dry before proceeding.

Glue injector

Inject plastic-resin glue or wood glue into the blistered area with a *glue injector* or syringe, or apply with the edge of a knife blade or toothpick. Roll the area with a veneer roller or wallpaper seam roller to apply pressure and force out all excess glue. Clamp the repair if possible, or apply pressure with weights. Remove clamps after 3 to 4 hours. Allow glue to dry overnight.

Repairing Broken Veneer

Chests, tables and drawers are the most likely candidates to develop chipped veneer on their edges or ends. When a piece breaks off, save it and attempt to make the repair as soon as possible for the best results. A prompt repair will be easier to do and will prevent further damage from occurring. If the repair can not be done at the time of the break, place the veneer piece in a labeled envelope, in a safe place, so it will not be lost or damaged.

Broken and missing veneer.

The same piece after repairs.

Remove the old glue from the back of the piece of veneer and from the base wood of the furniture. Lightly scrape off the old glue with a knife blade or razor blade, being careful not to damage the edges of the veneer. Take your time and remove as much of the old glue as possible as it may prevent proper adhesion of the new glue or cause lumps under the repaired area. Dab the old glue with white vinegar, if necessary, to remove stubborn spots, and allow the wood to dry thoroughly. Apply a plastic-resin glue or wood glue to the piece of veneer and replace. Wipe off any excess glue with a damp cloth or paper towel. Clamp the repair or apply weight with a stack of books or bean bags until the glue sets. Remove clamps after 3 or 4 hours. Allow glue to dry overnight. Small gaps or seams can be hidden by filling them with wax or shellac stick (see pages 50-52) in a matching color.

If the veneer has broken, and the piece is missing, place a piece of wax paper over the area and carefully trace the shape of the missing piece. Cut out the shape to use as a pattern. Find an inconspicuous place on the furniture (usually the back, lower sides, or bottom) where you can remove a small piece of veneer for the replacement piece, or buy a small piece of veneer of similar wood from a lumber yard, or woodworker's supply store. Try to match the grain and color as carefully as possible. Remember, the wood will need to be finished after the repair, and most finishes will add some color to the wood. Dampen a corner of the veneer to get an idea of how it will look when finished. If you can not match the color, get veneer that is a lighter shade and stain it to match.

Clean any dirt and wax from the repair area with mineral spirits. Use white vinegar to remove old glue residue. Allow to dry thoroughly. Trace the pattern on to the veneer, and carefully cut it out with an X-Acto knife or new single edge razor blade. Check to make sure the veneer patch will fit into repair area. If the new veneer is not as thick as the old veneer, use the pattern piece to cut a piece of tissue paper to the proper shape. Glue the paper to the area and allow to dry prior to applying veneer patch. If tissue paper does not raise the veneer patch to the proper height, it may be necessary to use a small piece of balsa wood cut to shape, or two pieces of veneer.

If the patch is too thick, sand with the grain on the underside of the patch until it will sit flush with the surrounding wood. Make a holder for the patch to make the sanding easier. Form a ring of masking tape by folding it over your fingers and sticking the ends together. Place the right side of the veneer patch on to the sticky side of the tape. This will expose the underside of the patch for easy sanding.

Apply a plastic resin glue or wood glue to the veneer patch, and carefully apply it to the repair area. Clean off any excess glue with a damp cloth or white paper towel. Use clamps, or weights to apply pressure until the glue sets. Remove clamps after 3 or 4 hours. Allow glue to dry overnight. Apply a finish coat over the repair area, blending the edges. Allow finish to dry.

Any remaining small gaps or seams can be hidden by filling with wax or lacquer stick in a matching color (see pages 50-52).

Small pieces of loose or missing inlay can be replaced using the same techniques described for broken or missing veneer.

Chapter 4

Repairing Chairs

Chairs are subject to more use and abuse than any other kind of furniture, and as such are the most frequently repaired. Damage will usually occur in those parts receiving the most wear and stress. Leg posts are stressed when a chair is tipped back on its legs. The bottoms of feet may show extensive wear from being pushed and pulled across rough floors. Seat rails, and back posts suffer stress damage from pulling, twisting, and turning. But stretchers (also commonly called *rungs*) can potentially receive the most damage.

Round stretchers will almost always break at or near the tenon (the piece of wood that fits into the hole to form the joint) as that is the weakest point. Stretchers are usually no more than 7/8" diameter, and are not intended to individually support direct weight. Consequently, a break in the middle of the stretcher is usually evidence of improper use. Simply regluing this type of break is usually not sufficient to bear the stress of continued use.

Rectangular stretchers are made from thicker pieces of wood and do not break as frequently as round stretchers. When they do break, it is generally the tenon that will break and not the main body of the stretcher. The same techniques can be effectively used to repair either round or rectangular stretchers.

Back posts are most likely to break in the area where the two seat rails meet, because this is the area that receives the most stress and is the weakest area of the post. On an arm chair, back posts might also break where the arm is connected to the post.

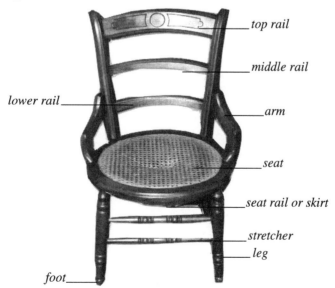

top rail

middle rail

lower rail

arm

seat

seat rail or skirt

stretcher

leg

foot

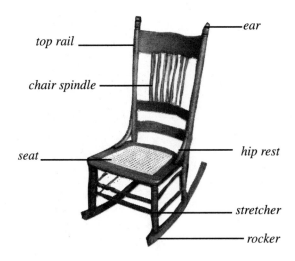

Routine check-ups and maintenance can prolong the life of your chairs, and knowledge of basic chair construction can alert you to potential problems and prevent unnecessary damage.

Chair back designs fall into two categories: those that are independent of the rear legs, and those that are formed by the two continuous rear legs extending from the floor up to the head rail.

Chair back is independent of rear legs.

Rear legs extending from the floor to head rail.

Continuous rear leg chairs were more expensive to produce, but offer a great deal more strength then the type whose back posts were simply inserted into holes drilled in the seat. The advantage of the latter type of chair, from a repair perspective, is that the posts tend to loosen before they break. Loose posts can easily be repaired at home with minimal equipment. Broken ones require more complex equipment and skill and should be taken to a professional.

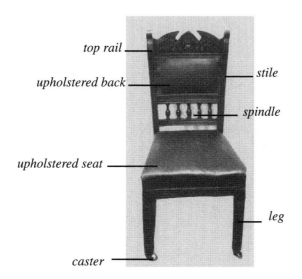

top rail

upholstered back

stile

spindle

upholstered seat

leg

caster

Dining chairs, occasional chairs, and over-stuffed easy chairs and sofas, all of which usually have padded seats with no underbracing, put a much greater strain on the chair frames than do wooden seats. These chairs are only as strong as the joints in the frames, and often have unstable front rails or side rails which are loose at their juncture with the back rail and legs.

Repairing Chair Spindles

Loose or broken chair spindles can start out as a minor repair and turn into a major one if not treated promptly. Spindles serve more than a decorative purpose in the design of the chair, and all spindles must be secure and in good repair for the chair to remain stable. When one goes, the others will soon follow. Loose spindles can be repaired in the same manner as loose chair stretchers. (See "Repairing Loose Chair Stretchers" page 66.)

Broken spindles create a bigger challenge. Most spindles or rungs will split along the grain. If the grain is angled enough to produce a long break once, it will probably happen again. The repair is easiest if the spindle can be removed from the chair prior to making the repair. Remove the spindle by gently twisting and pulling. Stubborn spindles may be loosened by applying white vinegar to the end of the spindle. Allow vinegar to soften the glue, then gently twist and pull the spindle.

After the spindle is removed, apply wood glue to the ends of the broken pieces and carefully match them together. Apply pressure with clamps to assure a good bond.

Small metal C-clamps work well for repairs on spindles and rungs because of their size, but can damage wood with their metal ends. To prevent damage, use hot-melt glue to attach caps from 35mm film containers to the swivel ends of the clamps. The caps will provide protection for the wood, and are easily removable.

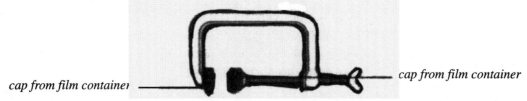

cap from film container ———————————— *cap from film container*

Allow the glued spindle to dry at least 24 hours. Replace the spindle to its position in the chair by applying glue to the inside of the hole (not on the end of the spindle) and reinserting the spindle. Apply pressure with clamps or tourniquets to assure a good bond.

If you do not want to (or are unable to) remove the spindle, some breaks can be successfully rejoined by applying wood glue to both broken ends, then carefully matching the two pieces back together. Apply pressure with clamps to assure a good bond. Any remaining small gaps and imperfections can be filled with lacquer stick, or one of the other methods used to repair dents in wood. (See "Removing Dents" page 49.)

Repairing Loose Back Slats
The slats in the back of a chair are usually supposed to "float"– that is, rest loosely in the slots they fit into. If the slat is glued into place, the wood's ability to expand and contract will be inhibited, and the wood may crack. If the loose slats rattle noticeably, and you feel that they must be immobilized, use a water soluble glue for the repair. Inject glue into the slot and apply pressure with clamps until the glue has set. Water soluble glue is less likely to inhibit the wood's expansion and contraction and will crumble and break away from the wood rather than keeping its bond and allowing the wood to deteriorate.

Chair-Loc (a wood expanding fluid used to swell wood and keep it permanently swollen) can also be used to stabilize loose slats. Squeeze a small amount into the slot and apply pressure. Immediately wipe off any excess that oozes out as it may leave a dark stain on the finish, and is difficult to remove when dry. (Chair-Loc is available at woodworking supply stores. See Appendix for sources.)

Stabilizing Chairs

One of the best ways of repairing unstable chairs is to add triangular corner blocks to the corners of the frame, securing them with glue and four countersunk screws– two on either side of the corner. The blocks should be at least 3" long on the 90° angle sides and at least 1-1/2" thick.

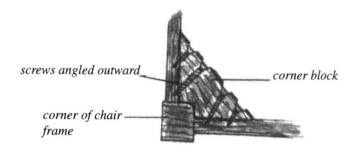

screws angled outward — corner block

corner of chair frame

It is important that the point of the 90° angle fit exactly into the corner, and the two abutting sides must meet the frame. Drill screw holes through the triangular reinforcement to penetrate the chair frame. These holes should not be straight in, but angled outward like the spokes of a fan for the best support. Each screw will probably be a slightly different length, because the holes are slanted differently. Apply glue to the holes, then thread in the screws. When the glue is dry, wooden plugs can be glued over the countersunk screw heads.

If the wobbly chair already has corner braces as part of its original frame, and the problem is not a simple case of loose screws, remove the screws and replace with the next larger size and apply new glue to the braces.

Replacing Hip Rests

Many old wooden side chairs had hip rests, a curved piece of wood which joined the seat and back at the sides. Hip rests act as a brace between the back of the chair and the seat, and help stabilize the chair. If they are broken or missing, the chair may become unsteady and the back side posts may break. Replacements can be purchased from many hardware stores or woodworking supply stores. Hip rests (replacement or the originals if you have them) are simply screwed to the chair's seat and back. Use the old screw holes to help with the proper placement.

Old screws will be less noticeable for this repair as the screw heads will show when the repair is complete. If old screws are unavailable, new ones can be aged by dipping in a commercial product made for this purpose, (available through woodworking supply stores and some hardware stores), or by home methods. One simple home method is to hold the screw with a pair of pliers and place it in a candle flame until it starts to discolor. Remove from the flame and wipe with a cloth until the screw is left with a slight discoloration. Top coat the screws with lacquer to seal in the discoloration.

The hip rest is attached to the stile with a screw here.

The hip rest is attached to the seat with a screw here.

Repairing Loose Chair Stretchers (Rungs)

One of the most common furniture problems is loose rungs stretching between the legs of chairs. Fortunately, it is also one of the easiest problems to fix. Loose stretchers are especially prevalent during winter months. Dry air and low humidity dry wood and deteriorate old glue causing stretchers to shrink and become loose in their sockets. Once loosened, they will cause additional stress on the remaining stretchers, increasing the chance that they too will fail. To prevent a minor problem from becoming a major one, loose stretchers should be repaired as soon as possible. Left unattended, a loose stretcher could lead to broken components or necessitate the complete rebuilding of the chair.

To check for loose stretchers, stand at the front of the chair and try to rock it from front to back and side to side. If any part of the frame rocks, or exposes some lighter colored, unpolished wood on the faces of the joints (no matter how small an amount) that section of the frame needs to be cleaned and stabilized to prevent further damage. If one joint has failed the rest will probably follow. It is a good idea to stabilize all joints at the same time.

Fill a syringe or glue injector with wood glue and insert the needle into the loose joint. Do not attempt to pull the rung and chair apart! If necessary, drill a small hole into the joint cavity to allow the glue to penetrate. It is important to remember to use wood glue for the repairs and *not* epoxy glues. Wood glue will expand and contract with the wood and will adjust to changing pressure. Epoxy glue will make the repair stronger than the wood itself and could result in a broken stretcher instead of a loose one.

If the wood has shrunken and no longer fills the cavity, thin pieces of veneer or toothpicks can be inserted next to the rung. Any excess wood protruding from the cavity can be trimmed off with a single edge razor blade or X-acto knife after the glue has set. Pieces of cotton balls can also be soaked in glue and pushed into the cavity. Or, wrap thread around the dowel, then coat it with glue to take up the slack.

Chair-Loc is a wood expanding fluid used to swell wood fibers and keep them swollen permanently. It works very well when the fit of the stretcher is not overly loose in the socket. Squirt Chair-Loc into the cavity surrounding the loose spindle or turning and then allow to penetrate. To prevent surface discoloration, wipe off excess liquid before it has a chance to dry. Chair-Loc works especially well on chair backs and delicate turnings where other types of repairs would be ugly or distracting. (Chair-Loc is available from woodworking supply stores. See Appendix for sources.)

Repairing Broken Chair Stretchers (Rungs)

If the end of the chair rung has broken off where it connects into the leg, the repair should be made as soon as possible. Failure to do so will put additional stress on the remaining stretchers resulting in additional breaks. Apply wood glue or hide glue to both of the broken segments and rejoin them exactly as they came apart. Clamp the repair until the glue has dried.

Measure 2" from the end of a 1/4" drill bit and apply a piece of tape. The tape will help to accurately gauge the depth of the hole. Drill a 1/4" diameter by 2" hole through the chair leg and into the stretcher, being careful to keep the hole centered and straight. Drill the hole until the tape touches the wood. Liberally coat a 2" by 1/4" wooden dowel with wood glue. Tap the coated dowel into the hole; countersink just below the surface. When the glue has dried, fill the hole with wax putty stick, or shellac stick (see pages 50-52).

Repairing Split Chair Stretchers (Rungs)

Apply glue to both of the broken segments and rejoin them exactly as they came apart. Apply pieces of scrap wood to the top and bottom of the rung to help distribute the pressure and protect the rung, and apply clamps. Allow the glue to dry completely. Any small gaps in the stretcher can be filled with wax putty stick or shellac stick (see pages 50-52) after the repair is complete.

Repairing a Cracked Rocking Chair Rocker

Chair rockers, and other curved furniture pieces generally break along the grain of the wood. To repair a broken rocker, lay the chair face down on the floor and gently scrape the break clean with a thin knife blade. Be careful not to remove surrounding wood. Spread a thin layer of wood glue or hide glue inside the break or inject glue with a syringe or glue injector. Reassemble the pieces exactly as they came apart. Wipe away any excess glue with a damp cloth or paper towel. Wrap the repaired area with wax paper, then apply thin pieces of wood to the top and bottom edges of the rocker on each side of the break. Apply clamps to provide pressure. Allow the glue to set for at least 4 hours, then release clamps. Any small gaps in the rocker can be filled with wax putty stick, or shellac stick (see pages 50 -52) after the repair is complete.

Rocking chair rockers usually break because of excess stress placed on the wood. Breaks will usually occur along the grain lines.

A severe break may require inserting a dowel into the repaired area to reinforce the rocker. To determine the depth of the dowel hole, measure along the side of the rocker. The dowel will be inserted from the bottom of the rocker, through the break, and two thirds of the way into the rocker. Mark the hole position with an awl. Use a drill bit the same size as the dowel (usually 1/4" to 3/8" diameter) and put a piece of masking tape on the bit to mark the depth of the hole. Drill a hole at the mark on the rocker, stopping when the tape on the drill bit touches the rocker.

Cut a dowel 1" longer than the depth of the hole and bevel one end slightly with some coarse sandpaper. Draw the dowel through the jaws of pliers to score its sides. This will allow excess glue and air to escape as the dowel is forced into the hole. Spread a thin layer of wood glue on the dowel. Place the beveled end of the dowel in the hole. Tap it in with a rubber mallet. Wipe away excess glue with a damp cloth or paper towel. Allow the glue to set for at least 24 hours.

Use a coping saw to cut the dowel flush with the surface of the rocker. Use medium sandpaper, then fine sandpaper to smooth down the dowel. Use a fine artist's brush to apply wood stain, oil paint, acrylic paint or other colorant to restore color to the repaired area. Allow sufficient drying time. Do a spot test in an inconspicuous area to determine the type of finish on the rocker. Apply one or more coats of finish with a fine artist's brush, feathering the edges so they blend with the existing finish. Allow sufficient drying time between coats.

Getting Rid of Squeaks in Wooden Chairs

Squeaks in most chairs are caused by moisture loss in the wood. As the wood dries, the dowels shrink and no longer fit properly in their cavities. Apply Chair-Loc (a wood expanding fluid used to swell wood fibers and keep them swollen permanently) around the loose furniture joints. It will absorb into the hole and expand the wood surface to make the joints fit tight. Wipe off any excess liquid to prevent possible finish discoloration. (Chair-Loc is available from woodworking supply stores. See Appendix for sources.)

Repairing Loose or Wobbly Chair Legs

Turn the chair upside down to check for loose corner blocks. If the old screws are loose and cannot be retightened, replace them with the next size screw.

If the wobble is due to loose stretchers or rungs, try to inject wood glue into the cavity or drill a small hole into the cavity and inject the glue into it. Pound the stretcher or rungs firmly into place with a rubber mallet and use a tourniquet to clamp the legs. As a last resort you may have to knock the legs apart with a rubber mallet. Clean the old glue off of the rungs and stretchers and out of the cavity, and reassemble the chair using wood glue. Apply pressure with clamps or a tourniquet until the glue is set.

Repairing Loose or Wobbly Legs on Bentwood Chairs

The most common problem with bentwood chairs is they tend to wobble. The back legs are usually fastened to the chair seat by nuts and bolts, often complicated by a rounded top bolt. These bolts can wiggle loose and cause the whole chair to become wobbly. To remedy this problem, set the chair upside down so that the seat rests on a flat surface at a comfortable working height. Grip the nut with a pair of pliers or a wrench and the edge of the bolt with pliers. Hold the bolt still with one hand, while you turn the nut with the other. If the nut and bolt seem immovable, add a drop of oil and a drop of turpentine, and try again. When the bolts are securely tightened, the chair legs should once again be steady.

Reshaping Split Bentwood

The process for producing bentwood furniture was developed in Austria during the early part of the 19th Century by Michael Thonet, and the technique is still in use today. The wood is steamed and then slowly bent into different shapes while being held with quick-release metal clamps. The resulting bent wood is used to make the various components of the furniture.

If the wood is allowed to dry out, it may try to straighten and begin to split at the curves. You will need heat and moisture, similar to what was used in the construction, to repair the split.

Use a thin knife blade and scrape the interior surface of the split until it is clean. Be careful not to cut or scrape the wood. Wrap a damp cloth around the split area, then steam the wood by applying a hot steam iron to the cloth on all sides. Steam the split for approximately 15 minutes, wetting the cloth as it dries. This will make the split wood pliable.

Unwrap the cloth and press the split wood against the curve. To hold the wood in place, position automotive hose clamps at each end of the split and tighten the clamps with a screwdriver, alternating from one to the other. Do not over tighten the clamps so that the edges cut into the wood. Allow approximately 24 hours for the wood to dry, then release the clamps.

Ease open the split and use a toothpick, a glue injector, or a syringe to apply wood glue. Cover the interior surfaces of the split with an even coat of glue. Press the split together again and wipe away any excess glue with a damp cloth or paper towel. Wrap the split with wax paper and re-clamp with automotive hose clamps. Allow the glue to set for at least 24 hours, then release the clamps.

It may be necessary to do some minor repairs to the finish after reshaping bentwood furniture. The moisture and heat involved in the reshaping process may damage the finish.

Bentwood chairs were produced in large quantities during the middle of the 19th Century, and many of these chairs are still around today. Paper labels were commonly applied to the underside of the seats identifying the manufacturer, where the chair was produced, etc. Few of these original labels remain intact, but it is still worth checking for them prior to attempting any repair. If you are lucky enough to find an original manufacturer's label take care to protect it, as it can help you identify and date the piece, and will add to its value. See "Preserving and Protecting Furniture Labels" page 234.

Repairing a Loose Chair Arm
Check the back of the arm to see if there is a little wooden button or plug concealing a screw. Gently pry the button out with a knife or screwdriver, or drill out the wooden plug. Tighten the screw but take care not to overtighten it as this could crack the surrounding wood. Apply wood glue to the edges of the wood plug, and replace the plug.

If tightening the screw does not secure the loose arm, remove the screw and replace it with the next size larger screw. Apply wood glue to the edges of the button and replace. If the wooden button was damaged when it was removed, replacements are available at most lumber yards and woodworking supply stores. Use the instructions on pages 34 and 35 "Repairing Scratches in the Finish" to match the color of the button with the rest of the chair.

Arms that are loose at the arm supports can also be injected with glue. Use wood glue for the repair, and clamp or use a tourniquet to apply pressure while the glue is setting.

Repairing a Split Chair Seat

Remove any old glue from the crack by scraping with a thin knife blade. Cotton swabs dabbed in vinegar can be used to remove stubborn glue. Apply wood glue or hide glue to both of the broken segments. Make sure the two surfaces and edges are exactly aligned. Apply pressure with clamps until the glue has set.

A tourniquet can also be used to apply the necessary pressure. Tourniquets can be made from soft rope or clothesline and a stick. Wrap the rope two or three times around the edge of the seat, using folded pieces of cardboard to protect the corners. Insert the stick into the rope and turn. This will tighten the rope and apply pressure on the chair.

Cleaning Leather Chair Seats

Natural leather is very rich-looking and beautiful, and is one of the strongest upholstery materials known to man. It will become even more beautiful with use if it is given proper care. Most leather seats can be cleaned by gently wiping with a mild solution of soap and water on a clean cloth that is wrung dry of excess moisture. Rinse with clear water using a clean, soft cloth, also wrung dry of excess water. Dry with a clean soft cloth. Use distilled bottled water and a white cloth for lighter colored leather furniture. Chlorine and residual minerals in tap water can cause discoloration on some light colored leathers.

White or light colored leather should be protected against permanent staining due to dye and ink transfer from newspapers, jeans, etc. *Do not* place leather furniture in direct sun or expose it to extreme temperatures. This may cause the leather to dry and crack. *Do not* allow grease or oil spills to remain on the leather. Use talcum powder or baking powder to absorb spills, then clean with a soft cloth moistened with a mild solution of soap and water. Wipe with a cloth moistened with clean water. Dry with a clean soft cloth.

To remove accumulated dirt and mild stains: Cut a fresh lemon in half. Rub the lemon on the leather chair seat. Wipe off lemon juice, then polish seat with leather conditioner.

Some manufacturers use vinyl on the less visible parts of leather furniture. This can be detrimental to the furniture in the long run because leather and synthetics age differently.

 Pro Tip:
You may occasionally come across a chair seat covered with suede (leather with a napped surface). Never use leather cleaning products on suede unless they are specifically designed to clean suede as well. Suede spots easily and absorbs dirt readily. To clean, gently rub against the nap, and then with the nap, using a soft brush. Some stains may be removed from suede by gently rubbing with a gum eraser.

Cleaning Vinyl Seats

Vinyl seats should be periodically cleaned to remove accumulated soil, but should not be oiled. Body oils, polishes, or even air-born oils from cooking can harden vinyl, making it impossible to re-soften, and causing it to crack. Built-up soil can be removed with a paste of baking soda and water. Scrub soiled area with a dampened cloth. Wipe with cloth dampened in clear water and dry thoroughly. White vinegar added to the rinse water will help reduce static.

A mild cleaning solution can be made by mixing 2 teaspoons liquid detergent with 2 cups of water. Dampen cloth with solution and wipe on soil. Wipe with a clean damp cloth. Dry thoroughly. Do not use abrasives, strong cleansers, or chlorine bleach to clean vinyl seats. Remove seat from chair frame, if possible prior to cleaning, to prevent damage from water or cleaning solution.

Re-covering Drop-In Seats

Drop in seats (also called slip seats or pad seats) are the simplest of all furniture to reupholster. They have no springs to disconnect and re-tie, and little or no decorative gimp or trim. Most pad seats are removable by simply unscrewing and removing the screws on the underside of the seat frame. Set the chair upside down on a sturdy work surface. Remove the screws from the corner blocks or from under the seat itself. Push up on the seat and it should dislodge from the frame.

screws attaching the seat are found under the seat in the corner blocks or in the seat itself _____

_____ *drop in seat*

Carefully remove the old tacks or staples from the underside of the seat by lifting out with a tack remover or screwdriver. *Never attempt to put a new seat cover over an old one.* This will make the seat too big, and can cause the seat rail joints to break when the seat is reinserted into the frame.

Gently lift off the old fabric, but do not disturb the padding underneath. Note how the fabric was pleated or cut to fit around back posts, legs or seat base. Lay the new fabric face down on a flat work surface. Iron the old fabric cover if necessary to make it lie flat, then trace its outline on to the new fabric with a pencil or tailor's chalk. Replicate the old cover's pleats and cuts as closely as possible to ensure the new cover fits properly. Remove the old cover and cut out the new cover with sharp scissors.

Set the new cover on a flat work surface with the right side facing down. Lay the seat on top of the new cover. Fold the fabric up around the seat, pulling it tight, and hammer in tacks or use a staple gun to hold the fabric temporarily. Pleat the fabric at the corners and tuck it in. Turn over the seat and check for pulled fabric or wrinkles. If there are any, remove the tack or staple nearest the wrinkle, pull the cover tight, and refasten. Cut away excess material from corner pleats. Drive tacks, or staples all around the seat at 1" intervals. Replace the seat into the chair frame, and replace screws and corner blocks.

Removing Impressions from Upholstered Seats

Velvet material and other materials with a nap, may develop lasting impressions as a result of heat or moisture and weight being applied to them. To raise the nap back to normal and remove the impression, lay a piece of woolen fabric over the spot. On top of that place a piece of dampened muslin. Heat an electric clothes iron to the "cotton/linen" setting and rub the iron back and forth over the muslin. The wool will protect the napped fabric, while the steam from the muslin passes through to soften the crushed nap. Remove the cloths and carefully brush up the nap with a toothbrush. Allow to dry thoroughly before use.

Take care not to over-dampen the fabric while attempting to remove impressions. Many older chairs were stuffed with horsehair or down, and some still exist today with the original marsh grass stuffing. These old materials could be damaged by excess moisture.

Polishing and Preventing Rust on Chrome Chairs

Chrome is easy to clean but the highly polished surface is easily scratched and can be discolored by strong chemicals. For general cleaning, wash chrome with detergent and water; rinse and polish dry to prevent water spots. Commercial liquid glass cleaner can also be used to remove grease and dirt. Spray liquid glass cleaner on the chrome and wipe with a soft cloth. Some stains may be removed from chrome by rubbing with a soft cloth dipped in baby oil. When stains are removed, polish with another soft cloth. Stubborn grime can be removed by rubbing with a damp sponge dipped in baking soda or cider vinegar. Rinse with water, and buff dry.

Automotive chrome polish can be used to remove built-up grime, and slight rust on chrome chairs. Pour a small amount of chrome polish on a damp cloth and rub lightly on the chrome. Work on a small area at a time. Buff with a soft cloth.

To prevent rust and to make the chrome easier to keep clean, apply a light coat of wax. Work on a small area at a time. Apply a thin coat of wax with a soft cloth. Allow to sit until the wax forms a haze, then buff with a soft cloth.

 Pro Tip:
If chrome chairs are to be put away for storage, coat the chrome parts with Vaseline to prevent rust and pitting. The Vaseline can be removed later by buffing with a soft cloth.

Chapter 5

Repairing Tables

Next to chairs, tables are among the most abundant pieces of furniture and one of the most often restored. Even though they run the gamut from small telephone tables and fern stands to massive dining tables, every table is basically a flat surface supported by legs. Table tops receive most of the "wear and tear" and abuse. But table bases can encounter broken stretchers, broken legs, damaged feet, or broken leaf supports. Most table repairs are not more complicated than repairs on other furniture, they just need to be done on a larger scale.

Table stretchers are no different from those found on chairs, and can be repaired in the same manner. (See "Repairing Loose Chair Stretchers" page 66 and "Repairing Broken Chair Stretchers" page 67.)

Table legs are generally not subjected to movement, and unlike chair legs they seldom break. When they do, it is not uncommon for the damage to be in the area of the feet, as it is the weakest part of the leg. A repair to the foot of a table will usually involve trimming the broken foot, creating a new piece on a lathe to recreate the missing or broken pieces, then reassembling and refinishing the table base. This is a job best left to the professionals. Minor dents in the feet can be repaired and small missing wood areas replaced by following the techniques for repairing dents. (See "Removing Dents" page 49.)

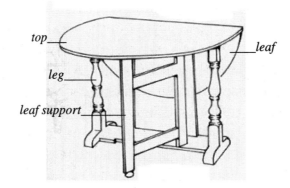

Repairing Broken Drop-Leaf Table Supports

Drop-leaf tables have pivots or leaf supports that either pull out or swing out to support the table leaves. These supports are subjected to a great deal of stress through daily use and can break on occasion. Remove the table top and make a reference point on the underside of the table so that it can be replaced in the same manner that it was removed. Mark the screws as they are removed so they will also be replaced properly. If at all possible, remove the table top with the leaves still attached – but be careful not to place unnecessary stress on the hinges or leaves.

If the support has suffered a clean break, remove the support from the table base. Apply wood glue to both of the broken pieces and rematch carefully. Apply pressure with clamps to assure a good bond. Allow glue to dry for at least 24 hours. Reassemble table taking care to replace table top and screws in their original locations.

If the support has not broken cleanly, a new one will have to be made. Remove the undamaged leaf support and trace its shape on to a piece of paper. Transfer the pattern to a piece of cardboard, and cut out the shape, cutting it just a little larger than the pattern. Fit the cardboard piece to the recess left by the broken support and trim where necessary. The original leaf supports may look similar, but because of different stress and wear may not be identical. Do not attempt to duplicate the remaining support without checking for differences. Cut a new support using the cardboard pattern, and replace on table base. Reassemble table taking care to replace table top and screws in their original locations.

Repairing Drooping Table Leaves

Wood dries out and shrinks with age. Over time, this can cause drop-leaf table leaves to appear to wilt or droop even when fully opened and properly supported. The wood of the table support or the wood of the table leaf may be to blame. To remedy the drooping problem, use wood glue to attach small pieces of veneer to the tops of the leaf supports. Apply pressure with clamps to assure a good bond. Multiple veneer pieces may be applied, if necessary, to attain the correct height. Allow sufficient time for the glue to dry between applications.

Straightening a Warped Leaf

Wood needs to have an equal distribution of moisture throughout its pores in order for it to remain flat. If moisture is able to penetrate one side of the wood and not the other because of a protective finish or if one side loses more moisture than the other, the wood will warp. To prevent warping, all flat wood surfaces should have a finish coat applied to both the topside and the underside. To repair a piece that has already warped, you will have to apply moisture to the dried out side. This will always be the concave side.

Warping problems are usually not permanent and even old warps or twisted warps can be straightened with time and patience. However, once the board is flat it must be held that way or it will eventually warp again as it dries. The time necessary to correct warping varies greatly with the type of wood and its age. Softwoods like pine will respond quickly, while hardwoods like cherry will respond more slowly.

The easiest way to remove a warp from a table leaf is to place the leaf concave side down on the grass in your yard and let the sun shine on it. The moisture from the grass and the heat from the sun should remove the warp in a few days. When the board looks straight, take it inside for a few days to see if the warp returns. If some slight warping reoccurs, put it back out in the sun for another treatment.

If the board is warped and twisted, you will have to apply weights on the high spots while applying the heat and moisture treatment. Keep in mind that while moisture will remove the warp from the wood it might also damage the finish or any water-soluble glue used to construct the furniture. You may have to do some minor regluing or touch up the finish once the board is straightened.

Straightening a Warped Table Top

When a finish is applied to only the top surface of a piece of furniture, it inhibits the absorption of moisture from the atmosphere, while the lack of finish on the other side allows for a great deal of absorption. The result of this will be warping, or to be technically correct, *cupping* so called because the wood edges tend to warp upward towards the finished side of the wood.

The top will need to be removed from the base to properly make the repair. Turn the table upside down if possible. Make a reference point on the bottom of the table so that it can be replaced in the same manner that it was removed. Mark the screws as they are removed so they will also be replaced properly. Take the top from the base. Place the table top in the sunshine on the grass in your yard with the concave side down, the same as you would to remove the warp from a table leaf. If extra moisture is required, a damp towel can be placed under the table top.

Table tops that are badly warped can sometimes be corrected by kerfing the wood; running a number of small lengthwise cuts 1" to 1-1/2" apart on the convex side of the board to eliminate the stress and therefore the warp. This can be difficult to do without cutting clear through the boards, and requires a table saw or circular saw, so this technique is probably best left to professionals if it is to be done at all.

After the warp is straightened, and the wood has completely dried, several coats of finish should be applied to the underside of the wood. Remember the warp was caused in the first place by unequal moisture absorption and the additional protective finish will prevent the problem from recurring.

Repairing a Split Table Top

Table tops splits are usually caused by one of two reasons: either the glue between the boards dries out and cracks breaking the bond between the wood, or, the wood dries out and shrinks while it is secured to the frame or base of the furniture. Eventually something has got to give and the wood will crack and separate. If dried glue is the problem, the boards will need to be cleaned, reglued and clamped. If moisture loss is the culprit, the moisture level in the wood will have to be restored to prevent any further damage. Then the warp, if any, will have to be straightened (See "Straightening a Warped Leaf" page 79 and "Straightening a Warped Table Top" at the top of this page.)

Small cracks in the table top can be filled with lacquer stick or shellac stick, or wood putty stained to match (see pages 50-52.). Very fine hairline cracks can be filled with beeswax. Rub the beeswax over the crack and wipe off excess with a soft cloth.

Larger cracks will have to be glued and clamped. Clean out the split. Remove as much of the old glue as possible, using white vinegar if necessary to remove stubborn spots. Brush undiluted white vinegar on the stubborn spots with a fine artist's brush. Give the vinegar sufficient time to soften the glue, then wipe away with rags or white paper towels. Allow the wood to dry thoroughly.

Apply wood glue to both sides of the split and allow to set according to the label directions. Use furniture clamps or pipe clamps (with clamp pads for protection) to supply proper pressure for a good glue bond. Use one clamp every 8" alternating the clamps above and below the table top to prevent the top from curling under the pressure. Remove any excess glue that may squeeze out and clean the wood surface. Allow 24 hours for the glue to dry. Remove the clamps.

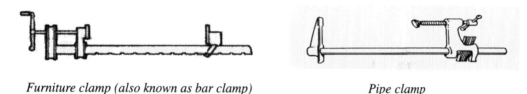

Furniture clamp (also known as bar clamp)　　　　*Pipe clamp*

Lubricating a Wooden Extension Mechanism

Extend the table top as wide as possible to expose the entire length of the wood runners. Use a sharp knife or chisel blade, and scrape the accumulated dirt, wax or lubricant from the runners. Take care not to gouge the wood. Use gum turpentine or mineral spirits on a soft cloth if necessary to remove wax or grease, then wipe with a dry cloth. Rub a block of paraffin or a candle in the runners to leave a thin coat of wax. Open and close the table a few times to help distribute the new lubricant evenly.

Wooden extension mechanism

Repairing a Sticking Sprocket Extension Mechanism

Extend the table top as wide as possible to expose the entire length of the mechanism. If the sprocket is loose, use a screwdriver to tighten the screw in the center of the sprocket. If the screw hole has become enlarged so that the screw no longer will tighten, remove the screw and sprocket. Fill the hole with flat toothpicks and wood glue. Allow the glue to dry at least 4 hours. Replace the screw and sprocket. The toothpicks will provide additional wood so the screw will fit tighter when reinserted.

If the sprocket is clogged with dirt, remove the screw and lift off the sprocket. Spray lubricant on the sprocket and scrub with a small brush or old toothbrush. Replace the sprocket making sure that the teeth mesh with the teeth on the tracks, and carefully spray the tracks with lubricant. Protect the surrounding areas to prevent damage from lubricant over-spray.

Cleaning and Redressing a Butcher Block Table

Butcher block tables are generally made from hardwoods – rock maple, sugar maple, beech and birch. Some tables intended for dining and uses other than food preparation are made of oak in the butcher block style. But, oak is not used for butcher blocks intended to be chopped on, because it is too porous. In fact, oak is not permitted for most commercial uses because the porosity makes it difficult to keep clean. Most butcher blocks are "*end-grain solid block construction*". This means that flat grain panels are glued so that the ends face up to form the cutting surface. Boards are cut thin and glued together to reduce the potential warpage that could result from using wide boards, and to add strength. End grain construction results in the least durable surface, but the best cutting surface.

The best and least destructive method of cleaning built up dirt and grease from a butcher block surface is by scraping. Use a wide blade scraper (available in most houseware departments or variety stores) and gently scrape the top, following the grain. Do not use excessive pressure, and take care not to remove any wood.

If the top is excessively dirty or greasy, you can use sandpaper to help cut through the layers, but you should always try scraping the surface first. Grease will load-up the sandpaper and you will have to change paper often. But, it will also act as a lubricant on the end grain and make the final surface very smooth. Use a sanding block to hold the sandpaper and make sure that you rub with the grain at all times. Fine sandpaper should have enough grit to smooth all but the most roughed-up butcher blocks.

After the wood is scraped or sanded, scrub the surface to clean it of any remaining dirt and grease and to remove any wood residue. *Use water cautiously!* Water can be very damaging to wood, especially end grain wood, and most glues used in the construction of butcher blocks are *water-resistant* not *waterproof.* Water will cause the wood to expand and may create or accentuate cracks in the cutting surface. Use as little water as possible, and *never* leave water standing on the surface. A small amount of soap or TSP can be added to the water to help dissolve grease and remove dirt. Make sure the soap or degreaser you use is not toxic and will not have any harmful effect on food.

Follow up any washing by rubbing a coat of oil into the wood pores. This will prevent cracking and prevent the wood from drying out. Use only oils that contain FDA approved ingredients. "Martens Wood Preservative" and "Chicago Cutlery Wood Conditioner" are two good examples of products that are FDA approved. These products and others for use on butcher blocks, are available from woodworking supply stores, variety stores, and some hardware stores.

Vegetable oil should not be used on butcher blocks. It provides minimal protection to the wood, and tends to leave a sticky surface that can turn rancid. Mineral oil should also not be used to condition butcher blocks because it will only provide short-term protection and may not be FDA approved.

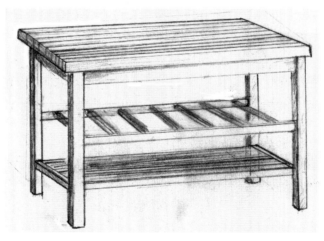

A properly oiled and maintained butcher block table will provide many years of service.

Opened joints or cracks that have formed in the butcher block surface are difficult to fill satisfactorily if the block is to be used as a food surface. Left unfilled, they can trap food particles, which in turn will breed bacteria and decay that will contaminate fresh food placed on the cutting surface. Wood putty can be used to fill smaller cracks. Choose a brand that is nontoxic when dry and follow the directions for application carefully. Smaller cracks can be filled with a paraffin mixture.

Use 1 part paraffin and 4 parts nontoxic mineral oil, and melt them together in a double boiler. Be careful – paraffin is very flammable! Apply the mixture to the cracked butcher block surface with a plastic scraper or spatula. Allow to set, then scrape off the excess with a plastic scraper. A windshield scraper or plastic pastry scraper works good for this. Rub the surface with the edge of the scraper to work the wax into the cracks and give the surface a nice sheen. Repeat this procedure approximately every four to six weeks.

Do not attempt to apply a clear finish or stain to a butcher block if it is to be used as a food surface. The finish will flake off and contaminate food. Wood stains generally do not penetrate well into maple, beech or birch (the woods traditionally used for butcher block construction) and may also contaminate the food surface.

A properly oiled and maintained butcher block will usually not develop stains from use. If a grease stain or other stain should penetrate the protective oil barrier, it generally will not penetrate very deeply. To remove stains, soak a white dishcloth or rag with bleach and lay it over the stained area. After 10 or 15 minutes, remove the cloth and rinse the area with clear water. If stains remain, allow the wood to dry thoroughly, then use fine sand paper to lightly sand with the grain to remove the stain. Wipe off sanding residue with a damp sponge or cloth. Allow the wood to dry, then apply a coat of protective oil.

Dents or small gouges in the butcher block surface can usually be raised the same as dents in other wood surfaces. See "Removing Dents" page 49.

Wax or gum can be removed from the butcher block surface by first applying an ice pack to the area to make the wax or gum brittle. Then use a plastic credit card, a plastic scraper, or a fingernail to remove it. Always scrape with the grain to avoid damaging the wood surface.

Maintainance of Marble Table Tops

Marble tops can be found on a variety of tables from small fern stands and lamp tables to large coffee tables and buffett tables. These beautiful tops are for the most part very durable, but their finish is not impenetrable. They can be damaged by dirt, rust, water and a variety of stains that can be acquired during daily use. For general cleaning of marble table tops, see "Cleaning Marble Tops" page 100. For stain removal see "Removing Stains from Marble Tops" pages 101 and 102.

Beautiful marble table tops can be found on both contemporary and antique tables.

Mahogany liquor cabinet.

Chapter 6

Repairing Chests, Cabinets and Desks

The most common repairs on chests, cabinets, and desks will be done to the drawers. Drawers are one of the few moving parts on furniture and are usually subjected to daily use. Stress is put on the joints every time a drawer is pulled out. When you consider the number of times a drawer is opened and closed during the course of its lifetime, it is easy to understand why a little maintenance may occasionally be in order.

A drawer slides in and out of the cabinet on a system of runners and guides. The drawer sides may be grooved, forming guides that slide along wood runners in the sides of the cabinet. In other pieces of furniture, the bottom edges of the drawer sides may serve as runners. Wide drawers may have a middle runner to help distribute the weight.

Drawer runner inside cabinet. *Middle runner inside cabinet.*

Repairing Broken Drawer Bottoms

Whenever possible, the original drawer bottom should be repaired rather than replaced. Remove the drawer and turn it upside down. Try to separate the crack slightly and dab in wood glue. Tap the side of the drawer lightly with a rubber hammer until the crack is closed. If this method does not repair the crack the bottom will probably have to be removed.

Check to see if there are removable nails along the back and sides of the drawer. If nails are visible, carefully remove them. If there are no visible nail heads, it is usually an indication the drawer was glued. Moisten the glue with small amounts of water or white vinegar to help loosen and dissolve the glue.

Slide the bottom out of the grooves. To repair, follow directions for "Repairing Split Panels" page 92. To replace, cut a new bottom piece from plywood or 1/4" oak, using the measurements from the old drawer bottom as a guide. Lightly sand rough edges. Slide new or repaired bottom back into place and replace nails or reglue.

A badly stained or otherwise abused drawer bottom may sometimes be reused by removing it from the drawer, turning it over, and replacing it in the grooves. Try this before replacing the old drawer bottom with a new one. Reusing the original bottom will retain the authenticity of the piece, and is a quick and easy repair.

Loosening Stiff Drawers

Drawers are usually stiff and difficult to move because the wood has become swollen due to exposure to excessive moisture or damp weather. Basically, the drawer is now too large for the hole that it fits into. If the wood feels damp, remove the drawer and allow it to sit in warm sunshine, or use a hair dryer on low setting to dry the wood. The heat will evaporate the excess moisture and shrink the wood back to the proper size. Use low heat, keep the hair dryer moving, and keep it at least three to four inches from the wood. Heat from a hair dryer will also help to dislodge drawers that are stuck and cannot be completely removed.

Next, determine whether the drawer is sticking on the sides or the bottom. Usually the friction from the wood rubbing will leave a shiny, almost waxed, appearance making it easy to find the problem area. If the sides seem to be dragging, rub the outside of the sides and bottom of the drawer with soap, paraffin, or a candle. If the drawer still remains stiff, remove a little of the wood by lightly sanding with the grain using medium grade sandpaper. Stop frequently to test the way that the drawer fits so you do not remove too much wood. Finish the wood with furniture oil to seal out moisture.

In some cases the sides of the drawer may be stiff because the joints have become loose. Use wood glue to reglue them but be careful to maintain the squareness of the drawer. Wax the sides of the drawer after glue has completely dried to help the drawer glide more easily and to seal out moisture.

If the bottom of the drawer is sticking, applying furniture wax to the drawer runner will usually make it move easily again. Sticking drawers are often caused by dampness. Remove the piece of furniture from the damp environment, if possible, to prevent the stiff drawers from reoccurring.

If the stiff drawer is in a painted piece of furniture, the problem could be caused by a buildup of paint on the drawer runners. Remove the drawer and carefully apply a chemical paint stripper. Use a metal scraper to loosen paint. When the paint buildup has been removed, clean the area with mineral spirits and allow to dry. Lightly sand the runners with fine sandpaper to smooth the wood. Then rub soap, paraffin or a white candle on the runners to help reduce friction.

Drawers will sometimes not work properly on large pieces of furniture (i.e.: chests or dressers, etc.) because the framework of the piece may have gotten out of plumb from moving or from standing on an uneven floor. You can check for this by using a carpenter's level. The top of the piece should be level and the sides absolutely plumb for the drawers to work most efficiently. Move the furniture to a more level location if possible or shim up the legs by wedging thin strips of wood or cardboard under the low side. Continue wedging until the piece sits perfectly level from front to back and side to side.

Wood will shrink as it dries, and some pieces of furniture may get out of plumb or develop loose components from lack of moisture. Applications of lemon oil will help to remoisten the wood. Make sure the undersides and backsides of the furniture receive a good coat of lemon oil as well. To prevent unnecessary drying of the wood, the furniture should be moved to an area with a higher humidity level.

the top of large pieces should be level ____

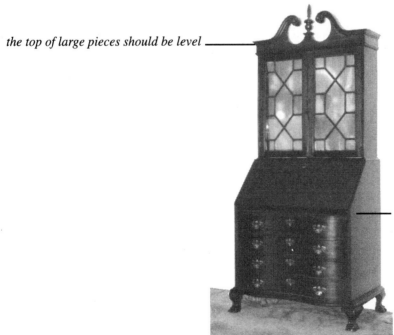

the sides should be absolutely plumb for the drawers to work properly

Fixing Loose Drawers

Drawers need to have something to slide on in order for them to work properly. For most furniture, the drawer guide serves this purpose. The most common cause of loose drawers is a broken, worn or missing drawer guide. Missing guides can be easily replaced with scrap wood and a few small brads or tacks. Measure the replacement wood and cut to fit. Secure with tacks or brads. Loose guides can be reglued with wood glue and set in the correct position. When the glue is dry, coat the guides with paste wax, paraffin or a white candle to help reduce friction.

Worn guides are often caused by the hardwood of the drawer sides rubbing on the softer poplar, pine, or fir of the drawer guides. The worn guides can be repaired with either Plastic Wood or Minwax High Performance Wood Filler. Use the Plastic Wood or High Performance Wood filler to build up any worn spots on the guides. Allow to dry completely then lightly sand until smooth. Coat the guide with paste wax or rub with paraffin or a white candle to help reduce friction.

If the bottom of the drawer is worn down and you have to lift the front of the drawer to push it all the way in, check the track the drawer slides on. Quite often the track will have become gouged from many years of use. The gouges can be filled with Plastic Wood or Minwax High Performance Wood Filler.

Clean off any accumulated wood dust and vacuum thoroughly. Build up the gouges with Plastic Wood or High Performance Wood Filler according to package directions. If the gouges are deep, apply more than one thin coat rather than one thick one. Lightly sand the surface after the repair has completely dried. Coat the track with paraffin or rub with a white candle.

If the wear is on the bottom of the drawer sides, raise the level of the track by gluing thin pieces of wood onto it with wood glue. To help determine what thickness of wood strip is needed, push a few thumb tacks into the trough of the drawer slide and try sliding the drawer in and out over the elevation of the tacks. Remove the tacks noting how deep they had to be driven in to accommodate the drawer, and use that measurement as a thickness guide for the wood strip.

If the drawer pushes in too far, the drawer stops on the inside framework may be missing or broken. Remove any broken pieces. Use broken pieces as a guide to cut new drawer stops. Use wood glue to fasten the new stops on to the old glue marks. Allow glue to dry completely before replacing drawer.

When a drawer is pushed completely in, and there is an uneven gap across the top, it is usually a result of either the framework of the furniture becoming loose or out of plumb (see page 89), or one of the drawer runners or guides becoming worn (see instructions at the top of this page).

Removing Odors from Musty Drawers

The interior wood on most older furniture (the bottoms and sides of drawers, the backs of dressers and chests, etc.) was very seldom sealed with any type of finish. Over the years, the porous bare wood absorbs odors and retains them. This includes both good odors, like the fragrance from perfumes and sachets, as well as bad odors, like musty smells from stuffy attics and damp basements.

You have three options when dealing with unwanted odors: attempt to remove them, attempt to hide them under a coat of sealer, or learn to live with them. The age of the piece of furniture and the odor itself will usually dictate your course of action.

If you are working on a true antique, you may not want to apply a coat of sealer if none has been there before. Some experts believe an application of sealer could destroy the authenticity of the piece. On the other hand, finishing off the unsealed wood could improve a piece that is not an antique.

In either case, start by removing any drawer liners and thoroughly vacuuming the inside of the piece of furniture. Use the hose attachments of your vacuum and clean the runners, the sides, the drawer bottoms, etc. If you live in a warm climate, set the drawers outside in the shade and allow them to "air-out" for a few days. (Remember to bring them in at night to avoid moisture buildup, which would trigger the odor problem all over again.) If you cannot put the drawers outside or prefer not to, try putting baking soda, kitty litter or other odor absorbent in the drawers, and allow to sit for a few days. Remove absorbent, vacuum thoroughly and wipe with a slightly damp cloth before use. Cedar chips can be placed in the drawers to mask any lingering odors or cedar oil can be rubbed into the raw interior wood. (Cedar chips and cedar oil are available from woodworking supply catalogs. See the Appendix for sources)

To seal the odor into the raw wood, brush a thinned coat of shellac or varnish on to the wood and allow to dry thoroughly.

Repairing or Replacing Dust Panels

Better furniture has a thin board between the drawers to keep dust and dirt from falling from one drawer to the next. These are known as *dust panels*. They are usually made from the same material as the back, and are quite often installed in slots in the rails. Unless the furniture has been subjected to extreme moisture or abuse, the dust panels will seldom require repairs. Occasionally one will warp so badly that it will interfere with the opening and closing of the drawers. Remove the warped board from the slots. Some warps may be removed by using the techniques for "Straightening a Warped Leaf" on page 79.

If the warping is extensive, the board will have to be replaced. Remove the old board. Use the dimensions of the old board for a pattern and cut a replacement board from plywood. Slide the replacement board into the slots. The board may be glued in place with wood glue if desired.

Cracked dust panels can sometimes be glued and repaired and will not need to be replaced. Follow the instructions for "Repairing Split Panels" on this page.

Repairing Split Panels

Understanding what made a panel split on the side of a dresser, cabinet, or door can prevent future splits from occurring. Many of these panels were designed to "float" within the frame and fit loosely in their grooves. This allowed the wood to expand and contract with changes in the temperature and humidity. Over the years an accumulation of varnish or an application of glue may have fastened them in place. This in turn inhibited the expansion and contraction of the wood and something had to give: the panel cracked. You should attempt to remove any accumulation and allow the panel to once again float freely, prior to making any repairs. If you don't, the problem will reappear and the panels will continue to split.

side panels ____

*Side panels were designed to "float" within the frame
to allow for expansion and contraction of the wood.*

Many panels are difficult to repair because they are still surrounded by their frame. If the joints of the framework are loose, the panel can be removed, repaired and replaced. If they are not, the panel will have to repaired in the framework. Use a sharp knife blade to loosen any accumulated varnish or glue. Clean any dirt or wax from the split. Attach two wood clamps on either side of the split. Wrap a piece of string or cord between each pair of clamps. Insert wood glue in the split using a syringe or glue injector, then tighten the "tourniquet" cords. This will pull the panels together. Be careful not to apply excessive pressure. Remove any glue from the surface by wiping with a damp paper towel or damp cloth. Allow the repair to dry at least 24 hours.

Do not attempt to shortcut this job by simply filling the crack in the panel with shellac stick, wax stick, wood putty, etc. The side piece will continue to expand and contract and the repair material will eventually fall out. This is one of those "do it right or don't do it at all" repairs.

Replacing Broken Backboards

Most furniture backboards are made from unfinished wood and are fastened to the back of furniture with either tacks or staples. Antiques usually have backs made of solid wood; either a solid panel or a series of boards that have been joined together. If the furniture has dust panels, the backboard is usually made from the same material.

Backboards help to keep dust and moisture out of furniture and provide support to keep furniture square and rigid. If allowed to dry and crack backboards may break free from the edges. The furniture will then shift out of alignment resulting in racking. This "un-squareness" can lead to a number of other furniture problems including sticking drawers, sagging doors, or loose joints.

If the piece is an antique, every effort should be made to salvage the original backboard. If it is warped, you may be able to remove the back, straighten the warp, and reassemble the piece of furniture. Follow the instructions for "Straightening a Warped Leaf" page 79.

If the backboard is cracked, you may be able to remove it, repair the crack and reassemble the piece of furniture. Follow the instructions for "Repairing or Replacing Dust Panels" pages 91-92.

If all else fails, the backboard will have to replaced. Remove the backboard, carefully removing tacks or nails with a screwdriver or tack puller. Be careful not to damage the wood frame. Use the old back as a pattern and trace the shape on to a piece of plywood or 1/4" oak the same thickness as the original piece. Cut the board along the traced lines. Carefully align the replacement back piece on the back of the furniture. Fasten new back to the piece of furniture with tacks or small nails.

Repairing a Stiff or Broken Roll Top Desk Lid (or Similar Slatted Door)

The roll top of a roll top lid is technically known as a *tambour*. When the top starts sticking or generally not working properly the most common cause is that the canvas backing on the inside of the tambour has dried out and separated from the slats. To solve this, the lid or door will have to be removed. First remove the entire top assembly of the desk. (This would be the unit that contains the cubby holes, the little drawers, and the grooves that the tambour slides in.) Remove the screws from underneath the desktop, and lift the top straight up. (Find a volunteer to help you lift the top off as roll tops can be quite heavy!)

Place the top on its back so that the tambour grooves point up. Pull the tambour all the way out. If the slats of the tambour have broken loose, they will have to be fished out of the grooves too. Check at the bottom of the back of the desk to make sure that you have all of the slats. Place them in order, canvas side up.

Carefully pull the slats out of the groove.

Place the slats on a flat surface in order, canvas side facing up.

Peel the canvas away from the slats. The old fabric will probably have lost its strength, and if you've gone to this much trouble already, you should make all the necessary repairs while the desk is apart. Use turpentine as a solvent if necessary to help remove the old canvas.

Cut a piece of heavy linen or heavy linen canvas (the kind used by artists) to the size of the lid or door minus 1/2" on each side to ride in the grooves. Coat the lid or door with contact cement. Then apply contact cement to the canvas. Following the directions on the cement, allow the cement to dry slightly, then carefully lay the canvas across the slats. Remember contact cement bonds "on contact" so take care to get it right the first time as it will be extremely difficult to remove. Press the canvas all over to ensure a good bond, then allow the cement to cure for a day or two before reassembling the piece. Coat the ends of the slats on the tambour with paraffin, prior to reassembly, to ensure it will roll smoothly.

Cleaning and Conditioning Leather Tops

Genuine leather tops are usually found only on quality furniture. To keep the furniture in top form, it should optimally be kept in a room with a temperature below 70° F and with a humidity level around 50%. Leather tops should be dusted regularly with a soft, dry cloth. Never use furniture polish on leather tops. The solvents in the polish may soften the finish and cause it to become sticky.

Leather tops, like other leather, need to retain a high proportion of water. The moisture can be sealed into the leather by applications of leather oils or leather polishes. Once the moisture is gone the leather will crack, and expose more unprotected leather to the atmosphere. This will weaken the leather further and cause additional deterioration.

**Follow these tips to prevent moisture loss
and other damage to the leather:**

• *Never keep leather objects in direct light. Leather can fade just like fabric.*

• *Never keep leather anywhere hot. Excessive heat will dry out leather.*

• *Never keep leather in a damp atmosphere because being organic, it tends to rot easily.*

• *Never dry wet leather quickly in a hot place– this will stiffen the leather. Allow it to dry naturally or pack it with absorbent material to help absorb excess moisture.*

If leather passes the "wet finger test", it can be cleaned by regular dusting and by wiping with a barely moist cloth. To test: touch the leather with a wet finger. If there's no absorption of moisture or darkening of color, proceed to wipe the leather with a cloth dipped in warm, soapy water and wrung almost dry. Rinse with clear water and, another clean, wrung-dry cloth. Lightly buff dry and allow to dry thoroughly. When completely dry, wax with a natural-base paste wax. Buff with a soft cloth after 24 hours.

If the leather can't pass the wet finger test, dust it with a soft, clean cloth and rub it with another. Then apply a light film of paste wax. Buff with a soft cloth after 24 hours.

If the leather is dirty and in good condition, it can be cleaned with saddle soap or commercial leather cleaner. To use saddle soap, clean all excess dirt from the surface by brushing with a slightly dampened cloth. Rub a moist cloth over the surface of the saddle soap to develop a lather. Work on a small area at a time and rub the lather into the leather. Wipe off the excess lather with a damp cloth. Allow leather to dry, then buff with a soft, dry cloth to develop lustre.

Saddle soap, paste wax, leather cleaner and Neatsfoot oil

If you prefer, you can make your own leather cleaner by using one of the following formulas:

Homemade Leather Cleaner #1

1 cup of warm water
1 teaspoon of liquid soap
1 teaspoon of vinegar.

Thoroughly mix ingredients together. To use, dampen a clean cloth with the mixture, then rub gently on leather. Follow by wiping with a clean cloth dampened with clean water. Wipe dry. Mixture can be stored in clean covered jar.

Homemade Leather Cleaner #2

3/4 cup isopropyl alcohol
1/2 cup white vinegar
1 -1/2 cups water.

Mix ingredients together thoroughly. To use, dampen a clean cloth with mixture and rub into leather until clean. Mixture can be stored in clean covered jar.

Before applying saddle soap or leather cleaner:
Do a spot test in an inconspicuous area,
on *each* piece of leather, *every* time.

After cleaning, a commercial leather dressing can be applied to protect the leather from future dirt and wear. Remember: a leather dressing should only be used on smooth, sound leather and no dressing should be used without testing first in an inconspicuous place.

Cracked or dried-out leather can be rejuvenated with Neat's Foot Oil (also known as "Neatsfoot Compound"). First, clean the leather with saddle soap to remove dirt and grime. Then, pour a small amount of Neat's Foot Oil on to a soft cloth and rub it into the leather. Work on a small area at a time, adding more Neat's Foot Oil to the cloth as necessary. Allow the leather to dry.

Leather can also be revived by applying a mixture of 2 parts denatured alcohol and 3 parts castor oil. Mix the ingredients together. Use a soft cloth to rub the mixture into the clean leather surface until it is absorbed. Let it sit for one or two days, then apply a light coat of castor oil alone. Rub into the leather until absorbed.

Pro Tip:
Leather that is painted or gilded should not be cleaned by an amateur as permanent damage or removal of the gilding or paint can occur.

Removing Wax Build-Up from Leather Tops

Most commercial leather cleaners and conditioners contain solvents that will help dissolve previous applications of wax, cleaners or polish. If older furniture has a wax buildup it can be removed by applying a solution of 1/4 cup white vinegar and 1/2 cup water with a soft rag. Wring out the rag to remove any excess moisture, and carefully wipe the leather. Remoisten and wring out the cloth often to remove wax from cloth. Be careful not to saturate the leather as it may dissolve the glue on the backing, or create water stains. Dry the leather carefully. Wipe the excess moisture from the surface, *do not* rub. Allow the top to dry completely before use.

*This unusual antique desk has a leather
writing surface.*

Removing Stains from Leather Tops

Some stains can be removed from leather tops by applying a thick layer of
Rubber Cement over the stained area. Peel off the cement when almost dry.
The cement will lift off the stain.

Grease spots and other difficult stains can often be removed from leather
with egg white. Separate an egg, and beat the white until stiff. Using a soft
cloth, apply stiffened egg white to leather and lightly rub until stain is gone.

If the leather has been burned or is badly stained it may have to be replaced. Many woodworking supply stores carry replacement leather tops and
replacement instructions are included. This can be a messy and expensive
project, and unless you are quite skilled, should probably be left to the professionals.

Removing Ink Stains from Leather Tops

Some ink stains can be removed from leather tops by brushing skim milk
over the stain. Allow the milk to penetrate the stain, then polish the leather
with a soft, dry cloth to work out ink. Repeat if necessary. Do not use excessive pressure when rubbing the dampened leather. This technique will also
polish leather giving it a soft lustre.

Removing Indention Marks from Leather Tops

Indention marks left by heavy objects can be removed from leather tops by applying lemon oil to the area twice a day for a week. This should be sufficient time to re-moisturize the leather and swell the fibers back to their original shape. A monthly coating of lemon oil or leather conditioner will help protect the leather and prevent future dents from occurring.

Cleaning Marble Tops

Marble is hard limestone that can be polished to a high shine. It is found in a wide variety of colors from pure white to many dark, exotic shades. Marble tops appear on a variety of different types and styles of furniture. The most valuable tops have fancy or scalloped edges. The second most valuable have plain edges with decorative corners. Straight line edging is the most common. The value of marble can also increase or decrease depending on the color; reddish, rose and brown are usually considered the most valuable, moving down to black, various shades of gray and then to white. But all marble is valuable and great care should be taken to protect it.

Marble may be hard, but it is not impenetrable. It is very porous, and stains easily. Because of this, marble tops should be routinely cleaned with a vacuum cleaner and a brush attachment to remove accumulated dust, soot, etc. Ideally speaking, the marble should be kept clean at all times so it never has a chance to become dirty or soiled. Do not dust marble tops with a cloth. Dust cloths can smear grime over the surface pressing it down into the porous stone, and scratching the smooth surface.

Great care should be taken when cleaning marble to avoid damage. Any liquid used on marble has the potential to carry foreign matter deeper into the stone, creating a stain or leaving a deposit that could discolor the piece. Light colored marble should be cautiously tested in an inconspicuous area before attempting a complete cleaning.

To remove localized grime from white marble, dip a wad of cotton into a mild solution of clear household ammonia and water (approximately 1 or 2 teaspoons per quart); wring out most of the fluid and apply the dampened cotton to the soiled area. (It is a good idea to wear rubber gloves as ammonia can be very irritating to skin.) Then lay a soft white cloth on top of the area to absorb the moisture. Do not rub the surface dry. *Do not use this solution on colored or variegated marble.*

Commercial marble polishes are available, and can be safely used on most colored marble. But some purists insist that a dusting of talcum powder, rubbed over the surface with a soft cloth until a gleam appears is the best and safest choice for white or light colored marble.

Removing Stains from Marble Tops

The longer the stain remains on the marble, the deeper it can penetrate, and the harder it is to remove. For best results, tackle them as soon as possible. Some experimentation may be necessary to find the proper solvent to remove a particular stain, unless the cause of the stain is known. Variegated marble is very susceptible to permanent damage when exposed to strong chemicals or stain removers, To prevent damage from occurring, all stain removers should be tested on an inconspicuous area, before each application, even if the product has been previously used on marble with successful results.

Marble tops often develop rings and food stains. Fruit juices can be particularly damaging because the fruit acid can eat through a coat of marble polish and dissolve the surface of the stone. If the damage is slight, careful polishing will usually restore the shine. Use powdered chalk or pumice powder, and rub in circles over the affected area with a slightly damp chamois or a thick clean rag. When the surface feels smooth, rinse off the powder with clear water. Blot the surface of excess moisture, then allow to dry completely.

Oil and grease stains can penetrate into the pores of the marble and are the toughest stains to remove. The grease that has been absorbed by the stone will have to be drawn out to remove the stain. Dampen a small piece of blotting paper with alcohol or acetone. Place the paper over the stain, and cover with a piece of plastic wrap to keep the poultice from drying out too quickly. Wait about 30 minutes, then check on the condition of the stain. It may be necessary to repeat this a number of times with fresh poultices.

Rust stains, if noticed immediately, can usually be removed by rubbing vigorously with a clean dry cloth. Once the stain is set, rust remover will have to be used. Follow the directions on the bottle carefully to avoid damage to the stone.

Fingernail polish can be removed by using acetone or nail polish remover. Apply a small amount with a cotton swab, then wipe the marble with a damp cloth. A little trisodium phosphate (TSP) and cold water, or hydrogen peroxide should remove blood stains from marble. Ink stains can be difficult to remove but may respond to laundry bleach or peroxide. Apply carefully with a swab, then wipe the marble with a damp cloth to remove. Most other stains can be successfully removed from marble by using a 35% solution of hydrogen peroxide and household ammonia. Always try a spot test on the underside of the piece, or in an inconspicuous area first. Carefully pour about a teaspoonful of hydrogen peroxide onto the stain. Immediately sprinkle a few drops of ammonia on top. This will make the peroxide start to bubble. When the bubbling stops, rinse at once with clear water, two or three times. Repeat if necessary. *Do not use this solution on dark colored or variegated marble.*

Repairing Loose Casters
Casters or castors are small rollers attached to the feet or base of a piece of furniture. Their original purpose was to make it easier to move the furniture around without lifting. Early casters were made of wood, later they were made of leather or brass. Today they are principally made of rubber and synthetic materials. At the height of their use, they were part of the design of the furniture. Today, they are often applied after the piece is completed which mars the design of the furniture and limits the usefulness of the caster.

It should be noted that very little furniture was actually designed to be regularly pushed or pulled, even if it was originally fitted with casters. In most cases the casters were intended to be more decorative than functional. A quick look at the size of the screws used to attach the casters should give you some idea of the intended purpose.

Small caster attached to antique chair leg.

Large caster attached to modern chair leg.

Old casters can be made inefficient by wear or can snag on carpet or an uneven floor, breaking the joint or splitting the leg. Because of the potential damage, most furniture with casters should be lifted, where feasible, and not pushed or pulled to prevent serious damage.

Furniture casters consist of a wheel, a stem or shaft that goes up into the leg and a tube-shaped socket that holds the stem in place and prevents the metal stem from wearing out the wood. Some casters have an optional hood over the wheel. The baseplate of the socket has sharp teeth that secure the socket to the furniture leg. If the wood shrinks, or the teeth loosen their grip, the socket and caster can become wobbly or fall out.

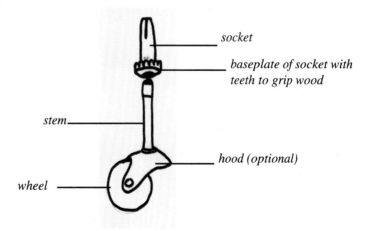

socket

baseplate of socket with teeth to grip wood

stem

hood (optional)

wheel

Remove the caster socket from the leg and coat the outside of it with epoxy putty. Be careful not to get any epoxy on the top end of the socket; it may interfere with the tip of the shaft. Tap the socket back into the hole, then, lightly grease the shaft, especially the tip and drive it into the socket. The grease will make insertion easier and will help to prevent the epoxy from accidentally adhering to the shaft. From time to time, as the epoxy cures, turn the shaft to make sure it is not being held by the epoxy.

A temporary caster repair can be made by winding steel wool or plastic tape around the socket to make it fit into the hole more tightly.

If you decide to permanently remove problem casters from a piece of furniture and do not replace them, there will be a noticeable difference in the height of the furniture. The empty sockets will present another problem unless they are also removed, as they can scratch floors and snag carpets. Save all of the removed sockets and casters so they can be replaced at a later date if you change your mind.

Repairing Chipped Enamel on Hoosier Kitchen Cabinets

Hoosier cabinets were staples in American homes for almost 70 years. The name comes from the fact that many of these "comprehensive kitchen cabinets" (as they are properly called) were manufactured in Indiana. One company is said to have called their cabinets "Hoosier Cabinets" and the name stuck and was commonly applied to all cabinets regardless of where they were manufactured or by whom.

Hoosier cabinets were made in a variety of styles and sizes, but most were made in two pieces – a base section with a porcelain table top and an upper section containing shelves and other storage. The two sections were connected with brackets designed to allow the table top to slide forward and back.

This slide-out top often developed chips on the flat work surface or on the edges. You can easily repair the damage with Duro White Appliance Touch-Up, DEVCON Appliance Touch-Up Paint, or similar products used to repair enamel and porcelain surfaces. Before attempting the repair, use a clean cloth or white paper towels dampened with mineral spirits to thoroughly clean the surface and remove any grease or dirt. Use the cap brush or a fine artist's brush to apply touch-up paint to the chipped area. Use thin, even strokes and feather the edges to blend the repair. Allow sufficient drying time before use.

For deep scratches or chips, apply several thin coats, not one thick one. Allow 10 minutes between each layer for drying. Let dry overnight for best results. Any excess touch-up paint can be cleaned up with lacquer thinner.

Cleaning Brass Hardware and Trim

Before attempting to clean hardware, make sure it is solid brass and not just brass-plated steel or iron. Use a magnet to test the metal. Brass will not be affected by magnetism, but the magnet will stick to iron or steel. Do not use brass polish on brass-plated metal. The polish may remove the brass plating.

Brass knobs, pulls or trim should be removed (if possible) before cleaning and polishing to prevent cleaning solvents from damaging the finish on the furniture. Corrosive metal cleaners can remove the wood finish from around the handle or trim piece and build up behind them, creating water damage and unsightly green residue. The damage will be compounded each time the hardware is cleaned.

If the hardware can not be removed from the furniture, try slipping a plastic credit card between the wood and the metal before applying polish. This will prevent the polish from damaging the finish. If there is not enough room for a plastic card behind the hardware apply a coat of paste wax or lemon oil to the furniture before polishing the hardware to protect the finish. Then, do not attempt to polish the brass right to the very edge. Instead polish the center areas that receive the most wear. Do not attempt to mask the wood with tape. When the tape is removed it may take some of the finish with it.

Drawer pulls are generally held in place with screws and nuts. Check the inside of the drawer and carefully remove the fasteners. Brass feet are generally held in place with small tacks which can be pulled out with needle nose pliers or a tack puller.

Brass hardware can be cleaned with any gentle, noncorrosive brass polish. Brasso, Wright's Brass Polish, and Simichrome Polish are very effective but gentle to the brass. Apply the polish with a dampened soft cloth or sponge and gently rub the brass. When the tarnish is removed, rinse all of the residue away with water. Distilled water has no chlorine or dissolved minerals and will leave no residue to cause chemical reactions. Dry the brass carefully. Spray with lacquer, if desired, for protection and to inhibit tarnish.

Tarnished brass can also be cleaned with ammonia. Place brass pieces in a dish or glass jar and cover with full strength household ammonia. Work in a well ventilated area as ammonia fumes can be irritating. Wear rubber gloves to protect your hands. Soak the pieces in the ammonia for 10 to 15 minute. After soaking, the blackened tarnish should disappear from the brass. Stubborn pieces may require scrubbing with 4/0 steel wool or a soft brush. (An old toothbrush works well for this.) Rinse the brass with water and dry thoroughly. Ammonia will remove blackened tarnish and dirt but will not polish the brass. Use brass polish to bring up the shine. Spray the polished brass with a coat of lacquer, if desired, to prevent tarnish. Allow lacquer to dry. Replace the hardware or trim.

You may prefer the brass on antique pieces to have a softer shine. To achieve this make a paste of rottenstone and boiled linseed oil. Wipe the resulting paste on clean dry brass. Rub to remove the tarnish. Polish with a soft dry cloth, changing the cleaning surface of the cloth frequently. Spray the clean brass with low gloss lacquer for protection, if desired.

Or, clean all traces of old polish from the brass pieces with denatured alcohol or lacquer thinner. Allow to dry completely. Then apply a very thin coat of paste wax. Allow wax to set, then buff to a shine.

Brass feet are held in place with small brass tacks on the sides of the foot.

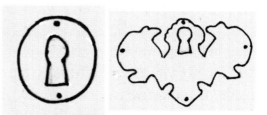

Escutcheons (decorative protection for the outside of the keyhole) are held in place with small tacks.

This type of pull ia held in place with small screws on the front of the pull plate.

This type of pull is held in place with two screws and nuts on the inside of the drawer. The handle will often seperate into 3 or more pieces when removed from the furniture.

This style of pull is held in place with one screw and nut on the inside of the drawer.

If the brass does not seem to be responding well to the cleaning efforts, it may be because it was coated with one or more applications of lacquer at some point. Lacquer can be removed with lacquer thinner. Wear gloves to protect your hands and apply lacquer thinner to the brass pieces with cotton balls, swabs, or a small soft rag. *Do not allow the lacquer thinner to touch the furniture finish* – it will damage almost all finishes. Rub the brass with lacquer thinner until the lacquer coating softens, then wipe it off the brass with 3/0 or 4/0 steel wool.

The composition of brass has changed over the years, and this has resulted in a change in color. If you need to replace a lost or broken piece, you may find a similar style but the color will often be quite different. Broken brass pieces can often be repaired. Contact your local antique mall, or check your local Yellow Pages for sources.

Replacement hardware is available from mail-order catalogs, many woodworking supply stores and from companies specializing in antique and reproduction hardware. Reproductions are often available in an antique or darkened finish, a highly polished finish, or a brushed, semi-gloss finish. Check the Appendix for a list of sources.

Chapter 7

Repairing Beds

Beds are usually one of the largest pieces of furniture in a home. In spite of their size they are often taken for granted. Bed frames are designed to be strong and flexible, but are still susceptible to wear and stress. The various parts of a bed should be periodically inspected to prevent a minor problem from becoming a major repair. Most bed repairs are relatively simple, do not require much time, and are easily done with basic tools.

Beds, are "knockdown construction", which means they are built to be taken apart. This allows them to be moved easily, and makes them easier to repair. Wooden bedposts are joined to the headboard and footboard with glued mortise-and-tenon joints. The side rails usually attach to the bedposts with metal hooks, concealed bolts, or wedged wood tenons. Together they form a frame for the removable mattress slats. Metal beds have metal side rails that usually attach to the headboard and footboard with knuckle and ball joints. The mattress support on a metal bed may be inserted wooden slats, or a web of metal and springs attached to the side rails.

Early 19th century beds usually have wooden pegs along the headboard and footboard and holes drilled into the side rails. Tightly strung rope was woven through the holes and used as a mattress support until the later part of the century and the invention of bed slats and bed springs. The early bedrails had to be hefty to resist the tension of the tightly strung rope and were often 3 inches thick. The invention of the box springs which could be supported on narrow boards attached to the inside of the side rails resulted in narrow side rails which were reduced to a thickness of about 1 inch, as they remain today.

Early mattresses were considerably thinner than the modern mattress and box springs sets to which we have become accustomed, and were often filled with corn husks, animal hair, cotton batting or straw. Feather filled mattresses were a very expensive luxury. Old beds often appear to be quite a bit higher off the floor than modern ones. This is usually due to a new mattress and box springs set in the place where a flat naturally stuffed mattress used to be.

Antique bed with bed springs.

During the 19th century, many bedroom suites were made from exotic woods and were elaborately decorated. These suites were very popular with the middle and upper classes who could buy them on credit. Less expensive furniture was made of cheaper woods (pine or oak instead of mahogany, rosewood, or walnut) and had less expensive decoration (usually paintings or decals rather than inlay). Many headboards from this time period still exist today with their original painted panels. The panels frequently showed a farmhouse scene, a castle scene or other European settings, or still life scenes of fruit or flowers. These original panels add to the current value of the furniture, and care should be taken not to damage them during repairs.

Canopy beds and four-poster beds have been around since the Byzantine and medieval periods and remain popular today. The use of a canopy bed was once considered a status symbol, and only the head of the family could sleep in a bed with a full canopy. Other family members had either half canopy beds or no canopy at all. The canopy served some useful functions and was not just used for status or decorative purposes. In the winter, heavy fabric was hung from the *testers* (the framework of boards attached to the four posts) to protect the occupants from the cold and drafts. In the summer time, lighter fabric was hung from the testers to keep out insects. The canopy could also be used to provide privacy.

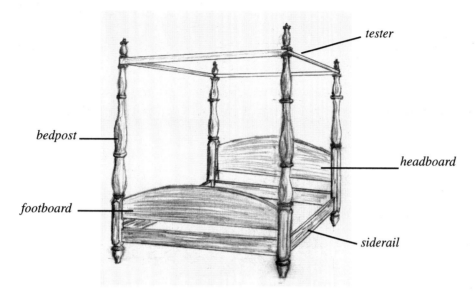

Canopy bed

It is not uncommon today to find older beds in all styles that have been modified from their orginal state. Older beds were often rebuilt to accomodate taller people or larger rooms. Taller beds were often shortened to fit into rooms with lower ceilings. During the 1920s four-poster mahogany beds were commonly "modernized" by cutting down or replacing the canopy to create a half canopy or torchére. Many older oak beds have been widened, lengthened and reduced in height to adapt them to changing tastes and needs.

Repairing a Cracked Side Rail

Minor cracks in a side rail can be successfully repaired. Severely cracked or damaged side rails should be replaced instead of repaired. Remove the damaged side rail from the headboard and footboard. Remove fastener hardware if necessary. Use toothpick or glue syringe to work wood glue into the crack. Place a clamp on the top and bottom edges of the side rail, inserting pads, cork or tops from 35mm film containers between clamp and wood to protect the wood and finish from the clamp. Tighten the clamp just enough to bring the crack together. *Do not over tighten!* Wipe away excess glue with a damp cloth or paper towel. Allow glue to set for 3-4 hours. Remove clamps, and allow repair to sit undisturbed for 24 hours. Replace fastener hardware.

Siderail attached to footboard

Straightening a Bulging Side Rail

Lift out the mattress, box springs and bed slats. If bed slats are 1" x 4" or wider they can be used to help straighten the side rail. If not, cut three boards 1" x 4" to the width of the existing bed slats. Lightly sand ends to prevent scratching the finish on the side rails.

Place the boards, evenly spaced, between the headboard and the footboard. Use two pipe clamps and place across the side rails, inserting cork, padding, or tops from 35mm film containers between the clamp and the side rail to protect the wood and the finish. Tighten the pipe clamps until the side rails straighten and each of the three slats is 1/8" from the inside surfaces of both side rails. This will ensure that the side rail is pulled in squarely.

Mark the edges of each slat on the edge with a pencil, then remove the two outer slats. Use an awl to punch two screw position marks on each end of the remaining slat. Drill 3/32" holes at the position marks and into the ledge below. Countersink each hole with a countersink bit. Drive a No. 8 wood screw into each hole. Replace the remaining two 1" x 4" slats and install in the manner described above. Remove the clamps. Replace the bed slats, mattress and box springs.

Replacing Damaged Bed Slats

Damaged bed slats are usually caused by a flaw in the wood. Slats that are unevenly spaced on the bed frame cannot adequately support the weight of the mattress and box springs and are also prone to damage.

To replace damaged slats, lift out the mattress, box springs, and damaged slat. Measure the dimensions of the damaged slat and use them to cut a replacement slat out of hardwood. Lightly sand the cut ends to prevent damage to the finish on the side rails. Set the new slat into the bed frame. Evenly space all slats equally within the frame. Replace the box springs and mattress.

*Bed slats should be evenly spaced in the
bed frame to prevent damage to the bed.*

Re-gluing a Wood Joint on a Headboard or Footboard

To repair a loose joint on a headboard or footboard, lift out the mattress, box springs, and slats. Detach the headboard and footboard from the side rails and place the piece to be repaired on a padded surface to protect the finish.

Completely separate the joint by pulling it apart by hand or carefully tapping it with a rubber mallet. Scrape out old glue and dirt from the glue hole with a small, sharp knife. Be careful to remove only glue and not the surrounding wood. White vinegar may be used to help dissolve built-up glue deposits. Apply vinegar to dowel hole, allow to soften glue, then wipe out with swabs or paper towels. Allow vinegar to dry before attempting to re-glue. Thoroughly remove all old glue and dirt to assure a good glue bond when the repair is complete.

Spread a thin coat of wood glue on the dowels and insert into the dowel holes. Lightly tap the joint together with a rubber mallet. Apply pressure to the joint with a pipe clamp to assure a good glue bond. Use small pieces of cork, padding, or the tops from 35mm film containers on the ends of the clamp to prevent damage to the wood or the finish. Tighten the clamp only enough to close the joint. *Do not overtighten!* Wipe off excess glue with a slightly dampened paper towel. Allow at least 24 hours for glue to set, then remove the clamps. Reassemble the bed.

Silencing a Squeaky Wooden Bed Frame

If a wooden bed frame makes a squeaking noise when weight is put on the mattress, it is probably caused by the wood surfaces of the frame rubbing together. To correct this problem, remove the mattress and box springs. Melt a small amount of paraffin over a double-boiler. Pour paraffin into all of the joints and corners of the bed frame and allow it to cool completely. When it hardens, the paraffin will act as a lubricant between the wood surfaces and will silence the squeak. Melt more paraffin and reapply if necessary.

Repairing Iron Beds Trimmed with Brass

Painted iron beds with brass trim were very popular in the United States from the late 1800s through the 1930s. The beds were referred to as "iron" but were usually made of steel because of its strength and durability. During the late 19th century, it was a common belief that excessive decorations in the bedroom could be harmful to one's health. Iron beds became quite popular because of their simple lines and because they were thought to be easier to clean than traditional wooden styles.

White was the standard color for most iron beds and it was thought to harmonize well with painted furnishings and golden oak or other light colored woods. Black was a popular choice for beds purchased for servant's use. The enamel paint, called "Japanning" in the Montgomery Ward and Sears and Roebuck's catalogs during the late 1800s, was also available in blue and maroon. The top rods and decorative knobs and finials on the headboards and footboards were made of brass. These beds were not only beautiful, but were also very durable, and are still in abundance today.

If the brass has been painted to match the bed, the paint can be removed by following the directions for "Removing Paint from Brass Beds" page 117. Small brass trim pieces can often be unscrewed and removed from the bed to make paint removal and polishing easier.

It is not always necessary to strip off old paint from the bed before applying a new coat of paint. Remove brass trim. Test the paint in an inconspicuous area to ensure the new paint and old paint are compatible. Sand the paint to dull the finish and smooth over any chipped areas. Spray or brush on thin, even coats of paint, allowing sufficient drying time between coats.

Because of the popularity of this style of bed, reproductions have been manufactured for many years. The newer beds are coated with an electrostatically applied baked on "powder-coat" finish that is chip-resistant and fade resistant. If you should discover chips or defects in the finish contact the store where you purchased the bed as many of these finishes are covered by a manufacturer's warranty. The finish *can not* be repaired or removed like a regular painted finish.

Pro Tip:
Carefully check iron bed frames for rust spots prior to repainting. If rust is discovered, it should be treated with Naval Jelly or other rust remover and neutralized. Use steel wool or a metal brush to scrape off any rust flakes. Allow the metal to dry completely before repainting. Untreated rust will continue to deteriorate metal under a new coat of paint and may eventually structurally weaken the bed.

Removing Blackened Tarnish from Brass Beds

Brass beds were thought to be the perfect complement to dark walnut and mahogany furniture, and became a staple in homes around the turn of the century because they were so easy to keep clean. They had simple lines and few decorations but the highly polished brass more than compensated for the lack of decoration. The brass used in the construction of many beds was not solid, but rather brass tubing fitted over cords of steel. The steel added extra strength to the bed and reduced the price.

A coat of lacquer was often applied to the brass to prevent tarnishing and to prolong the shine. Lacquered brass should never be polished, soaked or washed with hot water. The solvents in the polish or the rubbing action will damage the lacquer finish or remove it.

Even under ideal conditions, use and age will cause lacquer coatings to wear off leaving tarnished or blackened age spots on the brass. When this occurs, it is best to remove the lacquer finish with lacquer thinner and steel wool, polish the brass, and apply a new protective coat of lacquer.

Before attempting to clean the brass, determine whether it is solid brass or brass-plated steel or iron. Use a magnet to test the metal. Brass will not be affected by magnetism but the magnet will stick to iron or steel. Do not use brass polish on brass-plated metal. The polish may remove the brass plating.

The best way to remove the black tarnish from brass is with 4/0 steel wool and ammonia. Work in a well ventilated area to avoid damage from the ammonia fumes and wear gloves to protect your hands. Pour some ammonia in a dish. Moisten a small piece of steel wool pad with ammonia and rub a small area of the brass until the black is removed. Wipe with a cloth dampened with water and dry thoroughly. Do one small area at a time and then move on to the next. Ammonia will remove tarnish but will not polish the brass. After all of the brass has been cleaned, polish the brass with Brasso or other brass cleaner. If the brass is antique, do a spot test in an inconspicuous area before polishing. Spray the clean brass with a coat of lacquer, if desired, to prevent tarnish and corrosion and provide extra protection.

If you prefer brass with a softer shine make a paste of rottenstone and boiled linseed oil. Wipe paste on clean dry brass. Rub to remove light tarnish. Polish with a soft, dry cloth, changing the cleaning surface of the cloth frequently. Spray the clean brass with a coat of low gloss lacquer for protection if desired.

Removing Paint from Brass Beds

You can remove paint from brass with the same paint strippers that you would use on wood. Do not use metal scrapers to remove the stripper as they may scratch the brass. Instead, use a small piece of wood to help remove the paint sludge. Wipe with paper towels or soft cloths to remove any residue. Steel wool dipped in paint stripper can be used to clean off any remaining film.

Repairing Metal Beds

Steel beds have been popular since the 1930s. They are very durable, require low maintenance, and are often used in children's rooms and for institutional use. They consist mostly of tubular steel parts, and often have flat center panels of sheet metal on the headboard and footboard. Most beds were originally painted solid colors. But some older beds were more highly decorated, with the center panels painted to resemble walnut or other woods, or to resemble caning.

Small dents in the metal can be repaired with Bondo Glazing and Spot Putty or other similar automotive products used to fill dents in car bodies. Clean the dented area thoroughly to remove all dirt and grease. Apply a thin coat of Spot Putty to the dent with a plastic spreader. Allow each coat to thoroughly dry before applying a second coat. When the dent has been filled, lightly buff with fine grit sandpaper. Clean off sanding dust with a tack rag prior to repainting. If spot painting, feather the edges of the repair to blend with the existing painted finish.

Rusted areas should be treated and neutralized prior to painting. Untreated rust will continue to deteriorate metal under a new coat of paint and may eventually structurally weaken the bed. Treat rust spots with Naval Jelly or other commercial rust remover. Wear gloves to protect your hands and work in a well ventilated area. Apply Naval Jelly with a disposable, natural bristle brush. Wait 5-10 minutes, then sponge off the Naval Jelly with water. After the rust has been removed, and the area has been thoroughly rinsed, dry with paper towels or cotton cloths and allow to completely dry before repainting.

Old paint does not always have to be removed prior to repainting but a spot test should be done to insure that the new paint and the old paint are compatible. Use fine sand paper to scuff the finish to give "tooth" to the new coat of paint. Thoroughly remove paint dust with a tack rag.

New paint can either be sprayed on or brushed on. Work from the top of the bed to the bottom whenever possible. To achieve an even finish coat, apply two to four thin coats instead of one thick one. Allow sufficient drying time between coats.

Metal beds are still manufactured today and remain a popular choice for those looking for a durable, low maintenance bed at a reasonable price. Contemporary metal beds are usually made from tubular steel and are often coated with a baked on powder-coat finish. This finish is chip-resistant and fade - resistant under normal conditions, Should chips or other finish problems occur, contact the store where you purchased the bed. Powder-coat finishes *can not* be repaired like a painted finish.

Extending Bedrails on Antique Beds

Antique beds were made in sizes similar to the modern double, 3/4 and twin size beds. However, you may have difficulty getting an antique bed to accept a modern double mattress and queen and king sizes are almost always out of the question. Some antique beds can be converted and still retain the original design. Other beds may need to be redesigned by attaching the headboard and footboard to a new bed frame. Any modifications can detract from the antique value of the bed. The old rails should be saved, even if they are not used, so the bed can be returned to its original design in the future.

Most antique iron or brass beds were originally sold with iron side rails. Care should be taken when working with old metal bedrails as the knuckle and ball joint connectors on them vary from piece to piece, and the rails are nearly impossible to replace. Metal side rails can be taken to a local welding shop and metal extensions can be added to lengthen the rails. With the proper equipment, you can do this job at home.

Wooden beds are easier to convert. Purchase wood that is of a similar type and size to the original bed rails. Cut new side rails to the desired length. Remove hardware from the old side rails and attach it to the new ones. Reassemble the bed. Save the old wooden side rails for future use.

If the bedrails are damaged or missing, the headboard and footboard can be bolted onto a new bed frame. Use an electric drill to drill holes in the skirt of the headboard and footboard. Use bolts and nuts to attach the headboard and footboard to a purchased bed frame. This will reduce the bed's antique value but the missing rails reduce the bed's usefulness.

"Orphaned" headboards that are missing their footboards and rails can often be found in attics or garages or can be purchased quite inexpensively at garage sales or flea markets. They can be attached to purchased bed frames in the same manner described above. This is an effective way to get the look of an antique bed, with the comfort and convenience of a larger modern mattress.

Victorian demi-arm chair with caned seat woven in Spider Web pattern

Chapter 8

Repairing Wicker, Woven Seats, and Bamboo Furniture

Wicker is not a material. It is a generic term referring to furniture woven from a variety of materials such as *rattan, willow, reed,* and *seagrass.* The term *wicker* is believed to be of Swedish origin (*wika,* to bend, and *vikker,* meaning willow). Chairs woven from a variety of materials, and referred to as "twiggen chairs" can be found listed in English household inventories as early as the 15th century. Wicker furniture became extremely popular in the United States between 1850 and 1900, and the term *wicker* came into common usage. Before that time, most trade catalogues used the terms *rattan* or *reed* to describe this type of furniture. The popularity of wicker furniture in the United States was sparked by a Massachusetts grocer named Cyrus Wakefield.

Ships bringing goods from Asia often used rattan as ballast. Once reaching port, the rattan was either dumped into the harbor or left to rot on the docks, Cyrus Wakefield became intrigued by the abundance of this product, and experimented until he devised a way to recycle it. He found that rattan could be woven to produce useful and inexpensive furniture, and in 1855 the Wakefield Rattan Company (which was later renamed Heywood-Wakefield) introduced wicker to the masses.

Wicker objects have been used by man for thousands of years, and during that time numerous styles of furniture have been created. But the process of weaving and constructing the furniture remained pretty much the same until 1917, and the invention of the Lloyd Loom.

The Lloyd Loom allowed wicker furniture to be "machine made" out of strands of paper fiber. The fiber was woven to form flat sheets of wickerwork which were then wrapped and fitted around pre-assembled furniture frames. This process eliminated much of the labor involved in producing and weaving wicker from reed and enabled manufacturers to use less expensive material for the weaving. In 1912 only 15 percent of all wicker furniture was made of fiber. By 1920 that number had jumped to about 50 percent.

The new machine-made furniture was strong and durable, lightweight and easy to move around, required little maintenance and was very comfortable. The lower price of fiber furniture also made it much more affordable to the average household, and no porch or lawn was considered complete without a piece of wicker furniture or two. Unfortunately, along with the low price, came the loss of the intricate detailing that could only be produced by skilled craftsman.

Machine-made wicker was not as weather-resistant as its natural counterpart and was designed for indoor use and sun porches. It was quite often coated with one or more layers of paint to increase its durability. The factory paint choices were often bright colors such as blue, green, red or white.

Furniture made from natural materials is easier to clean and repair than its machine-made counterpart. If you think you may have a machine-made wicker piece in need of repair, consult a professional specializing in wicker/rattan restoration to ensure the repairs are done properly and the value of the piece does not decrease.

Rattan is the most common material used in the production of wicker furniture. It is derived from the rattan palm and grows in Borneo, Sumatra and Malaysia. The plants (which more closely resemble vines than palms) grow in dense forests and can attain heights of six hundred feet even though they rarely exceed a width of an inch and a half. After the rattan is cut and harvested, it bears a resemblance to young bamboo but rattan poles do not have hollow centers and do not have ridge marks.

Cane is produced by splitting off the hard outside bark of rattan vines into thin strips. It has been a very popular seat weaving material since the seventeenth century, and reached its greatest popularity in the 19th Century with the development of bentwood furniture.

Caned seats are either *woven* or *pre-woven*. Woven cane (also called *hand woven)* is woven right on the chair. The frame of the chair or other piece of furniture will have a series of holes in it through which the cane is woven. Pre-woven cane (also called *machine cane* or *webbed cane*) is purchased ready-made and is forced into grooves in the frame, then held in place with a piece of *spline*.

Hand-woven cane is quite common on antiques and very old furniture. But machine-cane can also be found on quite a few pieces dating back to the turn of the century. Most furniture manufactured today uses pre-woven cane. When the caning needs to be replaced, the type of cane you use is dictated by the presence of either the groove or the holes. Pre-woven cane can not be applied to a seat with holes and woven cane can not be applied in a frame with a groove.

Cane is available in two qualities and six sizes. *Blue Tie* is first quality cane. It is the best available and should be used whenever possible for re-caning antique chairs and other older pieces. *Red Tie* cane can be used for most other projects. For a list of caning sizes, see the chart on page 148.

Plastic Cane is also available from some caning and wickerwork suppliers. It does not require soaking prior to use, is strong and costs slightly less than natural cane. It has more "give" than natural cane so it tends to spring back into shape rather than sag and it is not affected by chemicals. Plastic Cane has a smooth, shiny surface that complements newer furniture. It should not, however, be used on antiques or older pieces. (Plastic Cane is only available in three sizes: Fine, Medium and Common.)

Re-caning a seat is not as difficult as it may appear. The only requirements are a very methodical approach and a few tools and supplies. Do not start on an antique or valuable piece to learn how to cane. A small square or oblong stool is a good beginner's project. Kits are available from most caning supply stores.

Natural *binder cane* is similar to strand cane in that it is made from the outer bark of the rattan vine but it is cut thicker and wider. It is used as a wrapping material on wicker and rattan furniture, as a seating material and to cover the holes in a hand caned project. See the chart on page 148 for sizes.

Once the outer cane covering has been stripped from the rattan, the remaining core, (called *reed*), is cut by machine into round, oval and flat shapes. Machine cutting insures precise diameters and guarantees maximum smoothness. *Round reeds* are used for manufacturing and repairing wicker and reed furniture. *Half Round Reeds* are easily confused with *Flat Oval Reeds* but upon examination they differ in appearance and function. Half Round Reeds are more rigid and are used as weavers in seats and the backs of wicker furniture. Flat oval reeds are more flexible and are used for seat weaving. Reed is very porous and can be easily painted, stained or dyed.

Willow comes from willow trees and is a very flexible and versatile weaving material. It has the appearance of blonde-colored twigs and is hard to distinguish from reed. During the early 1900s willow furniture was in such high demand that willow was planted and cultivated as a farm crop for various wicker manufacturers. It is still a popular weaving material today because it is easy to work with and can be successfully finished with either paint or stains.

Early craftsmen in Europe and American pioneers both used whatever materials were on hand to weave seats. *Natural rush* (produced from cattails and other swamp grasses) was a traditional weaving material on both continents then and is still used by purists today.

Rush leaves are harvested and then allowed to slowly dry. Then, because the leaves are usually too short for weaving, they are twisted together to form weavable lengths. The resulting "rope" is used to weave the seat. Natural cattails will shrink at least a third as they dry and cure, so plan to gather an abundant supply if you harvest your own.

Natural rush is available on a seasonal basis from a limited number of caning and wicker supply stores for those who do not choose to or are geographically unable to gather their own rush. It is generally harvested in July or August and supplies seem to be at their best at this time.

Natural rush is rather expensive and can be difficult to work with but makes a very durable seat that can last up to 50 years. Most seats can be re-woven using less than one bolt of rush and a minimum number of tools. The weaving process is simple and can be easily learned.

Keep an eye out for old chairs with damaged or missing rush seats. They can often be purchased very inexpensively and the addition of a new rush seat can increase both their value and appearance. Most antique dealers and appraisers would strongly discourage replacing the rush on a chair that is a true antique, unless repairs would be impossible. The antique value of the chair will be greatly reduced if the original rush is removed. If the seat must be replaced, genuine rush should be used (not fiber rush) to preserve the authenticity of the piece. Rush seats are not limited to use on older furniture and can also add an attractive rustic look to modern furniture.

Fiber rush is a loosely twisted, soft textured, pliable cord made from tough-grade paper fiber. Brown, green and yellow are blended in a random pattern to duplicate genuine marsh-grown cattails. Dark brown fiber rush is also available to simulate the patina of older seats. It is difficult to match old fiber rush with new because the color of the paper will fade with time. If new fiber rush is used for a repair it may need to be stained or have other coloring applied to blend it with the old rush.

Fiber rush is easier for the nonprofessional to work with and less expensive than natural rush. There is also a tremendous savings in time because, unlike natural rush, there is no collecting, drying, soaking, flattening and twisting required. Fiber rush makes a very durable seat and can last an average of 15-20 years.

Oriental seagrass (sometimes referred to as *China Seagrass* or *Hong Kong Seagrass)* is a strong, natural, twine-like material that is twisted to resemble a rope. It has been used for hundreds of years by the Chinese.

The natural color of seagrass is a variegated combination of green and tan but it has a tendency to darken and turn more brown with age. It does not take dyes well and should not be colored at home. Commercially colored seagrass is available from some cane and wicker suppliers.

Seagrass will vary in size and texture because it is handmade. Thicker seagrass has a more coarse texture and makes a good substitute for rush seating. The finer grades of seagrass are usually used on more modern furniture.

Prairie Grass was used on some wicker pieces between 1910 and 1930 but never really received widespread use. Its appearance is similar to seagrass but it is not as durable as seagrass or other wicker materials. Repairs on prairie grass seats should be left to a professional. If the seat needs to be replaced, seagrass or rush can be substituted.

Raffia is obtained from the leaves of the raffia palm of Madagascar. The tough outer transparent skin is peeled off and dried to form long strands. It can be found on Victorian wicker furniture and was used as a wrapping material.

Splint seats are woven from long, narrow, very thin strips of wood from ash or hickory trees or from the core of the tropical rattan palm. These distinctive seats are usually found on simple, spindle chairs such as American ladderback chairs. Splint is woven around the seat rails in a pattern to form the seat.

Danish Cord is predominately found on chairs made in Denmark or Sweden. It can also be used to re-weave seats on Japanese furniture and similar woven cord seats from other countries. Danish cord is approximately 1/8" in diameter and is made from specially treated paper that has been twisted into a 3-ply strand. There are two types of Danish Cord available: *Laced Danish Cord* and *Unlaced Danish Cord.* Laced Danish Cord has a more defined, rope-like appearance and the three strands of twisted paper are clearly visible. Unlaced Danish Cord has a much smoother appearance and the strands are not as noticeable.

Seats with Danish Cord are not difficult to re-weave but you should carefully study the original seat before removing it and make notes as to how it was originally done. Polaroid pictures may also be helpful as a reference. The more you know about how the chair was originally done, the easier it will be to duplicate.

Other materials may also be used for weaving chair seats. Macramé twine, cotton twine, rope, nylon yacht cord, venetian blind cord and plastic clothesline are just a few examples you might encounter. The weaving materials may change but the basic weaving patterns remain the same.

Cleaning Wicker

Painted wicker furniture should be dusted regularly with a damp rag. The brush attachment on a vacuum cleaner can be useful for removing recessed dirt. Use care around intricate turnings to avoid breaking the wicker.

To remove accumulated dirt and grime, clean the furniture as needed with a sponge and a mild detergent and water solution. Wipe with a sponge dampened with clean water to rinse.

Natural unpainted wicker can be washed to bring up its color and remove accumulated dirt and grime. Mix a small amount of peroxide and vinegar in a pail of water. Apply the solution to the wicker with a sponge. Rinse with clear water, then allow the furniture to dry thoroughly away from direct sunlight.

Pro Tip:
Check carefully for manufacturer's labels on the furniture prior to cleaning or painting. These labels will add to the value of the piece and should be carefully protected. Cover the label with paper or plastic and masking tape. Do not allow the tape to touch the label!

Unpainted wicker can be lightened and some stains removed by washing with a mild solution of laundry bleach and water. Test the bleach solution on the underside of the furniture first to make sure you will be happy with the results. Allow the wicker to completely dry to get an accurate idea of the color, as damp wicker will appear darker than it is.

Wicker chairs were often used as photographer's props before the turn of the century.

Table salt applied to your finger or a soft cloth and lightly rubbed over the wicker will help to remove stubborn stains. Rinse with clear water and allow to dry thoroughly.

Wetting down wicker furniture – both painted and unpainted – will help bring back the wicker's natural elastic qualities, prevent it from drying out and splitting and prevent a "creaking" noise when the furniture is used The wetting down can be done inside by placing the furniture in the shower, or in the yard (away from direct sunlight) with the spray from a garden hose. Once the furniture has been thoroughly moistened it should be allowed to dry out of direct sunlight.

> **Pro Tip:**
> *Furniture made of fiber wicker or Oriental seagrass should not be exposed to water. Excessive moisture may cause the furniture to deteriorate or unravel. If cleaning is necessary, use only a slightly damp cloth.*

Wicker peacock chair

Re-wrapping Wicker

If the wrapping on a chair leg (or other easily accessible part) begins to unravel it is a fairly easy repair job. Unraveling *binder cane* is the most common problem with damaged wicker furniture. Cut a small piece of the damaged cane and buy a strip of binder cane to match. Check your local craft store for caning supplies or wickerwork supplies, or check your local Yellow Pages. Several mail order sources are also located in the Appendix of this book.

When ordering by mail, ask for a catalog or mail a photograph of the furniture item with a clipping of the material you need. A photograph and sample will ensure that the new cane will match the old cane.

Soak the new cane in water for a few minutes to make it supple. Turn the chair over if necessary and clip off any damaged cane with heavy scissors or nail clippers. Unwrap the damaged cane (or loose cane) until you reach a point where the cane is firmly secured to the furniture and is in good shape. Then, using 1/2" to 3/4" nails, fasten the end of the existing cane to the inside of the chair leg where it won't show.

Overlap one end of the new strip of cane over the existing cane and use a nail to fasten it in place. Carefully wrap the cane evenly up the leg. When you get within 1/2" of the end of the leg nail the cane on the inside of the leg and trim off the excess. Seal the ends with white glue to prevent the cane from splitting. For a tighter hold, apply white glue to the leg prior to wrapping the cane.

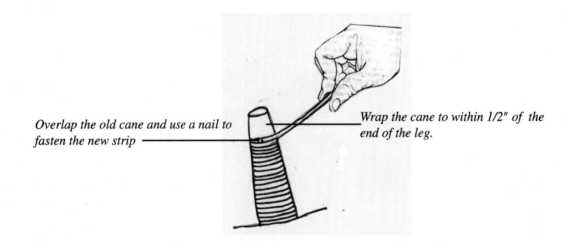

Overlap the old cane and use a nail to fasten the new strip

Wrap the cane to within 1/2" of the end of the leg.

Replacing Broken Wicker Spokes
Replacing missing or damaged vertical spokes on wicker furniture is not as complicated as it may appear. Study the pattern of the spokes before attempting the repair as you will need to duplicate it. Upon examination you will notice the spokes are angled in one direction at the front and in the opposite direction in the back on most furniture.

The vertical spokes are angled in one direction on the front and in the opposite direction on the back. Notice the broken spoke (marked by the white arrows) in the center of the picture.

You will need to buy reed the same diameter as the damaged spokes to make the repair. Reed is available at crafts stores, or wickerwork supplies dealers. See the Appendix in this book for mail order sources or check your local Yellow Pages.

Reed will need to be soaked in warm water prior to use to make it pliable. The soaking may take anywhere from 3 to 20 minutes depending on the thickness of the reed. While the reed is soaking, cut off the broken vertical spoke behind the third or fourth row of horizontal weaving at both the top and the bottom.

After the reed has soaked, insert a strip of reed into the lower horizontal weaves. Bend the reed slightly and insert the other end into the top horizontal weaves. (Clip the end of the reed to a point, if necessary, to make it easier to insert.) Follow the original pattern when replacing spokes. Remember that the front and back spokes slant in opposite directions.

Secure the repair with an application of white glue on each end and allow to dry completely. The replacement reed will stiffen as it dries making the repaired area more secure.

The new reed may need to be touched-up to help blend the repair with the old reed. See "Touching-up Wicker" for complete instructions.

Touching-up Wicker

Wicker, like other furniture, may occasionally show nicks and light scratches. If this happens to unpainted furniture, apply light colored stain to the nick with a swab or small artist's brush or lightly dab lemon oil or boiled linseed oil on the area.

Wicker furniture generally does not have a clear finish applied to it. If yours does, and the scratch is in the finish, a repair can be made by lightly spraying the damaged area with clear lacquer. Small nicks in the finish can be repaired by dabbing them with clear nail polish.

Nicks in painted wicker furniture, obviously need to be repaired with matching paint. Check your local craft or hobby store for small bottles and jars of paints in a variety of gloss and colors. Take a sample piece of the wicker with you, if possible, for an exact color match.

Wipe the nicked area with mineral spirits to make sure it is free of grease, dirt, oil, or wax prior to the repair. Lightly brush paint over the nicked area using a small artist's brush. Feather the edges of the repair to blend the paint into the original color and make the repair less noticeable.

Painting Wicker Furniture

Antique wicker furniture in its natural unfinished state is considered the most valuable. One reason for this is with the passage of time few antique pieces remain that have not been subjected to one or more coats of paint. In most cases, an old or antique wicker piece with a natural finish should not be painted.

Pro Tip:
Check carefully for manufacturer's labels on the furniture prior to cleaning or painting. These labels will add to the value of the piece and should be carefully protected. Cover the label with paper or plastic and masking tape. Do not allow the tape to touch the label!

Wicker furniture should be thoroughly cleaned before painting. Vacuum the piece with a brush attachment. Clean the wicker (see "Cleaning Wicker" page 111) and allow to dry completely. Remove any flaking paint by lightly rubbing with a stiff brush. Hose down the furniture to remove paint chips from the weaving and allow to dry.

Oil-based paint should be used on wicker – do not use latex paint. An oil-based paint will provide better coverage over a previous coat of paint, is more durable and will give better protection. Do not use house paint, even on wicker exposed to the outdoors. House paint will oxidize as it ages and dry out the fibers. Wicker should be spray painted for easiest application and best results. Cans of spray paint can be used, but a compressor and spray equipment would make the job easier and more cost-efficient for larger projects.

Turn the furniture upside down and paint the underside first. When the underside is finished, turn the furniture right-side up and continue painting. Apply light coats of paint and allow to dry completely between coats. Several thin coats will provide better protection than one heavy one.

Removing "Wicker Whiskers"
Wicker tends to develop "whiskers" – fuzzy fibers that become roughed up from wear. The roughness can be removed by lightly rubbing the whiskers with very fine (3/0) sandpaper, carefully following the lines of the grain.

Cleaning Rushwork
Rushwork consists of woven stalks of rushes or reeds. While other weaving materials may appear on a variety of pieces of furniture, rushwork is used primarily for chair seats.

Rushwork can be quite delicate and can be splintered by almost any kind of friction. Do not attempt to wash it! Excessive moisture may cause the rushwork to sag, mold or rot. In most cases, damaged rushwork can not be repaired or patched and will have to be cut away and replaced

To clean rushwork, dust the seat carefully, then wipe clean with a slightly dampened cloth. Once or twice a year rushwork can be coated with a thin coat of shellac (a mixture of 50% shellac and 50% denatured alcohol) for additional protection. Shellac will help preserve the color of the rush and smooth-out frayed or chipped fibers. Orange shellac will add a golden brown color to the rush, while clear shellac will accentuate the natural color. Carefully line up any loose ends before applying shellac. The shellac will hold them in place once it dries.

After the shellac has dried, wood stain can be used to get a closer color match to the rest of the chair, if desired. Apply stain with a brush. Allow the stain sufficient time to penetrate the rush, then gently wipe off excess with white paper towels. Choose your stain color carefully! Start with a light color, as you can always apply a second coat or use a darker color if the end result is not to your liking. Rush is very absorbent and in many cases will drink up the stain quickly. If the resulting color is too dark it can not be lightened or removed.

Stained rush will need to have a top coat applied to prevent the color from rubbing off on clothing while the seat is in use. Allow the rush to dry for a minimum of 24 hours before applying a coat of varnish or shellac.

Rush can also be sealed by applying a mixture of 50% turpentine and 50% linseed oil. Brush the mixture onto the seat so it can penetrate the rush. Allow sufficient drying time before use.

Loose strands of rush can also be held in place with a thin application of white glue.

Repairing a Sagging Rush Seat
Older rush seats have a tendency to sag. This is caused by the rushes drying out and breaking down. If the rushes are simply dry and not badly broken, the sag may perk-up by lightly spraying the seat with water and then leaving it to dry in an area with good air circulation, but away from direct sunlight. This should tighten the rushes and reduce the sagging look. If, after the seat has completely dried, it has not tightened up to your satisfaction, repeat the procedure. If no noticeable improvement has been made, the seat will have to be replaced.

Weaving a Rush Seat

Instructions will be given for weaving a fiber rush seat. Genuine rush is more difficult to work with, more expensive to buy and harder to find but the weaving process remains basically the same.

For the best results when weaving a rush seat, make sure the chair has front and back rails that are on the same level as the side rails. Rush will not weave properly on a chair with uneven rails. The angle of the rails may cause the rush to slip and bunch up on the lower rails.

To re-rush a seat you will need:

• one 2 lb. coil of rush (this will be enough to do one average chair seat approximately 14" x 16")

• a small knife or pointed nail clippers

• a medium-sized shuttle (or bodkin) to help hold the strands at right angles at the corners and to open the way for the weaving in the final stages.

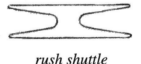

rush shuttle

• a smooth, wedge-shaped piece of wood to press the strands of rush together and for stuffing the seat with old rushes for filler.

See the Appendix for sources for rush and other supplies.

Pro Tip:
The color of rush may vary slightly from shipment to shipment, so order enough for all chairs at one time if you plan to re-rush a set of chairs.

Before cutting away the damaged seat, make notes or take Polaroid pictures to use as a reference in replicating the old seat.

Cut away the old seat using a sharp knife or razor blade. Try to keep the seat intact for reference purposes. Be careful not to damage the wooden frame.

Repairs to the frame should be done prior to re-rushing the chair. Make sure the wooden rails are smooth so they will not cut or scrape the new rush. Repair the finish on the chair rails if necessary as they may not be completely covered by the new seating.

As a point of reference, the left front corner will be called "A" and the right front corner will be called "B". The back right corner will be called "C" and the back left corner will be called "D". The rails are numbered 1 to 4.

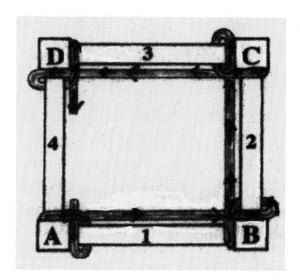

The weaving consists of simply wrapping the rush first around the rail to the right and then around the rail to the left of each leg, in turn. The seat gradually builds up from the corners, to the middle. The idea is to keep the strands at each side of the leg at right angles to each other so that the diagonal line between them is maintained as a straight running line towards the center of the seat.

Tie one end of the cord in the middle of the chair seat frame on the left hand side (between D and A). Make sure the cord is anchored securely and that the knot is facing the inside. Pull the cording forward and over and under the front rail (1) at the left hand corner (A). Then over and under the side rail (4). Pull the rush to the opposite side rail (2) and go over and under the rail at the lower right-hand corner (B) and then pull the rush over and under the front rail (1). Continue around the opposite corners (C) and (D) in the same manner.

Build up each corner by pressing the rows together with smooth, wedge-shaped piece of wood. Take care not to overlap the rows of rush, and make sure the diagonal line of the weave remains straight.

As the seat begins to develop, you will notice pockets beginning to form on each side of the diagonal line. Use the wooden wedge to stuff trimmings from the new rush or from the old rush seat into these spaces to fill them.

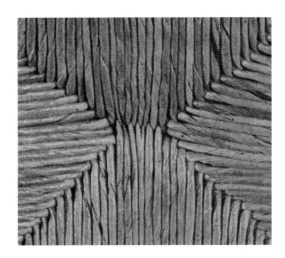

If the seat is perfectly square, the four diagonal corners will meet at the center. If the seat is oblong, the diagonals will end when the shorter rails are completely filled, but there will still be unfilled spaces left on the longer rails. To fill these empty spaces, weave forward and back through the middle of the seat in the form of a figure eight, going over and under the front rail, then over and under the back rail.

As the space becomes smaller, a shuttle (or bodkin) may come in handy to help open the way through the seat. (See illustration page 121.) When the seat has been completely woven, tie off the ends and trim the loose ends. Use the wooden wedge to stuff the knotted ends into the seat. Use rush clippings to stuff into the weaving to make the seat firm and even in appearance. Push the filler in gently so you do not damage the rush strands or knock them out of alignment.

Replacing a Seagrass Seat

Seagrass is a natural, rope-like material that has been used for hundreds of years to create very durable seats. It is not as smooth to weave or sit on as natural rush or fiber rush, but can be used as a substitute when an old rush seat needs replacement. Seagrass is less expensive and easier to use than natural rushes. It is sold by the coil and comes as one continuous length so there is no joining as there is with natural rush.

The following instructions for weaving seagrass can also be used for weaving seats with Macramé twine, rope, or other cords.

The weaving process involves wrapping seagrass around the seat rails from back to front and then weaving from side to side. Chairs with round seat rails are the best candidates for re-seating with seagrass because the round shape allows the seagrass to wrap snugly around the rail. Rails that are straight rather than curved, and of a similar length, are best for keeping the strands in place. The seagrass will slip if the side rails slant so the front rail is more than 3 inches wider than the back. To prevent slippage, the corners will need to be filled (as with rush seats).

To re-weave a seagrass seat you will need:

• about 2 pounds of seagrass (this will be enough to weave a seat approximately 14 inches square)

• upholstery tacks

• string

• strong thread

• 1/2" diameter wooden dowel (optional)

You will also need the following tools:

• a knife or scissors to cut the seagrass

• a smooth wedge shaped piece of wood to press the strands of seagrass together

• tack hammer

• pencil

• ruler

• a heddle (a weaving aid to hold the seagrass). You can easily make a heddle. (See illustration) Cut a piece of cardboard, so it is about 12 inches long and 6 inches wide. (Make sure you cut it so that the corrugation runs the long way.) Cut a slit on one of the short ends to hold the end of the seagrass. Wrap seagrass around heddle.

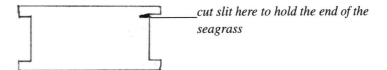

cut slit here to hold the end of the seagrass

See the Appendix for sources for seagrass and other weaving supplies.

Remove the old seat from the chair. Refinish or repair the chair, if necessary. All repairs or finishes should be allowed to dry completely prior to reseating.

Seagrass seats are usually done in either the woven pattern or the rush pattern. Directions will be given below for the woven pattern. If you choose to use the rush pattern, use the same directions for "Weaving a Rush Seat" page 123.

Seagrass can be moistened, if desired, to make it more pliable and easier to weave. Sprinkle it with warm water, or dip the heddle in a small pan of warm water until the seagrass is wet but the cardboard is still firm.

Before you begin weaving, mark the center of the front rail and the back rail with a pencil. This will help you to weave an equal number of strands on each side. Use one of the tacks to fasten the end of the seagrass near the left-hand corner on the inside of the frame.

 Pro Tip:
Place a thin wooden dowel (about 1/2" diameter) across the top of the frame before you start to weave. Then weave the seagrass over the dowel. The thickness of the dowel will help you achieve the proper tension in the first step, and enable the second set of strands to be easily woven.

Bring the seagrass up and around the front rail twice, then pull across the underside of the frame to the back rail. Wrap around the back rail twice. Wrap the next four strands straight around the frame, and then repeat the two wraps around the front and back bars. Do not pull the seagrass too tightly, or the next stage of weaving will be quite difficult. Proceed in this manner across the remainder of the frame. Check the number of strands on both sides of the center mark to be sure they are equal. End the same way as you began, by wrapping two strands around the front rails and two strands around the back rails.

If you have used a dowel for tension, remove it before beginning the side to side weaving. Bring the end of the seagrass up by the side of the frame. Remove the seagrass from the heddle if you have been using one. Wind the grass over your arm and hand to make a long loop. Leave about one yard of seagrass unwound so you will have some to work with. Tie string around the looped seagrass to keep it wound.

The seagrass will now be woven over four strands and under four strands as you weave across the frame. Wrap around the side bars twice between each set of four strands. This will add strength to the seat and help keep the rows straight. The weaving can be made easier on the topside of some seats by weaving a wooden dowel through the strands first, then pulling the seagrass through the space that has been opened by the dowel. Use the wedge of wood to periodically push the seagrass strands together. Weave the underside of the seat the same as the top, by weaving over four strands and under four strands. (Some weavers prefer not to weave the underside of the seat, and pull the seagrass straight across the bottom of the seat, and proceed with the top weaving. Weaving the underside is highly recommended, as it creates a double seat that is stronger and more durable.)

When it becomes necessary to join a new piece of seagrass to the weaving, be sure it is done on the underside of the seat so it will not show. Splice the new seagrass strand with the old one by pulling open the twist of the old strand about two inches from the end. Thread the new piece through, then thread it back again about an inch further down. Thread the end of the old piece into the new piece in the same manner.

Or, the old strand can be joined with the new strand using a *reef knot* on the underside of the seat. (See illustration below.) Make sure you pull both ends with equal tension when tightening the knot.

Continue weaving, keeping the strands pushed together, until you reach the back posts. To complete the weaving, weave a few inches across the underside. Cut the seagrass leaving a four inch end. Tuck the end into the pocket between the top and bottom of the seat. Use strong thread to tie square knots to secure the end to the nearby warp strands.

A close-up view of a finished seagrass seat.

Cleaning Canework

Remove soil from canework by wiping with a sponge dipped in a mild, soapy water solution, and wrung out nearly dry. Rinse by wiping with a sponge dipped in clear, warm water. Allow canework to dry thoroughly, away from direct heat or sunlight.

After the clean seat has completely dried, a thin coat of varnish or shellac may be applied to provide additional protection. Brush the finish on the top and underside of the seat and allow to dry for a minimum of 48 hours.

Caning can be found on headboards, tables, and a variety of other pieces of furniture. The caning on these pieces can be cleaned and protected with the same methods previously described.

Repairing Sagging Cane Seats

Machine woven and hand-woven caned seats both have a certain amount of stretch or sag woven in to allow for the stress of someone sitting on them. After months or years of use, the seat may not retighten and the sag may remain. When the cane can no longer stretch effectively it may also begin to rub on the edge of the chair frame or break in the center.

An application of glycerin and water can help remove the sag and get the cane seat back in shape. Mix 1-1/2 oz. glycerin into 1 pint of warm water. Turn the chair upside down and brush or sponge the solution onto the bottom of the caned seat. The underside of the cane is rough and will absorb moisture, but the top side is shiny and relatively nonporous. Allow the solution to penetrate for a few minutes until the cane is well soaked. Avoid wetting the wood surrounding the cane or you may damage the finish.

Use clean rags or white paper towels to mop off any excess solution Turn the chair upright and allow to dry. *Never* put the chair in the sun to speed up the drying process. Caning will shrink and tighten as it dries, and the sagging seat should tighten noticeably. Severely sagging seats may need to have the process repeated several times.

Replacing a Pre-Woven Cane Seat

Pre-woven cane is glued into a groove around the perimeter of the chair seat or back. The groove is then filled with a strip of larger cane (called *spline*) which helps to hold the woven cane in place.

To replace a pre-woven seat you will need the following supplies:

• wood glue or white glue

• a piece of pre-woven cane (measure from groove to groove at the widest points, then add one inch to each of the four sides. For example: If the seat measures 14" x 14" at the widest points you will need a piece of cane that is at least 16" x 16")

• a piece of spline the length of the perimeter groove plus 2". (To determine the size needed, use a ruler that shows 32nds of an inch or 64ths of an inch and match the width of the groove with the "Spline Sizing Chart" on page 130. Spline is easier to apply, will hold the cane more securely and give longer wear if it is the proper size.)

Width of Groove	Spline Size
5/64 "	#6
3/32 "	#6 - 1/2
1/8 "	#7
5/32 "	#7- 1/2
11/64 "	#8
3/16 "	#8 -1/2
7/32 "	#9
15/64 "	#9 -1/2
1/4 "	#10
17/64 "	#10 -1/2
9/32 "	#11
5/16 "	#12

You will also need the following tools:

• a small chisel or awl

• a hammer

• scissors

• single edged razor blades

• some softwood wedges
(hardwood wedges can break the cane)

• a few toothpicks.

See the Appendix for sources for cane and other supplies.

Softwood wedges (shown on the right) are made of sugar pine. Hardwood wedges (shown on the left) are made of oak. Softwood wedges can be used to push the cane into the groove by hand. Hardwood wedges are usually used by more experienced caners and are hit with a hammer to push in the cane.

spline placed
into groove —

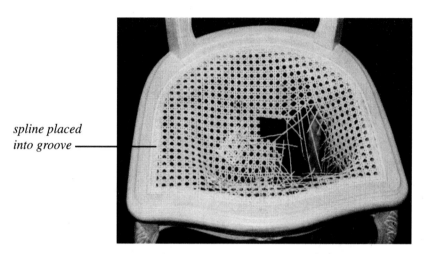

A pre-woven cane seat in need of repair.

Cut away the old cane seat using scissors or single edged razor blades. Be careful not to cut into the wood on the chair frame. Use a small sponge to moisten the spline with a mixture of vinegar and water. Allow the mixture to penetrate the spline to soften it and to start dissolving the glue holding it in the groove. Keep moistening the spline until it becomes pliable. Take your time! Soaking the spline makes it easier to remove and prevents splintering the sides of the groove.

After the spline and been soaked and is softened, place a small chisel on the inside edge of the spline and tap lightly with a hammer to loosen the spline from the frame. Go completely around the frame, first on the inside and then on the outside. Lift the loosened spline out with the end of the chisel. Take your time and do not force the spline out of the groove. If you encounter a stubborn spot, apply more of the vinegar and water mixture and allow it to soak some more. Carefully pry the spline out of the groove. Do not chip the wood on the chair frame!

Use a small chisel or awl to scrape the groove until it is completely clear of all cane, binder cane and dried glue. The cleaner the groove, the easier the new cane and spline will go in. Use an eye dropper to apply full strength white vinegar to the groove, if necessary, to remove stubborn glue or cane. If vinegar is used to clean the groove, allow the wood to dry before applying cane to prevent the vinegar from affecting the adhesive quality of the new glue. The chair is now ready to re-cane.

Pre-woven cane is available in traditional open patterns and contemporary patterns.

Soak the sheet of cane and the binder cane in lukewarm water for approximately 15 minutes, or until pliable. The amount of soaking time varies with the size and pattern of the cane and with each caner's personal preference. Shake excess water out of the cane. Lay the cane over the seat making sure it is straight on the chair. Trim the cane with scissors so that it is approximately 1" past the groove all the way around the chair.

Moisten one of the wooden wedges. Use a hammer on the wedge if using hardwood wedges or the heel of your hand if using softwood wedges, and press the cane into the groove in the center of the back. Leave the wedge in place. Pull the cane snugly across the seat with your fingers to the front of the seat. Moisten a second wedge and use it to press the cane in at the center front. Leave the wedge in place. Use your fingers to pull the cane snugly to the left side of the seat. Moisten a third wedge and use it to press the cane in place. Leave the wedge in the groove. Use your fingers to pull the cane snugly to the right side of the seat. Moisten a fourth wedge and use it to press in the cane, and leave it in the groove. Moisten a fifth wedge and use it to work the rest of the cane into the groove, working alternately on the front and back and from side to side. Press the cane firmly into the bottom of the groove, but take care not to break the cane. When the cane has been securely pressed into the groove all around the chair frame, carefully remove the wedges.

Use a single edged razor blade to carefully cut the cane just under the top of the outside of the groove. Do not pull the cane out of the groove while trimming! Remove the excess pieces of cane. If necessary, the narrow end of a wooden wedge can be used to tap the cane firmly back into the groove.

Squeeze wood glue into the groove all the way around the seat. Use toothpicks if desired to spread the glue but be careful not to pull the cane out of the groove. Allow the glue to set for about a minute, then use your fingers to press the spline into the groove. When the spline is in place, turn a wooden wedge on its side and place it on top of the spline. (The wedge will act as a buffer to prevent the hammer from denting or smashing the spline.) Lightly hit the wedge with a hammer as you work your way around the chair. Use nail clippers, wire cutters, or a single edged razor blade to cut the spline to size so that the ends meet properly.

Use a damp sponge to clean away any excess glue from the cane or chair frame. Allow the seat to dry indoors for 48 hours at room temperature. Do not dry a newly caned seat in the sun! The seat will sag and appear loose if the cane dries out before the glue has a chance to set.

A finished pre-woven cane seat.

Replacing a Hand Woven Cane Seat

Chairs that have holes drilled through the frame and around the opening in the seat require the cane to be hand woven. Hand weaving is not difficult. All that is required are a methodical approach and a few simple tools and supplies. Make sure the chair is in good condition and that all necessary repairs have been made prior to caning.

Remove the old seat by carefully cutting with a single edged razor blade or nail clippers. Clear the holes of all old cane and dirt. If the holes are blocked, use an ice pick or awl to clear them. As a last resort, drill the holes to clear any blockage.

To replace a hand woven seat you will need the following supplies:

• strand cane

• binder cane

• a plastic dishpan or large bowl for soaking cane strands

• several dozen caning pegs or plastic golf tees
(Do not use painted wooden golf tees, as the paint may wear off onto the chair or caning during the weaving process!)

• clothespins or plastic clips

You will also need the following tools:

• scissors or pointed nail clippers
(small pointed wire cutters can also be used)

• a caning awl or ice pick

See the Appendix for sources for cane and other caning supplies.

Cane sizes are numbered from 1 to 6. The thinner the cane the smaller the number. The most commonly used sizes are 2 and 6. It is not, however, unusual for two different sizes to be used on one project.

The size of cane to use can be determined by the distance between the holes in the frame. The usual distance between holes is 1/2". If the holes are closer together, the cane will become crowded and be more difficult to weave. Use size 2 or 3 cane to make weaving easier on projects with holes closer than 1/2". (Size 1 and 2 cane is usually used for finishing off chairs seats.)

Take a sample of the old cane with you when buying cane and get a similar size. If you can't determine between two sizes get the smallest of the two as it will be easier to weave. Cane is sold by the bundle (or *hank*), and one bundle will usually be sufficient to do one chair or a comparable sized project.

If the caning on your potential project is missing or severely damaged, the following charts will help you determine the size cane you will need. Match the dimensions of the holes in the frame with the sizes listed on the chart below.

Hole Diameter	Center to Center	Cane Size
1/8 inch	3/8 inch	Super Fine #1
3/16 inch	1/2 inch	Fine Fine #2
3/16 inch	5/8 inch	Fine #3
1/4 inch	3/4 inch	Narrow Medium #4
1/4 inch	3/4 inch	Medium #5
5/16 inch	7/8 inch	Common #6

Cane Size	Metric Width	Actual Width
Super Fine	2 mm	▬▬▬▬▬▬
Fine Fine	2-1/4 mm	▬▬▬▬▬
Fine	2-1/2 mm	▬▬▬▬▬
Narrow Medium	2-3/4 mm	▬▬▬▬
Medium	3 mm	▬▬▬▬
Common	3-1/2 mm	▬▬▬▬

Binder cane is similar to strand cane, but it is wider and thicker. After the seat has been woven, binder cane is used in the final step to cover the holes. In most cases, "Narrow" binder cane is used when sizes Super Fine, Fine Fine, or Fine strand cane are used. "Medium" binder cane is used when Narrow Medium, Medium, or Common strand cane are used.

Binder Cane Size	Metric Width	Approximate Size
Narrow	4 to 4-1/2 mm	▬▬▬▬
Medium	5 to 5-1/2 mm	▬▬▬
Large	6 to 6-1/2 mm	▬▬▬

The strand cane will need to be prepared prior to weaving. Carefully pull one strand of cane out from the looped end of the hank of cane. Do not tangle the cane. Select the longest strands first. The shorter ones can be used in the final steps. Do not walk on the cane or bend it unnecessarily. This will cause the cane to split and make it unusable. Roll each strand into a coil approximately 5 or 6 inches in diameter, and secure with a clothespin or plastic clip. Make 5 or 6 coils to begin with and then coil more as you need them.

There are many different caning patterns— from the basic Seven Step Pattern to the beautiful and intricate Spider Webs, Lace Patterns, and Daisy Chains. The following instructions are for the Seven Step Pattern. It is the most commonly used pattern and is the easiest to learn.

Weaving the Seven Step Pattern

Step One: Place one of the coiled strands of cane in a plastic dishpan or large bowl. Pour several inches of lukewarm water into the bowl. Allow the coil to soak for about 20 minutes. It is difficult to say exactly how long the cane should soak. Heavy cane will require more soaking time than finer cane and older cane will require more soaking time than fresher cane. But, too much soaking will cause the cane to shred.

If your work gets interrupted before all of the wet coils are used, simply remove them from the water and let them dry. Soak them again when needed. Once the weaving has begun, use a wet sponge or damp cloth to keep the weaving strand damp. Cane should always be kept moist when weaving as moist cane is much easier to work with than dry cane.

After the coiled cane has soaked, remove it from the water and shake off any excess. Place a dry coil in the water so that it can start soaking. A new dry coil should be put in the water every time one is removed.

Count the number of holes in the back rail. Place one end of the strand into the hole nearest the center leaving 3 or 4 inches of cane below the rail and secure it with a caning peg. The shiny side of the cane should be up at all times. Make sure the strand does not twist as you proceed with the weaving process.

Count the number of holes in the front rail. Place the other end of the strand through the center-most hole, making sure to keep the shiny side up. Pull the cane through until it is taut, but not tight. Hold the strand in place with another caning peg. Caning will shrink as it dries and the seat will tighten somewhat, so you do not want to weave it too tightly. The strand should now look straight in the frame from front to back and should not run crookedly to one side or the other. If it does not look straight, remove the second peg, and take the cane out of the hole. Place it in the correct hole so that it looks straight in the frame. It is critical to ensure that the first strands are straight or the entire seat will end up woven incorrectly.

Bring the end up through the next hole on the right on the front rail. Make sure the cane lays flat against the underside of the rail and does not twist in the hole. Use a peg to hold the cane in place. Pull the cane over the frame again and down through the next hole in the back rail. Use a peg to hold the cane in place.

 Pro Tip:
There is no need to use a new peg every time. The second and third peg can be alternately used until you reach the end of the strand. Each new strand should be pegged in the same manner.

Bring the end up through the next hole and pull it across to the front rail. Continue in this manner, working across the right side of the chair frame. Start new strands as needed. Do not use the corner hole! It will be used later.

You will find that most chairs have more holes in the front rail than the back rail. Because of this, separate strands will have to be used that will go from the front rail to a hole in the side rail. These strands must be parallel, and be an equal distance as the first strands. Some of the holes in the side rail may have to be skipped to accomplish this. Make sure the holes on the underside of the rail remain uncovered so they can be used later.

When the right side is complete, go back to the center of the seat, and work towards the left side of the seat in the same manner as before. When the left side is complete, you have finished Step One.

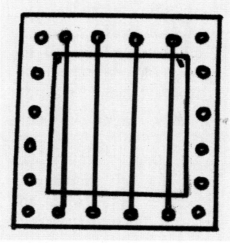

Step One

Step Two: Start Step Two in the back of the chair on the left side rail. Use the hole just below the corner hole. Use a caning peg to hold the strand of cane in place. Take the other end across the seat to the corresponding hole in the right rail. This piece of cane will lay on top of the strands from Step One. Use a caning peg to hold the cane in place. Continue across the seat, going side to side, in the same manner as in Step One. Some chairs have a curved front, and you may need to use an additional strand to make the pattern appear even. Make sure it is parallel and an equal distance as the other strands in Step Two. *Do not cover up any holes with this strand!*

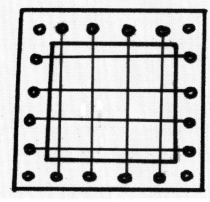

Step Two

Step Three: Step Three is done exactly as Step One. These strands will lay over the top of the strands from the first and second steps. You may reuse the same pegs. Remove the peg to put in the new strand of cane and then replace it. Be sure to keep the first end taut.

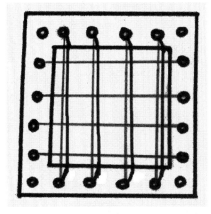

Step Three

Pro Tip:
Try to lay the strands in Step Three to the right of the strands from the first and second steps. This will make the Step Four quicker and easier to do.

Step Four: Step Four is where the actual weaving begins. In order for the cane to weave smoothly and easily through the other strands, it is important to take a minute and feel the strand of cane to determine which way the grain runs. Run your finger down the length of the cane and then in the opposite direction. The grain will cause the strand to feel rough when rubbed against the grain, just like a piece of wood. If the strand is woven with the rough side pulling against the weaving it will catch on the other strands and not weave smoothly.

Start Step Four by pegging the first strand on the left rail just below the corner hole in the back of the seat. (This will be the same hole where you started Step Two.) Make sure the cane strand does not turn or twist, and holding the end weave it under the strands from Step One. Make sure you weave in front of the cane from Step Two. Weave the strand over the cane from Step Three, then under the next strand from Step One. Weave about 1/4 to 1/3 across the seat and pull the strand until it is taut and straight. Be careful the cane does not turn and make sure the smooth side of the cane is facing upward.

Pro Tip:
A caning awl can be used to lift up the strands to make the weaving easier. Bending the end of the cane so that it points upward, can also help speed up the weaving. When the cane is woven under the strand, the bent end will point up and stick out so you can grab it easily. This eliminates the need to reach under the seat to poke the cane through.
A caning needle can also make the caning a bit easier. The needle is woven through the cane strands, then threaded with the cane and pulled back across the frame.

Continue weaving across the seat in this manner until you reach the corresponding hole on the right side rail. Use a caning peg to hold the strand in the hole. When you look at the completed row, you will see that you have woven under all of the vertical strands of Step One and over all of the upper vertical strands of Step Three. Then weave up through the next hole towards you. Make sure that your weaving is in front of the strand in Step Two. If the cane strand turns or you find that you make another mistake, use an awl to help remove the cane so that you can re-weave it. It is very important that Step Four be done properly so that you will not have difficulty with Steps Five and Six.

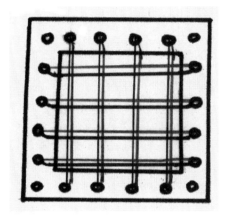

Step Four

Step Five: Use a sponge to moisten the cane prior to starting Step Five. Straighten the rows using the narrow end of a caning peg to help line them up if necessary. Make sure the cane is not overly wet. Overly wet cane will tend to bind up as it is woven.

Step Five is the first diagonal row. Start by pegging a strand of cane in the back of the seat in the right corner hole. Check the cane before weaving to make sure you will be pulling with the grain. Weave the cane strand over the vertical pairs and under the horizontal pairs. Then weave down over the next vertical pairs and under the horizontal pairs.

As before, weave about 1/4 to 1/3 across the seat, pull the strand until it is taut and straight, then proceed. Pull gently on the strands to prevent breaking, and take care not to let the strand twist or turn. Continue to weave the strand towards the front rail. If the seat is square, you will end up at the opposite corner hole. If the seat is not square, weave towards a hole where the diagonal looks the straightest. Use a caning peg to hold the strand in the hole, then push the cane up through the hole to the left. Continue to weave towards the back of the chair. The more strands you weave, the more you may find it necessary to put a strand in a hole you previously used.

When all of the diagonal strands towards the back are done, start a new strand in the hole where you originally started the diagonals and hold it in place with a peg. Weave under the horizontal pair first and then over the vertical pair. Continue in this manner until all of the diagonals are done.

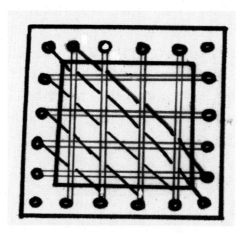

Step Five

Step Six: Step Six is the second diagonal step. Use a caning peg to hold a strand of cane in the back left corner hole. Make sure the cane has the shiny side facing upward and the grain is running in the right direction. Weave the cane under the vertical pairs and over the horizontal pairs, working towards the back of the seat, then towards the front.

Step Six (darkened for reference)

Step Seven: Step Seven is the finishing step. The binder cane is now used to cover the holes. Soak the binder cane and several strands of strand cane for about 20 to 30 minutes. Start at the center of the back rail and lay the binder cane over the holes. Skip the first two holes, then use a piece of the strand cane to lace the binder cane down. Put one end of the strand cane through the hole and allow it to hang about 3 inches below the seat rail. Put the other end of the strand in the same hole, wrapping it over the binder cane, then pull the strand cane from under the seat so that it lays tightly against the binder cane. Go to the next hole to the left and bring the strand up through the hole. Lace the strand over the binder cane and back down through the same hole. Continue in this manner as you work your way around the seat. Use additional strands of cane if necessary. When you reach the last two holes, lay the binder cane so that it overlaps the other end of the binder cane. Cut the binder cane so that the end will not be seen when the last hole is laced over with the strand cane.

Pro Tip:
If the holes in the rails are very close together it is not necessary to lace the binder cane down at every hole. Every other hole will usually be sufficient.

Tying Off the Ends: The ends of the cane can be tied-off during the weaving or after the seat is complete. Some weavers feel the seat will be tighter if you wait until after Step Seven has been completed to tie the ends. There are several ways to tie the ends. Try them all and see which one you prefer. One tie-off method is to wind the end of the cane under an adjacent loop on the underside of the rail. Do this twice. Use your caning awl to lift the loop so you can slide the end under.

Another tie-off method is to knot the end around an adjacent loop on the underside of the rail. Pull the end tight, and trim any excess so it will not show from beneath the seat.

A third method is to trim the ends of the cane so they will stick up into the next hole. The hole is then plugged with a piece of wood. The end of a caning peg can be used for this. Push the peg firmly into the hole. Use nail clippers or wire cutters to cut the peg so the plug is flush with the underside of the chair rail.

A fourth tie-off method is to trim the ends so they stick up into the next hole and then apply a bead of wood glue or white glue to hold them in place.

The seat should be allowed to completely dry, out of direct sunlight, before use.

Woven cane on two antique child sized rockers.

Replacing a Splint Seat

Splint seats are made from long, thin strips of wood woven into a variety of different patterns. Chairs need to have seat rails to accept a splint seat, as the splint will need to be wound around the rails during the weaving process. Splint is usually found on chairs that are very simple in design, such as Early American ladder-back chairs. It is often used on chairs that have side rails higher than the front and back rails. Do not use splint to re-seat a chair if the side rails slant so the front of the seat is more than 3 inches wider than the back. These chairs should be re-seated with rush or seagrass. Splint can also be used to re-seat chairs that have previously had woven seats made of rush, seagrass or wide binding cane.

To weave a splint seat you will need the following supplies:

• splint: for a seat 14" wide x 12" deep you will need:

> 3 coils* of 5/8" wide splint,
> *or* 4 coils* of 1/2" wide splint,
> *or* 8 coils* 1/4" wide splint)
> * Coils usually contain 6 strands, approximate footage per coil: 36'.

• glycerin

Approximately 1 cup for every 10 cups of soaking water to help the splint retain moisture, and prevent cracking.

You will also need the following tools:

• scissors

• pencil

• a ruler or measuring tape

• keyhole saw

• plastic dish pan or large bowl (for soaking the splint)

• sponge or towel

• 6 small clamping clothespins

• string to fasten the end of the strand

• staple gun and staples

(list continued on page 158)

(continued from page 157)

• needle-nosed pliers

• razor blade

• a screwdriver with a blunt end (to force the splint in place)

• a stick of wood approximately 1/4" thick and approximately 18" long

• a piece of cardboard from which to cut the shape of a of carpenter's square should be approximately 18" and the short end approximately 6" and fit between the chair rails.

See the Appendix for sources for splint and other supplies.

Remove the old seat from the chair. Cut it off in one piece, if possible, and save it for reference purposes. Remove any nails or tacks from the chair rails, and clean off any dirt or dust. Check to make sure the side rails are glued securely and that the wood is in good condition. The tautness of a fresh woven seat may cause the side rails to warp or break, or cause old glue to deteriorate. Make any needed repairs and allow sufficient drying time, before re-seating.

Pull one of the pieces of splint from the end of the hank near where it is tied. Do not untie the hank! Shake the hank of splint as you pull to prevent the splint from tangling.

Splint has a smooth side and a rough side. Weaving will be easier and the finished seat more comfortable if the smooth side is facing up. To help determine which is the smooth side bend a piece of splint. If the wrong side is facing up the splint will splinter and break. If the smooth side is facing up the splint will bend.

Wind the splint into coils, with the smooth side out, so it fits into the into the soaking pan. Fasten the ends with clamp clothes pins so the coils do not unwind. Prepare 3 or 4 coils in the same manner.

Mix the glycerin and water and pour into the soaking pan. Place the coiled splint into the soaking pan and allow to soak for about 30 minutes or until the splint is soft and pliable. Each time you remove a coil from the pan add a new coil so it can soak while you work.

Pro Tip:
*You can speed up the soaking process by using warm, **not hot,** water in the soaking solution.*

Splint seats are woven in two directions. First, the splint is wrapped around the seat rails. This is called *warping*. Warping is usually done from the back to the front of the chair, or the long way of the opening. The second step is done from side to side, or across the short way of the opening. This second step is called *weaving*. Both sides of the seat are woven so they are identical when finished. If the front of the seat is wider than the back, weave the center first and fill in the corners later with shorter lengths of splint. All splints woven one way on the top of the seat are at right angles to those woven the other direction.

Pro Tip:
If the back of the chair needs to be woven, wrap the strands the long way (up and down). Weave across from the bottom of the chair back to the top, so you can easily push the splint strands in place.

Take the cardboard carpenter's square you have made, and fit it closely against one of the back posts of the chair, parallel with the back rail. Use a pencil to mark the front corner of the square on the front rail. Repeat on the other side of the seat. Check to make sure you will have enough space for the width of the splint on the outside edge of the mark. If the chair seat area is out of square and the two sides vary, make adjustments by marking a slightly greater allowance on the shorter side and less on the longer side. Measure the center between these two marks, and use a pencil to mark the spot on the front rail, then mark the center on the back rail.

Take one of the coils of splint from the soaking water, and remove excess water with a sponge or towel. (Remember to place another coil in the soaking water so it can start softening.)

Do not cut or break the splint – work with the full length of the piece. Use a piece of string to tie one end of the splint to the left side rail, making sure that you keep the smooth side of the splint on the outside. Pull the splint under the back rail, then up and over the back rail. Keep the splint close to the post, and in the exact position and shape you want it to be in when dry. Pull the splint to the front rail making sure the outside edge is exactly at the pencil mark. Pull the splint over and under the front rail, then return it to the back rail.

Continue in this manner, keeping the splint taut, until you have used all of the piece of splint. Temporarily secure the end to the seat with a clothespin. Push the wet splint strands together so they will not slip on the chair rail. Splint will shrink in width as it dries, so it is very important to keep the strands pushed as close together as possible to avoid gapping spaces later on.

 Pro Tip:
Periodically wipe the seat and the working strand with a damp sponge during weaving. This will keep them moist and pliable, and make the weaving easier. If your weaving gets interrupted, the seat and working strand should be re-dampened prior to resuming weaving.

Join the new piece of splint on the underside of the seat. Place the new piece under the old, with the right side facing down. Lay the wooden stick across the chair rails, under the splint, and staple the splint together in three places. Leave enough of the old splint to provide support for the new piece, and trim the excess. (Do not allow the splint to form a double thickness where it will wrap around the chair rail.)

Pull the splint away from the stick and use the pliers to flatten the ends of the staples. Most of the staples will be covered up during the weaving process. Staples that remain uncovered can be removed later.

Staples were not used to join splint strands on older seats. They were joined using a more time consuming method of either cutting notches in the side of the two strands so they could be interlocked or trimming one of the ends to a point (like an arrowhead) which would be inserted into a hole cut in the other strand. (See illustrations below.)

After joining, pull the new piece of splint under and around the rail. Continue wrapping the splint until you reach the center mark. Count the number of strands to make sure you will have the same number of strands on the other side of the seat. Wrap the strands until you reach the pencil mark on the right side of the seat. Use a clothespin to temporarily hold the strand to the seat.

Count the number of wrapped strands (warp strands) on the back rail. The weaving step will be easier if this number is evenly divisible by the number in the design you want to use. For example, if you have 20 strands and the pattern you choose is two over and two under, or if you have 21 strands and the pattern is three over and three under.

If the number is not evenly divisible, the weaving pattern will have to be modified by either:

(A) starting the pattern off-center (i.e.: if you have 23 strands and a pattern of three over and three under, weave over one strand to start the row, continue across until you have used 21 strands, then weave over the first strand.)

or

(B) plan on using a diagonal design, which will divert the eye away from the side rails where the pattern may alter, and draw less attention to the seat if the side rails are uneven.

The weaving pattern forms the design in the seat. The choice of which design to use can be based on the size and shape of the seat, the width of the splint you will be using, the number of warp strands on the seat and whether this number is odd or even.

The most common design is formed by weaving 2 over and 2 under. Other common variations are: • 2 over and 3 under

 • and 3 over and 3 under.

It is difficult to achieve a close weave on the seat with a pattern less than 2 over and 2 under.

Larger seats, or seats woven with narrow splint strands that are 3/8" wide or less may be woven: • 4 over and 4 under

 • 4 over and 2 under

 • or 5 over and 3 under.

All of these variations can be reversed for variety. For example, the pattern could be 3 over and 2 under, 2 over and 4 under, etc.

Before beginning the weaving step, make sure the piece of splint is long enough to weave across the top of the seat and to join on the other side. Remove the clothespin and loosen the last warp strand over the back rail. Bring the splint strand from the front, under and over the back rail and under the preceding strand. Bring the strand diagonally in front of the back post, under the side rail and turned so the right side is down. Weave across the chair from right to left, in the desired pattern. Pull the strands tight. When you reach the opposite side rail, pull the weaver over the side rail and weave the underside of the seat, going under and over the same warp strands, in the same manner as the top.

When it becomes necessary to join pieces, join on the underside with staples, or one of the other joining methods. If you use staples, be sure to flatten the ends with needle nose pliers so they will not damage the splint as you weave.

Use a screwdriver (or similar tool with a blunt end) to force the strands close together, as you weave the strand through the seat and across the rails. The second row is woven in the same pattern but one warp strand to the left of the first row. (Weave to the right if you want the diagonal in the same direction as on the top of the seat.)

Once you have woven far enough to have established the design, and have the space, cut off a piece of splint for a warp in the corner of the seat. Hook about 3 inches over the weaver strand which will continue the design near the back of the seat. If the piece will fit snugly, it can be tucked in rather than hooked over the weaver strand. Bring the warp strand to the underside of the seat and fasten it there. (If necessary, strands may be joined on the top of the seat as long as the joining is hidden under the warp strands.)

The first strand should be held in place by the weaving at this point and the string used to secure it in the first step may now be cut and removed. Use short pieces of splint to weave the corners. A screwdriver may be helpful for lifting the splint as you get closer to the front of the seat. Continue weaving the pattern, joining pieces as necessary, until you reach the front rail. Finish the underside of the seat by weaving as far as you can, then tuck the end into one of the warp strands.

When the weaving is complete, use a razor blade to trim off any whiskers from the splint. Splint seats are usually left in a natural finish, and are seldom stained or top coated. If you wish to color the seat, a *blending seat stain* is recommended. (Blending seat stains can usually be purchased where you buy your splint or check the Appendix for sources.)

Penetrating oil stains can also be used to add color and seal splint, or polyurethane finishes can be used as a top coat. Allow stains or finishes to dry thoroughly between coats. Do not use varnish finishes on splint, as they tend to dry out the splint and cause it to crack.

 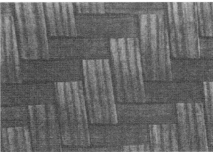

A close-up view of two woven splint seat patterns.

Replacing a Danish Cord Seat

Danish cord is predominately used on chairs manufactured in Denmark or Sweden, but can be used to re-weave seats on Japanese furniture and to replace woven cord seats on furniture from other countries.

Danish cord is made from specially treated paper that is twisted into a 3 ply strand. It is available in two types: *Laced Danish Cord* and *Unlaced Danish Cord*. Laced Danish Cord has a more defined, rope-like appearance and the 3 strands of twisted paper are clearly visible. Unlaced Danish Cord has a much smoother appearance and the strands are not as noticeable. Both laced and unlaced cord are about 1/8" in diameter and are equal in strength. They are sold in coils, usually 2 pounds (360') per coil. One 2 pound coil will do an average chair seat (approximately 16" x 16").

Laced Danish Seat Cord

Unlaced Danish Seat Cord

It is not difficult to weave a Danish Cord seat. They can be woven in just a few hours with a minimal amount of tools and materials. Chairs need to have side rails to accept a Danish Cord seat, as the cord will need to be wound around the rails during the weaving process. Most chairs with Danish Cord seats have split side rails. The cord is wrapped through the split rail on this type of chair. It is wrapped over and around a solid rail. Directions will be given for weaving both split rail and solid rail seats.

Before you remove the original seat, study it carefully and make notes as to how it was woven. If you have access to a Polaroid camera, take some pictures of the seat (both top and underside) to use as a reference. Take note where the chair was started, how many sets of strands go from the front to the back, how many sets from side to side, how many times the rail was wrapped to make the space between the front and back strands and where the weaving ended.

To weave a Danish Cord seat you will need the following supplies:

• a 2 pound coil of Danish Cord

• Danish Nails* (optional)

* Danish Nails are special "L" shaped nails used to hold the Danish Cord to the seat frame. They are available from seating supply dealers.

You will also need the following tools:

• a hammer

• a screwdriver or block of wood to help push the cord strands together

• #4 tacks

See the Appendix for sources for Danish Seat Cord and other supplies.

Carefully remove all of the old cord from the chair. **DO NOT REMOVE any nails or hooks from the inside of the chair frame.** These are the "turn-around" hooks. The Danish Cord is looped around the hooks to change the direction of the weaving. If the nails are missing, replace them with Danish Nails. Danish Nails are generally available in two sizes: 1" and 1-1/4" long. Take one of the original hooks or nails with you when you purchase your seating supplies (or send one in with your order if you are purchasing supplies by mail) to ensure you get the correct size.

Repairs to the chair frame should be done prior to re-seating with Danish Cord. Make sure the side rails are smooth so they will not cut or scrape new Danish Cord. Repair the finish on the rails if necessary, as they may not be completely covered by the new seating.

Weaving a Split Rail Seat

Unwind about 1/3 of the coil of Danish Cord (approximately 100') and cut it. **DO NOT** untie the coil. Ideally you want a piece of cord long enough to use, but not so long that it will become knotted or tangled. The fewer pieces used, the fewer ends you will have to tack off. Danish Cord is woven "as is"– **DO NOT SOAK** Danish Cord prior to use.

Step One: Start the weaving on the left side as you face the chair. Use the hammer and #4 tacks to fasten one end of the cord to the inside front rail. Pull the cord under the front rail, around the top and over the top of the back rail. Loop the cord around the nail or hook, then come back over the rail. Keep sufficient tension on the cord to make it taut but do not overtighten. Likewise, do not allow the cord to sag. Bring the cord back to the front rail and go over the top and loop the cord around the nail or hook. Repeat this process until you have woven four strands (or the same number of strands as on the old seat).

Wrap the cord around the front rail as many times as necessary to create the proper spacing between the front and back strands. (Refer to your notes from the old seat or look at the Polaroid picture to count the correct number.) Keep proper tension on the cord while wrapping and keep the strands close together, without overlapping. Use a hammer to tap on a block of wood, or a blunt end screwdriver to help push the strands together.

Repeat the front to back strands, repeat the wrapping on the front rail, then repeat the front to back procedure. Continue in this manner until all of the front to back strands have been done and the front rail is covered. This completes the first step.

Step Two: The second step involves wrapping the back rail. Take another long piece of cord (approximately 1/3 of the coil) and tack one of the ends to the inside edge of the back rail. Wrap the cord over the rail to the outside. The back rail is wrapped using the same procedure used on the front rail: wrap the back to front strands, wrap the back rail to create the spacers, then repeat the back to front procedure.

Continue in this manner until all of the back to front strands have been done and the back rail is covered. This completes the second step.

Step Three: The third step is where the actual weaving begins. The cord will now be woven from side to side. Remove the last of the cord from the coil. This should be a piece approximately 100' long. Fold the cord in half and pull the looped end through the split rail to your left (as you face the chair). Tack it to the inside edge of the front rail. The remainder of the cord should be to your left. Pull the cord until it is taut, then wrap over the lower half of the split rail and down around the bottom of the lower rail. Then come up the inside edge through the split. Pull the entire length of the cord through. Pull both strands over the top rail, over the first set of 4 strands (or the number of strands in the original seat pattern) and under the next set of two. Then over and under in this pattern through the remaining sets of strands until you get to the right side of the seat.

At the right side, pull both strands of cord over the last set of strands and down the outside edge of both right side rails. Pull all of the cord through. Wrap the lower side rail with both strands of cord and come up through the split rail and over the top rail.

Begin weaving again, under the first set of strands and over the next two. Continue in this manner until you run out of cord, or finish weaving the seat. If you run out of cord, tack the old piece to the nearest side rail. To start a new piece of cord, tack one end to the inside of the rail and continue weaving. When the weaving process is complete, tack the end of the cord at the inside edge of the back rail.

Weaving a Solid Rail Seat

The weaving process is the same as for split rail seats except on these chairs you will weave with a single strand of cord and after wrapping around the side rail, you will loop the cord around one of the nails or hooks then return it to the other side.

Chair seats woven with Danish Cord are usually not sealed with shellac or varnish. If you feel the seat requires extra protection, spray on several thin coats of "Scotchguard" fabric protector. Scotchguard will repel moisture and soil and help the "new" look last longer. For best results, cover the wood surrounding the seat before spraying to prevent possible damage to the finish from over-spray and allow sufficient drying time between coats.

Replacing a Shaker Tape Seat

Shaker tape is a heavy-duty cotton canvas webbing. It has remained a popular seating material since the 1830s, but is probably best known for being the traditional seating material of Shaker communities, Shaker tape was preferred for use by the Shakers over cane, rush or wood splint because it was so functional. It does not dry out, stretch or break, and will not snag clothing or pinch during use. It can be easily woven into a strong, long-lasting seat that is not only comfortable but colorful as well. Shaker tape seats can be woven in a single color, but a popular traditional technique is to weave two contrasting colors to form a checkerboard pattern. The weaving process is so simple, a beginner can weave a new seat in less than two hours using simple tools.

Shaker tape seats are woven in much the same manner as splint seats, with two exceptions: they are sewn together instead of stapled, and they are woven over a cushion or batting. The Shakers traditionally used cotton batting for their seats but many people today prefer to use foam.

Shaker tape is available in two widths: 1" and 5/8". To determine the correct amount of yardage for one seat: measure the front rail between the two posts. Next measure straight across from the center of the back rail to the center of the front rail. Multiply these two numbers together. Divide the resulting figure by 9 and that will give you the total yardage required for one seat woven with 1" tape. To determine the yardage for 5/8" tape, use the above formula but divide by 5.3 rather than 9.

If you wish to weave the seat in two colors, buy half the number of yards per color. Shaker tape is sold by the roll. One inch tape is usually available in 5 and 10 yard rolls. Five eighths inch tape is usually available in 5, 10 and 20 yard rolls.

To weave a Shaker tape seat you will need the following supplies:

• Shaker tape

• foam cushion or batting

• thread in color to match tape

• size #3 carpet tacks

You will also need the following tools:

• needle

• scissors

• tack hammer

See the Appendix for sources for Shaker tape and other supplies.

Remove the old seat from the chair. Refinish or repair the chair, if necessary. All repairs or finishes should be allowed to dry completely prior to reseating.

The seat will be woven in two directions. First the tape is wrapped around the seat rails. This step is called *warping*. Warping is usually done from the back to the front of the chair or the long way of the opening. The second step is done from side to side or across the short way of the opening. The second step is called weaving.

Step One: To begin, tack the end of the tape to the left hand rail, as close as possible to the back corner. Pull the tape towards the front of the chair, keeping the tension taut but not overly tight. Wrap the tape around the front rail, then pull the tape back again towards the back rail. Continue to wrap the tape around the front and back rail until about half of the warp strands have been woven. Insert the foam cushion or batting. Continue to wrap the wrap strands over the cushion and finish off by sewing the end on the underside of the seat. Add new tape as necessary by overlapping the old strand and the new one and sewing them together. Make all new additions on the underside of the seat.

Step Two: Begin this step on the underside of the seat. Sew the end of the new tape to one of the warp strands under the seat. Weave the tape over one strand and under the next one. Continue across the top, then wrap over the side and weave across the bottom. Add new tape as necessary, joining on the underside as in Step One.

The second row on the top of the seat will be done the opposite of the first row. Weave under one strand and then over the next. Continue in this manner across the seat and over the side. Weave the bottom and then bring the tape up and over the side to the top.

Continue to weave, alternating the weaving patterns until the weaving is complete. Secure the end of the final weaver by either tacking it to the inside of the front rail or sew it to one of the warp strands on the underside of the seat.

Shaker tape seats may be coated with "Scotchguard" fabric protector if you feel the seat will require extra protection. Scotchguard will repel moisture and soil and help keep the seat looking "new". For best results, cover the wood surrounding the seat to prevent possible damage to the finish from over-spray, and allow sufficient drying time between coats.

Bamboo Furniture

At the end of the 19th century people in the United States and Europe developed a fascination with the Orient and with objects that looked Oriental. Few people from the Western world had been able to acquire items from the Far East since the ports were closed to trade in the 17th century. Commodore Matthew C. Perry returned from Japan in the early 1800s with an agreement, signed by the Japanese, to reopen the ports to trade with the West.

Japanese and Chinese furnishings (both originals and replicas) became popular accent pieces in fashionable homes on both sides of the Atlantic. Bamboo quickly became a popular material for unique furniture items. However, many of the resulting furnishings had only the most superficial basis in Eastern designs and were produced for Western homes and life-styles.

Not all "bamboo furniture" was made from bamboo. Maple wood was substituted for bamboo by some manufacturers because it was more durable and easier to work with. Furnishings with legs, stretchers, frames, or applied decorations resembling bamboo or incised carvings that resembled bamboo stalks were also common.

Bamboo furniture was mass-manufactured in the Far East, France, England and the United States. By 1900, more than 100 factories in America and Europe were producing bamboo furniture. Unfortunately, the quality of the Western-produced furniture could not match that produced in the Far East and few of these pieces remain today. Most of the furniture produced was small: card tables, racks, stands, étagéres and other accent pieces. Only a few manufacturers were able to produce large pieces such as cabinets, fall-front secretaries and bookcases, and the majority of these were of Western origin.

The quality of antique bamboo pieces is easy to determine, although the decorations may vary widely. The finest pieces were made in Japan and incorporate lacquer panels, usually in deep tones of black and red. The lacquerwork on pieces the Japanese produced for their own use (and not intended for export) usually contained more layers and had a harder finish. The lacquerwork on pieces intended for export was not as high-quality, but was still harder and thicker than lacquerware panels produced in China or Europe.

Bamboo pieces of lesser-quality often incorporated woven rush matting, or embossed paper painted and sealed to simulate leather, in lieu of the lacquer panels. Both the matting and the paper had a tendency to separate when wet or exposed to high humidity and were not very durable. These lesser-quality pieces were also made from thinner bamboo stock and often had burnt or brush painted decorations. (The burned or painted decoration on legs and shelves is a distinguishing characteristic of American pieces.) The legs and finials on lesser-quality furniture were often finished with thin, nailed-on metal caps instead of bamboo rootwork. Whether of high-quality or lesser-quality, antique pieces are difficult to find and can be quite valuable, so great care should be taken to preserve them.

Bamboo furniture is still popular today. It blends easily with modern or traditional furniture styles and compliments casual life-style. Bamboo pieces can be used on covered patios or porches, or inside the home. They are reasonably priced, and available at most import stores and some department stores or furniture stores. Newer bamboo furniture generally has simpler lines than its older counterparts, less decoration and is not constructed as carefully.

A modern bamboo chair.

Bamboo is unique from other natural furniture materials because of the way it grows. When a tree grows, it grows from the inside out and gains a new layer on the outside of the previous growth each year. Bamboo starts as an outside tube and grows inward. The hollow tubes are intermittently closed off at each growth ring. Bamboo is not a strong material because of its hollow structure and should be handled with great care. When damaged, it seldom breaks cleanly and tends to split into fibrous splinters.

The protective surface skin is the strongest part of the bamboo. Be careful not to damage the smooth, glossy finish on bamboo furniture or permit anything to enter the exposed hollow ends. Moisture or other contaminates can severely weaken the core of the bamboo and structurally weaken the furniture.

From a furnituremaker's perspective, bamboo is far from the perfect medium. It resists glues, splinters when cut with most types of saw blades and cracks when penetrated with nails and screws. These same tendencies can also make repairs on bamboo more difficult than similar repairs done on wood.

Cleaning Bamboo Furniture

The only care bamboo furniture needs is regular dusting and an occasional wiping with a damp cloth. A light coat of natural-base wax can be applied to help prevent marks and stains and to freshen up the finish on an older piece. Apply wax sparingly, allow to dry, then buff to bring up the original luster of the bamboo.

Repairing Cracks and Splits in Bamboo Furniture

Cracks and splits in bamboo furniture are usually a result of the bamboo drying out. The dry air in overheated homes, direct sunlight and placing furniture too close to heaters, or fireplaces can remove necessary moisture from bamboo and cause it to shrink and crack. Bamboo furniture should optimally be kept in a room with 50 percent humidity to maintain its natural moisture level.

Small hairline cracks in bamboo furniture can be filled by lightly brushing semi-gloss lacquer or glue into the crack with a fine artist's brush. Allow to dry completely. Repeat if necessary. When the repair is complete, lightly rub over the repaired area with 4/0 steel wool to blend the repair to the surrounding area and make it appear less noticeable.

Larger cracks requite a little more effort to repair. Hot steam applied to the cracked area will often relax the bamboo enough to close some of the gap. A small travel steamer (the type used to remove wrinkles from clothing) is ideal for this purpose. A tea kettle of boiling water can also be used. Point the steaming spout towards the cracked area.

If the crack is on a leg, place a brick in a bucket of water, and rest the cracked leg on the brick. Make sure to keep the furniture above the water line. Allow the cracked leg to remain in this humid environment for at least 24 hours. The crack should close enough so that it can be filled with semi-gloss lacquer or glue using the same methods for filling small cracks.

Re-wrapping Bamboo Furniture Joints

The joints on bamboo furniture are often wrapped with *binder cane* to strengthen and support the joint, and to conceal it The binder cane may dry out, shrink and become loose, or the small nail attaching it to the furniture may split the cane or fall out. This results in the binder cane unwinding from the joint. Fortunately, this is a very simple repair. The joints on rattan furniture are also commonly wrapped with binder cane and the same techniques can be used for repairs.

Binder cane can be purchased from cane and wicker supply stores. See the Appendix for a list of sources or check your local Yellow Pages for a source near you. Most furniture is wrapped with size "Large" binder cane, but it is a good idea to take a sample piece from your chair with you when you buy the new binder cane, or send a sample with your mail order, to ensure that you receive the proper size. The Binder Cane Size chart on page 136 will help to identify the proper size needed.

You will need the following supplies:

• binder cane

• 1/2" wire nails

• white glue or wood glue

> **You will also need the following tools:**
>
> • a tack hammer
>
> • scissors

Re-wrapping a T Joint

The T joint is the most common joint found on bamboo and rattan furniture. Soak the binder cane for 20 to 30 minutes in warm, *not hot* water, to soften the cane. Use scissors to cut the cane into pieces large enough to cover the joint vertically on both sides of the joint, plus a little extra. See illustration 1 at the bottom of this page.

Use the tack hammer to drive wire nails into the ends of the cane to hold them in place. Placing the nails slightly off-center will often help to prevent splitting the cane.

Cut a piece of cane long enough to wrap around the bamboo 4 or 5 times. Use a nail to attach one end to the underside of the joint (or another inconspicuous area). Wrap the new strand over the ends of the cane until they are covered. See illustration 2 below.

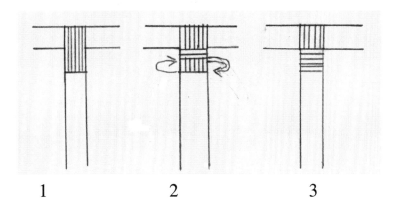

1   2   3

Trim the excess cane and use a nail to attach the end of the cane to the bamboo, in a place where it will not be readily seen. Illustration 3 shows the completed joint.

Re-wrapping an Elbow Joint

Elbow joints are much more decorative than T joints, but they are not as common. Use a wire nail to attach a long piece of soaked cane near the center of the joint. Wrap the cane around, and under one pole, as close to the joint as possible. Then wrap around the other pole to form a "figure 8".

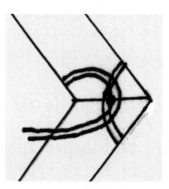

Continue to wrap in this manner until the joint is covered. Make sure the strands lay close to the strands next to them without overlapping. Trim the excess cane and use a nail to attach it in place where it will not be readily visible. The illustration below shows a completed elbow joint.

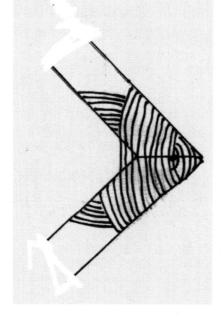

Chapter 9

Repairing Trunks and Cedar Chests

Some old trunks were made completely of leather, but most trunks consist of a wooden frame covered with thin sheets of wood, canvas, leather or tin. Each type of outer covering requires a different restoration method.

Most trunks were originally lined with printed paper that was glued to the interior of the trunk. These paper linings often featured fancy medallions, pictures or trademark designs. Some of the better made trunks additionally had a layer of printed cloth applied over the paper. These old linings can add to the value of the trunk. Try to preserve them whenever possible.

Thoroughly clean the trunk before attempting any repairs. Vacuum the inside and outside of the trunk, using attachment tools to reach into the crevices and corners. Be careful that you do not cause any damage to loose or fraying areas of the lining while vacuuming.

If the trunk has been stored in an attic or garage, or has not seen use in some time, it should be fumigated to kill spiders, silverfish, etc. prior to repair or use. Take the trunk outdoors. Raise the trunk lid and spray the interior liberally with insect spray. Be careful not to spray insecticide directly on old cloth or paper lining. Close the lid and allow to sit overnight. Open lid to air out the interior of the trunk, then proceed with repairs or put the trunk in use.

Removing the Musty Smell

Carefully wash the interior of the trunk with a mild solution of household cleaner mixed with water. Avoid wetting the paper lining if it is to be salvaged. Allow the trunk to dry out of direct sunlight. Spray the interior of the trunk with aerosol room freshener if desired. Or make your own air freshener by filling a small spray bottle with a solution of 50% water and 50% rubbing alcohol with few drops of a fragrant essential oil added. Shake the bottle to mix and then lightly spray the trunk's interior. (This mixture can also be used to freshen rooms, closets, etc.)

Cleaning Leather Trunks

If the leather is in good condition it can be cleaned quite easily. If it is in poor condition, a professional should be consulted. Leather can be extremely thin on old trunks and can often become brittle with age. The glue attaching the leather to the framework (probably hide glue) may be water soluble and may deteriorate or dissolve when exposed to water. Take care not to use excessive moisture, or allow leather to get overly wet.

Thoroughly clean the leather with saddle soap, working on a small area at a time. Moisten a piece of soft cloth with water and rub across saddle soap to work up a lather. Gently rub the leather, then when dirt has been removed, wipe off excess with a clean dry cloth. Apply a second coat of saddle soap, let dry. Buff the leather with a dry cloth.

To remove stains from leather trunks, see "Removing Stains from Leather Tops" page 99.

Cleaning Canvas Trunks

Canvas trunks consist of a canvas covering glued to a wooden frame. They were built to be durable and affordable and are usually less decorative than wooden, leather or tin trunks. Canvas trunks can be cleaned by scrubbing with a mild solution of household cleaner mixed with water and a soft scrub brush. Don't use excessive pressure when scrubbing and do not scrub areas where the canvas may be loose. These areas may be carefully cleaned using a sponge instead of the brush. Allow canvas to dry thoroughly away from direct sunlight.

When completely dry, loose canvas can be repaired. Dilute wood glue with water until you have a mixture of half glue and half water. Use a small artist's brush to apply the glue mixture to the back of the canvas. Carefully reposition the canvas, then apply masking tape over the repair if necessary to hold the canvas in place until the glue sets. Remove the masking tape slowly, and carefully to avoid damaging the canvas. Cleaned canvas trunks may be coated with shellac or varnish if desired to provide extra protection. Or, you may wish to spray on several thin coats of Scotchguard fabric protector to help the canvas repel dirt and moisture. Allow sufficient drying time between coats.

A metal steamer trunk before repairs.

The same trunk after repairs.

Cleaning Metal Trunks

Metal trunks can be cleaned with a mixture of household cleaner and water. Use a soft scrub brush to loosen dirt or rust. Rinse the trunk with cloths moistened in clean water and towel dry. Allow to completely dry away from direct sunlight before attempting any repairs.

When the trunk is thoroughly dry, check for rust spots. Use Naval Jelly Rust Remover to remove and treat rust. Wear gloves to protect hands. Apply Naval Jelly to rusted areas. Wait 5 to 10 minutes, then sponge off with water. In the case of severe rust it may be necessary to reapply Naval Jelly or allow a longer waiting time. After rust is removed, dry the area with towels and allow the trunk to completely dry before proceeding with repairs.

Liquid Steel may be used to fill small holes caused by rust damage. Larger areas can be filled with automotive metal putty or fiberglass filler. Obviously, if there are extensive repairs, the trunk will need to be repainted. If the repairs are minor the repaired areas can be painted to match the rest of the trunk.

Replacing a Trunk Bottom

If the trunk has casters on the bottom, remove them. Use the dimensions of the original trunk bottom and cut a new base from 1/4" plywood. Position the base on the trunk and attach it at each corner with long screws. The screws should go far enough into the corner posts of the trunk to firmly grip the wood. Lightly sand the edges of the new bottom, then paint or stain it to match the rest of the trunk. Replace casters or install new ones.

Loosening Rusty, Stubborn Casters

Turn the trunk upside down, or place it on saw horses. Scrub casters with household cleaner mixed with hot water, and a wire brush. This should remove any accumulated rust or dirt. Rinse with clean water. Towel dry.

If rust remains, use Naval Jelly to remove and treat rust areas. (See instructions on page 179.) Dry thoroughly. Spray the casters with WD-40 or other lubricant.

If casters are loose, see "Repairing Loose Casters" page 102.

Replacing Trunk Handles

Trunk handles withstand a lot of abuse and are often missing or damaged to the point of being unusable. Replacement handles can be purchased from leather supply stores, some woodworking supply stores, or companies specializing in trunk repair supplies. See the Appendix for a list of suppliers. The illustrations below show the two most common styles of leather handles

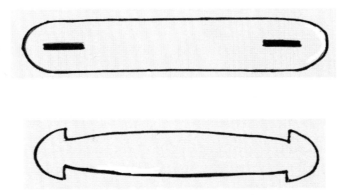

Handles are usually attached to the trunk with metal handle loops. The handle loops can enclose the ends of the leather handle, or straddle the leather handle and be secured with brads driven through the loop and the handle. Handle loops are available in a variety of styles and sizes, a few of which are illustrated below.

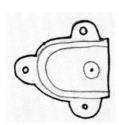

This style of handle loop encloses the end of the handle.

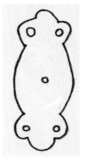

This style of handle loop straddles the handle.

The handle loops are attached to the trunk with nails. Remove the handle loop by prying out the nails with a tack hammer. Clean the handle loops if necessary with mixture of all-purpose household cleaner and water. Use Naval Jelly on rusted areas. Dry thoroughly. Polish metal or paint if necessary. Allow the paint or polish sufficient drying time before replacing handles.

Position replacement handle into handle loops on trunk. Attach to trunk using original nails, or use new nails of similar size.

Re-lining a Trunk

Most old trunks were originally lined with paper so it is the most authentic liner if you need to re-line a trunk. It is also the least expensive and easiest method. Reproduction lining paper can be purchased from some woodworking supply stores and stores specializing in trunk repair supplies. Good quality wallpaper with a small, all over print that is compatible with the trunk can also be used, but *do not* use vinyl-coated paper. An average roll of wallpaper should give you more than enough paper to line at least two average size trunks.

You will need the following materials:

• wallpaper or lining paper

You will also need the following tools:

• tape measure

• sharp scissors

• soaking tray for paper

• soft cloth or sponge

• single edge razor blades (optional)

• artist's spatula or dull kitchen knife

Before beginning, carefully measure the trunk. Measure the sides from top to bottom and side to side. Add 2" to the side-to-side measurement. Add 5" to the top-to-bottom measurement, if your trunk has a tray, and 1" if it does not.

Measure the front of the base, the back and the bottom as one unit. This will allow you to line all of those sections with one long piece of paper. *Do not* add any additional length or width to this piece. Next, measure the sides of the lid. Add 2" to the side-to-side measurement and 1" to the top-to-bottom measurement. Measure the back, top, and front as one unit.

Unroll wallpaper or lining paper and transfer the measurements to the paper. Cut out the pieces with sharp scissors. Cut 1" slits every 3" or 4" into both sides and the bottoms of the two pieces cut for the sides of the base. Do not cut any slits in the long piece that will form the back of the base, bottom and front. Do the same for the pieces for the lid. Cut 1" slits in the side pieces every 3"-4" along the edges that will form the top and side edges. Do not cut any slits on the long piece that will form the lid's back, front and top.

See the instruction sheet enclosed with your wallpaper to determine the soaking time for the paper and soak one base side piece. Lift paper out of water and drain quickly. Fit the piece into the trunk allowing the slit pieces to spread out onto the back, front and bottom. If the trunk has tray supports, press the paper around and over the supports. Use a soft cloth or sponge to smooth the paper and work out any bubbles.

You should have about 1" of paper sticking out at each of the supports. Cut away about 1/2" of the excess with a single edge blade or sharp scissors, and notch the rest to help eliminate some of the bulk. Use an artist's spatula or dull blade table knife to press the extra paper into the 1/8" space between the ends of the support and the front and back of the trunk. Repeat the process to cover the other side.

Soak the long piece of paper. Lift it out of the water and drain quickly. Press it into place on the trunk's front, back and bottom. Use a damp sponge or cloth to work out any bubbles that may form under the paper. The paper should now cover all of the wood on the interior of the base of the trunk.

Repeat the process for the lid of the trunk. Use the same method described above to recover the tray (if your trunk has one) or paint the tray to coordinate with the new lining.

Allow the open trunk to dry for several days, out of direct sunlight, before closing or using.

Cleaning and Replacing Trunk Hardware

Many trunks have shaped metal pieces covering their corners to provide extra protection from wear. These are logically called *trunk corners* and are usually made of brass or, on some newer trunks, brass plated metal. *Lid supports*, as their name implies, support the lid and hold it in an open position. *Drawbolts*, *dowells*, *surface locks*, and *set in locks* are used to close and lock the trunk. (See the illustrations on this page.)

Hardware in good condition can be cleaned using the techniques described on page 105 "Cleaning Brass Hardware and Trim". If the hardware is damaged or missing, reproduction hardware is available from trunk supply companies and some woodworking supply stores and hardware stores. Many antique stores also carry reproduction hardware. Check the Appendix for sources or check your local Yellow Pages.

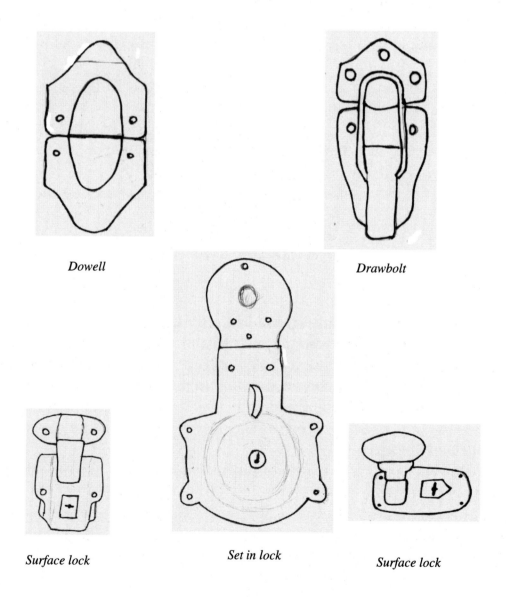

Dowell

Drawbolt

Surface lock

Set in lock

Surface lock

Removing Warps and Cracks in Wooden Trunk Tops and Chest Tops

Old flat top wooden trunks and chests often develop warped tops and cracked boards as they age. This is caused by lack of moisture in the wood. Some warps and cracks can be corrected by placing a large plastic container of water inside the empty chest or trunk, then closing the lid. The warping and cracking problems usually have not occurred over-night, and this technique is not an over-night solution. The water container will have to be left inside the closed trunk for several weeks before the positive effects may be noticed. The humidity created by the evaporation of the water will help to reswell the wood fibers and will straighten the warp and close the cracks. This technique works with varying degrees of success depending on the type of wood, how long the cracks or warp have been in the wood, and the age of the piece of furniture.

To prevent the warp or crack from returning and prevent future warping or cracking, move the trunk or chest to a room with a higher humdiity level and avoid placing near a heat source or in direct sunlight.

Restoring the Cedar Aroma in Cedar Chests

Time and use can cause cedar chests to lose their characteristic cedar aroma. This will, among other things, affect their ability to protect against moths and other pests. To rejuvenate the aroma, remove the contents of the trunk and lightly sand the unfinished interior wood with fine sandpaper. This will expose new wood and release the cedar oil. Vacuum the interior of the chest to remove any wood dust prior to use.

"Oil of Cedar Wood" can also be used to bring back the lost aroma in cedar chests. Remove the contents of the chest. Apply "Oil of Cedar Wood" to the interior of the chest with a clean cloth. Allow oil to penetrate, then wipe off any excess with a clean, dry cloth. "Oil of Cedar Wood" can be purchased from woodworking supply stores. (See the Appendix for sources.)

Repairing Brass Trunks

In general, brass trunks are intended for indoor decorative use or storage and unlike other metal trunks, are not intended for transportation of goods. The brass on the exterior of the trunk is easily scratched or damaged and the interior of the trunk is usually not sufficiently re-inforced to have the strength to withstand the abuse.

Shiny brass trunks are usually coated with several coats of lacquer to protect the polished lacquer and help retain the shine. The lacquer will eventually wear off with use and darkened tarnish spots may appear on the trunk. To clean and polish the brass, refer to the instruction for "Cleaning Brass Hardware and Trim" page 105-107.

Some brass trunks have been chemically treated to achieve an aged verdigris look. Scratches in this greenish finish can be touched up by using "Patina Creen" or other similar products. These finishing solutions are designed to "age" copper brass and bronze and are available from crafts supply stores and woodworking supply stores. See the Appendix for sources.

Do a spot test in an inconspicuous area to make sure you will be happy with the results of the application. The color will vary from piece to piece and may vary in different areas of the same piece. Colors may vary from blue to green and may have traces of yellow or reddish-brown. Do not use these products on iron, tin or steel and do not use on plated copper or brass – this may result in an over-all rusted looking reddish brown color instead of the intended greenish color.

Make sure the metal is free of all grease and dirt. Use a small artist's brush to brush the solution over the scratch until a dull film appears. Do not continue to brush the area and do not rinse or wipe the area once the film has appeared. Allow to air dry. Additional coats may be needed to achieve the desired color. Allow each coat to dry completely before applying the next one.When the desired color has been achieved, the area may be coated with lacquer for protection.

Chapter 10

Repairing Outdoor Furniture

Outdoor furniture comes in a variety of styles and materials. Your lifestyle and the climate for your particular area will usually help to determine your choice. Folding aluminum framed chairs with woven nylon webbing have been popular since the 1950s. They are portable, inexpensive and simple to maintain and repair. Another popular aluminum chair style, the vinyl-strap chair, features narrow vinyl straps across a tubular aluminum frame. These chairs are more expensive than woven-webbing chairs, but are usually sturdier.

Cast iron furniture has been used outdoors since the Victorian times and is still very popular today. It is made from painted pieces of ornate iron, held together by nuts and bolts. Cast iron furniture is extremely durable and when properly maintained, can serve one generation after another.

Redwood is one of the most popular natural materials for outdoor furniture. Its natural resistance to insects and weather make it ideal for picnic tables, lounge chairs and patio sets. Teak is also a popular wood for outdoor furniture. It is extremely durable and seems to improve with age and exposure, mellowing in color from a tawny brown to a weathered gray.

Directions for repairing furniture made from other natural materials including wicker, cane, rush, reed and bamboo are covered in Chapter 8.

Folding aluminum frame chair with web seat.

Cleaning Aluminum Chair Frames

Aluminum is often used for outdoor furniture because it is unaffected by rust, but it can be easily damaged by simple household cleaners and common tools. Strong soaps or detergents containing alkalis can pit aluminum. Glass cleaners and other household cleaners containing ammonia may darken the finish. Aluminum is also easily scratched and can be punctured by sharp objects.

To clean aluminum chair frames, mix a mild detergent with hot water, and use a sponge or soft brush to remove dirt and grime. Rinse well with clean water and dry thoroughly to prevent water spots. Baking soda is also a good nonabrasive cleaner for aluminum. Apply baking soda to the frame with a damp cloth. Lightly rub the soiled area. Rinse well with clean water and dry thoroughly. To remove stubborn grime, dip a 4/0 steel wool pad in kerosene and rub lightly. Rinse thoroughly and dry.

Older, dingy aluminum can often be polished to a shine by rubbing with a wadded-up piece of aluminum foil. Age spots and rust spots can often be removed by rubbing with crumpled aluminum foil dipped in cola. Rinse thoroughly and dry to prevent water marks.

The shine can be brought back to smooth aluminum by rubbing with the cut side of a lemon. Buff dry with a soft cloth.

A light coat of car wax will help keep clean aluminum shiny and protect it from corrosion. Apply the wax and allow it to dry until a haze forms. Then buff to remove excess wax.

Repairing a Vinyl-Strap Chair

Vinyl-strap chairs usually have stackable aluminum frames that are welded at the joints. Some of the more expensive styles are made with welded steel frames, and occasionally you will find folding aluminum frames. Plastic glides or caps on the bottom of the chair feet protect the legs from damage and prevent the metal feet from causing damage. The narrow strips of vinyl used to weave the seat are held in attachment slots in the frame. Expensive models have the vinyl strapping attached to the frame with plastic rivets.

Wash dirty straps with a solution of vinegar, mild detergent and water. Use a sponge or soft scrub brush to gently remove grime. Rinse with clean water. Dry to prevent water marks on shiny straps.

If the straps are broken or stretched out of shape they will have to be replaced. Repairs can be as simple as replacing one strap, or may involve re-strapping the entire chair. Replacement strapping can be purchased at most hardware stores or home improvement centers and should be the same width and color as the original strap.

To repair a vinyl strap chair you will need the following materials:

• vinyl strapping

• sheet metal screws
(size to fit into attachment slot in chair frame)
or

• plastic rivets

You will also need the following tools:

• sharp knife

• screwdriver

• tape measure

• scissors

• awl or ice pick

•bowl or dishpan large enough to soak strapping

• tongs or pliers

• rubber mallet (for inserting plastic rivets)

Turn the chair up-side down. Use a sharp knife to cut the strap where it enters the attachment slot. The piece of strap inside the frame should fall loose and leave the slot clear. If it does not clear the slot, use a screwdriver or other blunt edged instrument to gently push the piece of strapping in until the slot is cleared. Repeat on the other side of the strap. If the chair has plastic rivets, pry them out with a screwdriver. Be careful not to scratch the aluminum or chip the paint. For best results, the chair frame should be thoroughly cleaned before the strapping is replaced.

To measure for replacement strapping: Measure the distance from one attachment slot to the opposite attachment slot on the other side of the frame. Then subtract 1 inch so the strap will stretch taut when secured to the frame. Use scissors to cut the required length of strapping. Use an awl to pierce a centered hole, 1/4" from the cut end, of each end of the strap.

The strap will need to be softened so it can be stretched tightly across the seat frame. Soak the strapping in a bowl of boiling water for approximately 10 minutes. Wear rubber gloves to protect hands. Use tongs or pliers to remove strapping from boiling water. You must now work quickly to install the strap while it is still hot and pliable.

Push a sheet metal screw through the hole in each end of the strap. Use a screwdriver to drive the screw into the attachment slot in the chair frame. Pull the loose end around the frame until the second screw reaches the opposite attachment slot. Tighten the second screw to secure it to the chair frame. Repeat the procedure for any remaining straps.

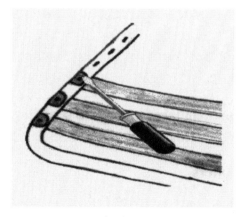

If you are attaching the strap with plastic rivets, insert the plastic rivets into the holes in the strapping instead of the sheet metal screws. Tap the plastic rivets into the frame with a rubber mallet.

If the chair frame has been painted, small chips may be touched up with enamel paint. Clean the surface thoroughly before painting. Allow to dry. Apply paint with small artist's brush and feather the edges to blend the repair.

Vinyl strap lounge chairs

Repairing a Woven-Web Chair

Woven web chairs have lightweight aluminum frames that fold for easy storage. The joints on these chairs are usually held together by screws and rivets. The webbing is usually either nylon or vinyl and is attached to the chair frame with screws or metal clips. Webbing is very inexpensive and is available at most hardware stores and home improvement centers. It can be purchased alone, or in a kit containing webbing and screws or replacement clips. In most cases, it is easier and cheaper to remove all of the webbing and re-weave the chair than to attempt to replace a few pieces of damaged or worn webbing. If the chair was a bargain piece to begin with, it may be cheaper to replace the chair rather than re-weave it.

To repair a woven-web chair you will need the following materials:

• webbing

• screws or replacement clips

• (optional) WD-40

You will also need the following tools:

• tape measure

• scissors

• awl or ice pick

Use a screwdriver to remove the screws from the back of the chair, or pry off the metal clips. Remove the webbing from the back frame. Stubborn or rusty screws can usually be loosened by spraying with WD-40. Allow it to penetrate, then remove the screws. Continue to remove all screws, clips and webbing. The chair frame should then be thoroughly cleaned prior to reweaving. (See "Cleaning Aluminum Chair Frames" page 188.)

To determine the correct length for the replacement horizontal strips, measure the distance from the attachment hole on one side of the chair frame, to its mate on the opposite side. Add 3" to this measurement if you will be attaching the webbing with screws. Add 1-1/2" if you will be attaching the webbing with clips. Cut the replacement webbing with scissors.

If you are installing the webbing with screws: Fold in the ends of the strap to make a point. Use an awl to punch a hole approximately 1/2" from the point.

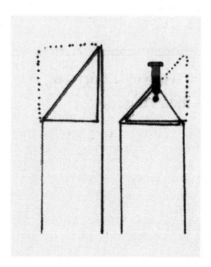

Push one of the screws into the hole and drive the screw into one of the attachment holes at the top of the chair frame. Pull the webbing tightly across the chair frame and repeat the procedure to attach the webbing to the opposite side of the chair. Repeat the process for each horizontal strap, working down the back and across the seat.

To determine the length needed for the vertical pieces, measure the distance from the attachment hole at the top of the frame back to its mate on the chair seat. Add 3" to this measurement if you are attaching the webbing with screws and 1-1/2" if you are attaching the webbing with clips. Use scissors to cut the webbing to the required length.

Fold in the ends of the strap to make a point. Use an awl to punch a hole approximately 1/2" from the point. Push a screw into the hole and drive the screw into one of the attachment holes at the top of the chair frame. Weave the vertical strap over and under the horizontal webbing on the back of the chair. Pass the webbing behind the bar at the seat back then weave it over and under the horizontal webbing on the chair seat. Fold the end to form a point. Make a screw hole with an awl as before, and attach the webbing to the chair frame. Install the remainder of the vertical straps in the same manner, alternating the weaving pattern.

If you are installing the webbing with metal clips: Wrap 3/4" of the webbing over the smooth edge of the rewebbing clip. Snap the clip onto the frame covering an attachment slot at the top of the chair. Pull the webbing tightly across the frame and repeat the procedure on the opposite side. This completes one of the horizontal straps. Work down the back and the seat using the same procedure for the remaining horizontal straps.

Fasten the first vertical strap to the seat frame by wrapping 3/4" of webbing over the smooth edge of the rewebbing clip and snapping the clip into one of the attachment slots. Weave the vertical strap over and under the horizontal webbing on the back of the chair frame. Pass the webbing behind the bar at the seat back, then weave it over and under the horizontal webbing on the chair seat. Wrap 3/4" of the webbing over the smooth edge of the rewebbing clip and snap the clip onto the attachment slot. This completes one of the vertical straps. Install the remainder of the vertical straps in the same manner, alternating the weave pattern.

Repairing Cast Iron Furniture

Cast iron contains a high carbon content and, unlike most metals, can not be shaped no matter how hot it is heated. Furniture pieces are formed by pouring liquid metal into molds, then allowing them to cool. Once cooled, cast iron becomes extremely hard and durable. The resulting hardness of cast iron and the low production costs, have made it a very popular furniture material since before the turn of the century. Cast iron furniture gained its initial popularity in the 1840s, and large quantities were produced in foundries all over the country until well after the turn of the century. Because cast iron furniture was almost always painted to help preserve it and protect it from rust, many chairs, settees and other pieces from this period have survived and have become quite collectible today.

Both indoor and outdoor furniture was produced, but the popularity of indoor cast iron furniture was rather brief. It remains a popular choice for patios and other outdoor use today. Cast iron furniture comes in a variety of styles from imitations of rustic wooden furniture to elaborately decorated Neoclassical designs.

White is the most popular color choice for cast iron furniture today, but it was not often used for furniture pieces during the early years. Green, brown, gray and other dark colors were more commonly used for cast iron pieces. When restoring an older piece of cast iron furniture, check for traces of the original color behind the skirt of the seat or inside the legs where newer coats of paint may not have reached.

The biggest enemy of cast iron furniture is rust. Rust can be kept under control by regularly touching up chipped spots with rust-resistant spray paint. If rust spots appear, treat them with Naval Jelly or other commercial rust remover prior to repainting. Wear gloves to protect your hands and work in a well ventilated area. Apply Naval Jelly to the rusted areas with a disposable natural bristle brush. Wait 5 to10 minutes, then sponge off with water. In the case of severe rust spots, it may be necessary to reapply the Naval Jelly or allow a longer waiting time. After the rust is removed and the area has been thoroughly rinsed, dry with towels, and allow to completely dry before painting.

If the furniture is extensively rusted, the painted finish may need to be removed with paint remover. Wear refinishing gloves and eye protection. Brush paint remover on the old paint with a natural bristle paint brush. Check the label on the can of stripper and allow sufficient time for it to work. Use a putty knife to scrape the paint to check on the progress of the stripper. If the paint comes off easily, use a putty knife, wire brush or old tooth brush to remove the paint sludge from the furniture. Use water, according to the stripper label's instructions, to remove any remaining stripper or paint. If the coating of paint was very thick and the stripper does not completely remove all of it, more stripper may have to be applied. When all paint has been removed, rinse off any remaining residue with water, then dry thoroughly.

Rusted areas should be treated with Naval Jelly or other commercial rust remover after the paint has been removed. Naval Jelly should be used outdoors, in a driveway or similar area. Do not apply Naval Jelly to furniture that is on or near grass or other plants as it may harm them. Spray on the Naval Jelly or apply with a natural bristle paint brush. Allow sufficient time for the rust remover to work. Use a wire brush or old tooth brush to get into cracks or crevices. To finish cleaning, rinse the furniture to remove any remaining flakes and loose rust and wipe dry.

If the nuts and bolts holding the furniture together are badly rusted, remove them and replace them with corrosion-resistant nuts and bolts made of stainless steel or galvanized metal. If the nut and bolt are rusted together, spray them with WD-40, wait 10 minutes, then remove them. Make sure all fasteners are tight before repainting the furniture.

Cast iron furniture should be painted with rust-resistant paint. The new paint can be either sprayed on or brushed on, working from the top of the furniture to the bottom whenever possible. You can achieve an even finish coat by applying two to four thin coats of paint instead of one thick one. Allow sufficient drying time between coats. Be sure to paint the undersides of the feet, arms, and chair seats to prevent them from rusting.

Ornate pieces of furniture should be periodically stripped of their multiple coats of paint even if they are not badly rusted. Paint will build up on the surface and eventually hide the fine details of the ironwork.

Repairing Wrought Iron Furniture

Wrought iron is nearly pure iron mixed with a glass-like material. Unlike cast iron, wrought iron is *malleable* and can be hammered into various shapes It also has a greater resistance to rust and corrosion than cast iron. Wrought iron furniture is usually painted or coated with a lacquer finish to provide the iron with additional protection.

If wrought iron furniture develops rusted areas, they should be treated with Naval Jelly or other commercial rust remover prior to repainting. Wear gloves to protect your hands and work in a well ventilated area. Apply Naval Jelly with a disposable, natural bristle brush. Allow Naval Jelly to remain on the affected area for 5 to 10 minutes, then sponge off with water. In the case of severe rust spots, it may be necessary to reapply additional Naval Jelly or allow a longer waiting time. After the rust is removed and the area has been thoroughly rinsed, dry with towels and allow to completely dry before repainting.

Wrought iron furniture should be repainted with rust-resistant paint. The new paint can be either sprayed on or brushed on, working from the top of the furniture to the bottom, whenever possible. An even finish coat can be achieved by applying two to four thin coats of paint instead of one thick one. Allow sufficient drying time between coats. Be sure to paint the undersides of the feet, arms and seats to prevent them from rusting.

Some newer wrought iron pieces are coated with an electrostatically applied baked enamel finish (commonly called "*powder-coating*") that is scratch and chip resistant. These finish coats can be colored and textured to resemble unfinished wrought iron, an aged verdigris finish, or are available in a variety of colors. If the finish should be accidentally scratched or chipped it *can not* be repaired or removed in the same manner as regular paint. Commercially available paint and finish removers will not remove a powder-coat finish or baked on finish. Many of these finishes are covered by a manufacturer's warranty, and the manufacturer or the dealer should be contacted in the event of a defective finish.

Nonabrasive cleaners should be used to clean a powder-coated finish. Window cleaner on a soft cloth or baking soda lightly rubbed on the finish with a soft cloth, followed with a rinse with clear water should remove most accumulated dirt and grime. Dry with soft towels to prevent water spots on a gloss finish.

A light coat of automotive wax can conceal minor scratches in the finish, help preserve the "new" look and give the finish added protection.

It is important to note that some newer wrought iron pieces may not be what they appear. Many pieces feature cast aluminum seats and backs in lieu of traditional heavier metals. The use of aluminum not only reduces the weight of the piece but also greatly reduces the price. The aluminum components are made using a sand-casting technique that duplicates the detail of traditional wrought iron. Table legs and bases on these pieces are usually made of cast iron for stability and added strength. The furniture is coated with a powder-coated finish to camouflage the two different materials and to provide a protective finish that won't rust, crack or peel and requires minimal care.

Tubular Steel Furniture with a Powder-Coated Finish

Many new pieces of patio furniture are made of tubular steel coated with an electrostatically applied baked enamel finish (commonly called a "powder-coated" finish). These modern finishes are extremely durable and are, for the most part, chip and scratch resistant. The chemical composition of these newer finishes differs from traditional painted finishes and they can not be removed or repaired with commercially available products. Many of these finishes are covered by a manufacturer's warranty, and the dealer or the manufacturer should be contacted if the finish should prove defective.

Gentle, but regular cleaning should be all the maintenance a powder-coated finish requires. A weekly washing with a mild soap and water solution, and thorough drying with soft towels should remove most accumulated dirt and grime. Stubborn spots can usually be removed with baking soda applied with a soft cloth. Rinse thoroughly and dry to prevent water spots.

A light coat of automotive wax may be applied to cover minor scratches in the finish. It will also help to preserve the "new" look and provide additional protection to the finish.

Steel and tubular steel "motel chair"

Repairing Steel and Tubular Steel Furniture

Steel and tubular steel furniture reached the peak of its popularity during the 1940s and 1950s and is enjoying a comeback today. At one time steel furniture was the most popular type of outdoor furniture and chairs like the one pictured above could be found on porches and patios from coast to coast as well as in front of motels all across America. Most styles of steel furniture are comfortable, very durable and require low maintenance.

The original chairs and tables had painted enamel finishes and are relatively easy to repair. Reproduction furniture is often coated with a factory applied powder-coated finish and can not be repaired. (See "Tubular Steel Furniture with a Powder-Coated Finish" page 197 for an explanation.)

If steel furniture develops rusted areas, they should be treated with Naval Jelly or other commercial rust remover prior to repainting. Wear gloves to protect your hands and work in a well ventilated area. Apply Naval Jelly with a natural bristle brush. Allow Naval Jelly to remain on the affected area for 5 to 10 minutes, then sponge off with water. In the case of severe rust spots it may be necessary to reapply additional coats of Naval Jelly or allow a longer waiting time. After the rust is removed and the area has been thoroughly rinsed, dry with towels and allow to completely dry before repainting

Steel furniture should be repainted with rust-resistant paint. The new paint can be either sprayed on or brushed on, working from the top of the piece to the bottom, whenever possible. An even finish coat can be achieved by applying two to four thin coats of paint instead of one thick one. Allow sufficient drying time between coats. Be sure to paint the undersides of the seats, table tops, and tubular arms and legs to prevent them from rusting.

Small dents in the metal can be repaired with Bondo Glazing and Spot Putty or other similar automotive products used to fill dents in car bodies. Clean the dented area thoroughly to remove all dirt and grease. Apply a thin coat of Spot Putty to the dent with a plastic spreader. Allow each coat to thoroughly dry before applying additional coats. When the dent has been filled, lightly buff with fine grit sandpaper. Clean off sanding dust with a tack rag prior to repainting. If spot painting, feather the edges of the repair to blend with the existing painted finish.

Repairing Iron Wire Furniture

Iron wire furniture gained its initial popularity in the early 1900s, and was produced in abundance by a number of manufacturers. The looped-wire furniture was sturdy, functional and often quite graceful. Iron wire chairs were popular in restaurants, cafés, pool halls and other public places, but are commonly referred to today as "ice cream parlor chairs".

The chairs consisted of twisted iron wire backs and legs, with seats made of either metal or wood. The wooden seats were attached to the chair frame with tacks and were made of a variety of woods from oak to plywood. Chairs intended for outdoor use usually had metal seats to make them more durable. Older chairs were generally painted, and were available in a variety of colors. Some chairs were left unpainted, exposing the gray iron and natural color of the wooden seat. Iron wire tables are not as common as chairs. Table tops, like the seats on chairs, were made of either wood or metal. Newer reproduction tables and chairs are almost always painted and are made of a lesser quality iron wire than their older counterparts. The reproductions may duplicate the style, but they do not duplicate the durability.

If iron wire furniture develops rusted areas, they should be treated with Naval Jelly or other commercial rust remover prior to repainting. Wear gloves to protect your hands and work in a well ventilated area. Apply Naval Jelly to the affected areas with a disposable, natural bristle brush. Allow to remain for 5-10 minutes, then sponge off with water. In the case of severe rust spots, it may be necessary to reapply additional Naval Jelly or allow a longer waiting time. After the rust is removed, thoroughly rinse the area, then dry with towels. Allow the piece to completely dry before repainting.

Iron wire furniture should be painted with rust-resistant paint. The new paint can be either sprayed on or brushed on, working from the top of the furniture to the bottom, whenever possible. An even finish coat can be achieved by applying two to four thin coats of paint instead of one thick one. Allow sufficient drying time between coats. Be sure to paint the undersides of the feet, arms, and seats, to prevent them from rusting.

Wooden table tops and seats may split and warp from age and use. To replace the damaged wood, turn the furniture upside down and remove the fasteners attaching the wood to the frame, then remove the damaged wood. Use the old top or seat as a pattern and cut a new one from a piece of wood similar to what was originally used. Lightly sand the edges, then paint or finish the wood as desired. Replace the fasteners in their original locations to attach the new wooden replacement to the frame.

Repairing Wooden Furniture

Wooden furniture designed for outdoor use is usually treated with some form of protective coating at the factory during production. The coating can be paint, varnish, or wood preservative. Certain woods like teak, mahogany, cedar, redwood or cypress are naturally decay resistant and do not have to be coated with a finish, but will look "new" longer if they are coated.

Some finishes will protect furniture from weathering and preserve the natural appearance of the wood. Semi-transparent stains will change the color of the wood without concealing the natural grain of the wood. Solid stains will obscure the grain and can be used to hide defects. Some stains can be mixed with a sealer or preservative in equal proportions to provide color change and protection. If you decide to use paint, check the label to make sure it is approved for exterior use.

Years of use and exposure to weather can cause almost any protective coating to deteriorate. When this happens, the coating will need to removed or repaired to prevent damage to the wood underneath. Unprotected wood exposed to the elements can change color, texture, and in extreme cases, the shape of the wood. With reasonable maintenance and adequate applications of wood preservative, paint or varnish, the life of outdoor furniture can be stretched from years to decades.

Most varnishes manufactured for outdoor use are synthetic. These exterior synthetic varnishes are easier to apply than natural varnishes and offer better protection. Most major brands are available in a variety of sheens from gloss to flat and can be purchased at any   )vement store, hardware store or discount store. The best choice for outdoor projects is Marine Varnish as it will provide the utmost protection and offer the most durability. **Do not use Spar Varnish on furniture.** Spar Varnish is made with a special formula and is designed to never dry completely.

There are four types of wood preservatives available: *creosote*, *pentachlocophenol* (*penta* for short), *copper naphthenate* and *zinc naphthenate*. Zinc naphthenate preservatives are the best choice for most jobs because they dry clear and do not add any color to the wood. Both zinc naphthenate and copper naphthenate are easy to apply and are considered the best choices for furniture that will come in contact with food or be positioned near edible plants. Copper napthenate will, however, discolor wood and leave a distinctive pale green cast after application. Creosote will stain wood a dark brown color and is highly toxic. It will also seal the wood pores sufficiently to prevent any future applications of paint or other surface coatings from adhering properly. Penta is difficult to mix, and like creosote, is highly toxic.

The best way to apply a wood preservative is to partially fill a container with preservative and then immerse the wood in it. This allows the liquid to soak into all of the tiny cracks and crevices in the wood surface. If the furniture is too large to be immersed, try to immerse the portions of wood that will touch the ground. Use a natural bristle brush to apply preservative and brush it on generously so it will penetrate deeply into the wood. Be sure to work in the shade so the preservative won't dry before it has a chance to penetrate.

Wood preservatives will delay weathering but can't retard it completely and will have to be reapplied periodically. A properly applied coating of zinc naphthenate should protect wood exposed to normal weather conditions for approximately 5 years. Copper naphthenate will give approximately 3 years of protection. Creosote or penta will need to be recoated twice in that amount of time.

Creating a "Weathered Look"

If you prefer wood with a weathered look, you can speed up the process and get a weathered look almost instantly by combining 1 or 2 cups of baking soda with 1 gallon of water. Scrub the solution into the wood surface, then rinse with clear water. Allow the wood to dry away from direct sunlight. The resulting degree of "weathering" will depend on the type of wood, its porosity and its age.

Teak Wood Furniture

Outdoor furniture made of teak wood is extremely durable and does not need chemical treatments to keep it looking beautiful. It is virtually rot and termite proof, and can stay outside for a lifetime no matter what the weather, and seems to just improve with age. Teak will begin to turn gray after about three months of exposure to rain and sun. Total graying, or "weathering" takes six to eight months, or longer depending on the weather conditions to which it has been exposed. Weathered teak wood can be cleaned by scrubbing with a brush and soapy water. Hose the furniture down after scrubbing to get rid of loosened dirt.

If you prefer the original tawny color of the teak wood, instead of the traditional weathered look, apply soapy water with a stiff polyester bristle scrub brush. Thoroughly scrub the furniture, working on a small area at a time. Hose the furniture down after scrubbing. Chemical preparations developed for cleaning teak boat decks can also be used to remove the grayish cast from the wood. These preparations are available from marine supply stores. Use according to package directions.

To maintain the tawny color of the wood, apply natural teak oil to clean wood when it is completely dried. Natural teak oil can be purchased from some woodworking supply stores and marine supply stores.

Scratches and minor scrapes can be removed from teak wood furniture by lightly buffing with fine sandpaper. Small cracks that may form in teak wood furniture are normal and harmless and generally need no repair. Small cracks are the result of the natural expansion and contraction of the wood.

Repairing Director's Chairs

Director's chairs are inexpensive, practical and readily available and can be used indoors or outdoors. The basic chair style is produced in several heights and is often available in lounge chair and bar stool styles. The finish on director's chairs is usually a durable lacquer. Small chips in the finish can be repaired by lightly rubbing over the chipped area with a small artist's brush dipped in lacquer thinner. If the chipping is extensive, re-amalgamation may restore the finish to its previous appearance. (See instructions for re-amalgamation page 31.) If re-amalgamating does not successfully restore the finish it will have to be removed and replaced.

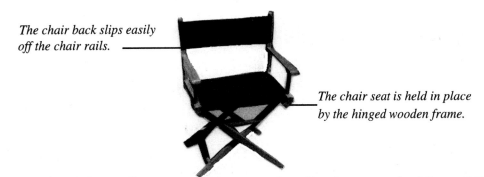

The chair back slips easily off the chair rails.

The chair seat is held in place by the hinged wooden frame.

The seat back is easily removed by grasping firmly on each side and lifting the canvas off of the chair rails. The seat can be removed by folding the chair slightly and removing the rolled edges of the canvas from the grooves that hold them in place. Replacements are available in a variety of colors and patterns at home improvement stores, discount stores, and from many catalogs.

Cleaning Canvas Seats and Seat Backs

Remove canvas pieces from the chair frame, and place on a firm, nonabsorbent surface. (The dye on the canvas may transfer to an absorbent surface once the canvas is wet. For extra protection, cover the surface with a plastic drop cloth.) Use a mild solution of detergent and cold water and a soft scrub brush to remove accumulated dirt. Rinse thoroughly with cold water. Return seat backs and seats to the chair frame while still wet. Allow to air dry away from direct sunlight.

The dry canvas can be coated with "Scotchguard" fabric protector if you feel it will require extra protection from stains and dirt. Scotchguard will repel moisture and soil and help keep the seat looking "new". For best results, cover the wood surrounding the canvas or remove the canvas pieces from the frame to prevent possible damage to the finish from over-spray. Apply several thin coats instead of one heavy coat, and allow sufficient drying time between coats.

Gluing Outdoor Furniture

Use only water-resistant or waterproof glue on outdoor furniture. Waterproof glue is usually more expensive, but is recommended for furniture that will be permanently exposed to weather.

Plastic resin glues (ureaformaldehyde adhesives) offer high strength and water-resistance, an unlimited shelf life and are considerably less expensive than *resorcinol* or *epoxy* glues. They are sold in a powder form and need to be mixed with water to form a thick, creamy consistency before using. Spread the glue on both surfaces, position the glued wood and then clamp securely. Setting time for plastic resin glue is 6 to 10 hours depending on the application. Curing time is approximately 24 hours.

Resorcinol resin glue is completely waterproof. It is sold as a two component product: a liquid resin and a powdered catalyst. When the two components are combined and cured they become an extremely strong adhesive. Mix only the amount needed; just before use. Use a disposable container to mix the glue. Apply the glue to one of the surfaces, then bring the surfaces together. Use clamps to apply pressure to achieve a good glue bond. Resorcinol resin glue sets well at temperatures above 50° F, but will not set properly at lower temperatures because of the slow chemical curing. Under ideal conditions, it will set in 6 to 10 hours and cure in 24. Two drawbacks of resorcinol glue are-it is expensive and it tends to leave a dark glue line on the wood.

Epoxy resin glues are two-part resin-catalyst products that are relatively new to the market. They contain a resin and a hardener which need to be combined just before use. Use a disposable container to mix the glue. Apply epoxy to one of the surfaces then bring the surfaces together. Clamping is not necessary with epoxy glue. Epoxies are waterproof and oil resistant when completely cured. They provide very strong adhesive qualities, but are best suited to small repairs. Care should be taken during application as epoxies are very difficult to remove when cured and hardened. Read the package label for the recommended solvent to remove excess glue immediately after application. Setting time for epoxies can be anywhere from 15 minutes to 12 hours depending on the application. Curing time is approximately 24 hours.

Hardware for Outdoor Furniture

All hardware used for repairs on outdoor furniture (screws, nuts, bolts, hinges, etc.) should be made of noncorrosive or *galvanized* metal to prevent rusted hardware and damage to the wood. The galvanizing process coats metal (most commonly iron and steel) with a thin protective coating of zinc or zinc alloy which prevents the metal from being damaged by corrosion. Iron and steel hardware that are not rust resistant should be painted, or have an application of clear finish (i.e.: lacquer, varnish, etc.) applied to prevent damage from exposure to air and moisture.

A thin coat of rust can be removed from iron or steel hardware by dipping the hardware in water, then scrubbing with a fine copper bristle brush. Rinse thoroughly, and dry completely. (Remove hardware from furniture first to prevent scratching the surrounding wood.) Once the rust has been removed, the dry metal should be given a protective coat of paint or other finish to prevent the rust from returning.

If the rust can not be removed using the method described above, remove the hardware from the furniture and apply Naval Jelly or other commercial rust remover to the rusted areas. (Wear gloves to protect your hands and work in a well ventilated area.) Wait 5 to 10 minutes, then sponge off the Naval Jelly with water. After the rust is removed, thoroughly rinse to remove any remaining Naval Jelly, then dry with towels. Allow to dry completely before painting or applying a clear finish.

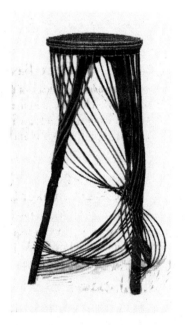

Chapter 11

Repairing Rustic Furniture

Rustic furniture is usually made of unhewn or unfinished parts of trees. Roots, logs, sticks, branches, twigs and tree stumps are all used, in different combinations, to create the various styles. Some Rustic styles also incorporate shells, animal horns and antlers, hides and other non-wood elements into the design. The bark is often left intact and little if anything is done to conceal any natural defects or disfigurations in the materials. Even moss attached to the bark is often preserved.

The style and type of Rustic furniture is usually determined by indigenous materials and the natural shape of the wood usually dictates the design. Most furniture styles manipulate or conceal the nature of the materials used. Rustic furniture is different; it is not sculpted or chiseled into a predetermined shape. The tree parts are joined, free-flowing and imperfect, just like in nature. Rustic styles imitate natural growth and attempt to make furniture appear as if it were still living. Rustic furniture covers a wide spectrum of styles; from delicate, lacey twig furniture that appears too delicate to withstand use, to huge, cumbersome styles made from stumps and roots.

The popular interest in Rustic furniture in the United States during the late 1800s was a reaction against, what people of the time believed to be, rapid industrialization and urbanization of their way of life. Rustic furniture offered the chance to go "back to nature" and represented a simpler way of life. Most people today associate Rustic furniture with summer camps, vacation resorts, the Adirondacks, the Appalachians or the Western frontier. But this natural style of furniture is not limited to a specific geographic region or way of life. It has appeared in regional variations and cultural interpretations across the United States and worldwide.

Rustic furniture was traditionally created by folk artists and untrained craftspeople who learned how to make the furniture "by doing it". But Rustic furniture is not limited to a select group of old, rare, or valuable pieces. Contemporary Rustic furniture and reproductions of 19th century factory-made furniture are being discovered today by a whole new generation of natural furniture enthusiasts, and it is readily available in many areas of the country. These styles are currently custom-made by more than 500 individual craftspeople in the United States alone, and produced by several companies, including The Old Hickory Furniture Company– the first commercial producer of Indiana Hickory style furniture.

American Rustic furniture can be divided into five different styles: **Indiana Hickory (or Factory-Made)**, **Northwoods**, **Southern Root and Twig**, **Western and Cowboy**, and **Antler and Horn**.

Indiana Hickory (also known as Factory-Made) is the most visible and widespread style. Rugged, comfortable furniture was produced from the abundant, young hickory trees that grew in the Midwest. This style was most popular from 1899 through the 1930s, and was at one time produced by ten companies in Indiana. The first, largest and most prolific of these companies was Old Hickory Furniture Company.

Indiana Hickory style (or "Factory-Made") chair and stool.

Old Hickory Furniture Company bent young hickory saplings into shape around a metal frame, then fitted the shaped pieces together to create tables, chairs, settees and other types of furniture. In 1922 their catalog listed over 125 different pieces of furniture and they produced approximately 2,000 pieces a week for 65 years. Every completed piece of furniture was marked with a brand on the rear leg or under the table top.

When Old Hickory Furniture Company finally ceased production they were flooded with requests to resume manufacturing. In spite of the popular demand, the industry sat idle for thirty years. Then, in the mid-1980s, Old Hickory Furniture Company once again began producing Rustic furniture.

The *Northwoods* style is more commonly, but mistakenly, called "Adirondacks". While this style of furniture was produced in the Adirondack region of upstate New York, it was also produced in other wilderness areas of the Northeast. Yellow and white birch, cedar, and hardwoods were commonly used to craft this style of furniture. Northwoods furniture was often decorated with twigs in intricate patterns commonly referred to as "mosaic". The Northwoods style is the most "untwiglike" of all rustic furniture and is usually very geometric in appearance.

Northwoods style chair

Southern Root and Twig style furniture (sometimes referred to as "Gypsy furniture") originated in the backwoods of the Appalachian Mountains and is made primarily from branches of rhododendron bushes. The branches were shaped into hooped or circle-backed chairs, rockers and other furniture items. Amish communities used young branches of willow to create similar circle-backed chairs. Cottonwood, poplar, alder and aspen are all included in the family of willows and were often used in lieu of willow depending on their regional availability. Weeping willows, while prolific and readily available, were seldom used as the trees provided an insufficient number of suitably sized limbs.

Southern Root and Twig Style Chair

Southern Root and Twig furniture is created from "benders" and "whips". Pieces from taller trees are cut and used to shape the backs of sofas and other larger pieces of furniture. These pieces are called "benders". Thinner branches are steamed and bent to form the hoops. These pieces are called "whips". Nails are used to secure elements on most pieces of furniture but some use only the natural tension of the wood to hold the pieces in place.

Root and Twig reached its peak of popularity between the 1920s and the 1930s, and there was a demand for this style of furniture all across the country. Southern Root and Twig is faster and easier to create than other styles of Rustic furniture and two or three chairs could easily be made by a single crafter in one day. Many people out of work as a result of the Depression crafted and sold homemade Root and Twig furniture as a source of income.

The *Western and Cowboy* style of furniture was originally constructed of lodgepole pine and juniper trees and made of "poles and slabs" of wood. The burls and knots characteristic to these woods give this style of furniture a very unique appearance. Western and Cowboy furniture often has seats and backs made of leather or rawhide and can be found decorated with tanned skins, fur, hooves or horns.

Western and Cowboy style rocker and footstool.

Many individuals (cowboys and otherwise) have produced Western and Cowboy themed furniture over the years. But Thomas Molesworth, a craftsman and furniture designer from Cody, Wyoming, is probably the most famous and prolific producer of Cowboy furniture to date. He began creating his cowboy inspired furniture in his studio in the 1930s. It was heavy, macho, "outdoorsy" furniture... and became an instant success. His furniture was ordered by owners of restaurants and resorts as well as private residences and he was frequently commissioned to design and build pianos, chandeliers and other amenities to complete the Western and Cowboy theme.

The *Antler and Horn* style of furniture was common in Europe between the middle 1800s and the early 1900s. American furniture builders used naturally shed antlers and horns of buffalo and longhorn steer to copy this style. Many craftsmen made use of horns salvaged from stockyards and slaughterhouses. The horns and antlers were used to create tables, chairs and other unique furniture and accessory items.

Antique Rustic furniture is quite valuable and many pieces were produced in very limited quantities. Most of these rare and valuable pieces are in museums. If you believe you may have a valuable, antique piece of Rustic furniture, contact a professional before attempting any repairs or maintenance procedures. As with other antique furniture pieces, genuine antique Rustic furniture should be appraised and insured.

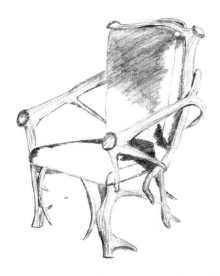

Contemporary chair made of antlers and cowhide.

Repairing Southern Root and Twig Style Furniture

One of the most common repairs to this style of furniture is replacing missing or damaged nails used to hold the furniture together. The nails are most often wire brads and generally range in size from 3/4" to 1". The brads should be just long enough to reach through the second piece of wood without the end of the brad protruding. (If the proper size brad can not be found, a longer brad can be used and the protruding tip can be snipped off with wire cutters.) To prevent the wood from splitting or breaking, larger sized common nails, finishing nails and wood screws should only be used on thicker branches of wood and only if wire brads are not available in a large enough size to do the job.

Pro Tip:
Keep in mind that brads used on green wood or wood that has not completely dried will work their way out of the wood as it shrinks and dries. If this should occur, simply use a tack hammer to tap them back into place.

Southern Root and Twig Style furniture is usually left in a natural state, and does not have a finish coat applied. A top coat will, however, help prolong the life of furniture kept outdoors or in a moist or damp environment. A linseed oil or tung oil finish will help keep internal moisture in the wood but a polyurethane finish (in an eggshell or flat sheen) is best for keeping external dampness and water from damaging the wood. The amount of potential moisture the furniture will be exposed to will usually determine the best finish to use.

Be sure to prepare the furniture prior to application: Make sure it is free of all dirt or grease. Old finishes which are cracked, blistered, checked or peeling should be removed. Glossy finishes should be dulled. Fill nail and screw holes.

For instructions on how to apply an oil finish see "Reviving an Oil Finish" pages 28-29.

For a polyurethane finish – prepare the furniture as described above, then apply the polyurethane with a synthetic bristle brush. Apply thin even coats, and work outdoors, out of direct sunlight whenever possible. Work from the top of the furniture to the bottom, and don't forget to do the underside. Allow the finish to dry for 3 to 4 hours, then check for beads of oil that may have weeped up from the wood. Gently wipe them off with a lint free cloth. Allow the finish to dry completely before applying another coat. The drying time will vary depending on the temperature, humidity and the thickness of the finish coat. Do not apply polyurethane in cold, damp conditions. Wait until the morning dew has dried before starting application and stop applying well before dusk.

Furniture left outdoors exposed to the elements will generally need to be re-coated with new finish about once a year. If it is protected by a patio cover or porch, it may only need to be re-coated every two years. Indoor furniture should not need a finish coat for protection but if one is applied it will generally last five years or more depending on the type of finish applied and the amount of use the furniture receives.

Repairing Indiana Hickory Style Furniture

Indiana Hickory style furniture is very durable because it is made from larger branches and fewer branches, than other styles of Rustic furniture. It is usually left in a natural state and does not have a finish coat applied. A finish coat will help prolong the life of furniture kept outdoors, or exposed to a moist environment. Applications of linseed oil or tung oil will keep the wood from drying out without giving it a "finished" look. Polyurethane varnish (in an eggshell or flat finish) will provide the utmost protection from exposure to dampness.

Be sure to prepare the furniture prior to application: Make sure it is free of all dirt or grease. Old finishes which are cracked, blistered, checked or peeling should be removed. Glossy finishes should be dulled. Fill nail and screw holes.

For instructions on how to apply an oil finish see "Reviving an Oil Finish" pages 28-29.

For a polyurethane finish – prepare the furniture as described above, then apply the polyurethane with a synthetic bristle brush. Apply thin even coats, and work outdoors, out of direct sunlight whenever possible. Work from the top of the furniture to the bottom and don't forget to do the underside. Allow the finish to dry for three to four hours, then check for beads of oil that may have weeped up from the wood. Gently wipe them off with a lint free cloth. Allow the finish to dry completely before applying another coat. The drying time will vary depending on the temperature, humidity and the thickness of the finish coat. Do not apply polyurethane in cold, damp conditions. Wait until the morning dew has dried before starting application and stop applying well before dusk.

Furniture left outdoors exposed to the elements will generally need to be re-coated with new finish about once a year. If it is protected by a patio cover or porch, it may only need to be re-coated every two years. Indoor furniture should not need a finish coat for protection, but if one is applied it will generally last five years or more depending on the type of finish applied and the amount of use the furniture receives.

Repairing Peeling Bark
The Southern Root and Twig and Indiana Hickory styles of furniture are usually constructed of wood with the bark left intact. To retain its bark, wood has to be cut in mid-winter when the sap is at rest and then thoroughly dried and "seasoned" for six to twelve months before being worked.

Changes in temperature and humidity or exposure to direct sunlight may cause the bark to separate from the branch wood. If this should occur, wood glue can be injected between the bark and the branch wood. Use toothpicks if necessary to work the glue as far into the opening as possible. Take care not to pry or push the bark or it may break off. Apply small "C" clamps to hold the wood and the bark together until the glue bonds. Automotive hose clamps can be used as an alternative to "C" clamps on smaller pieces of wood.

Repairing Northwoods Style Furniture
The most common repair problem with Northwoods style furniture is damage to the finish coat of paint or clear finish. To repair a chipped painted finish see pages 32-33. Polyurethane or varnish finishes are difficult to repair successfully, and, when damaged, should be removed rather than repaired.

The second most common problem with Northwoods style furniture is the fasteners used to hold the furniture together become loose or are missing. This style of furniture is usually held together with common nails or finishing nails, but many pieces may have been repaired over the years with various sizes of wood screws. If the fasteners need to be replaced, let the previous type of fastener be your guide as to what to use. If you need to use a larger fastener than the one previously used, pre-drill the hole to avoid splitting the wood.

Repairing Western and Cowboy Style Furniture

Older furniture constructed of lodgepole pine and juniper trees was most often left unfinished. Contemporary pieces are often coated with matte finish lacquer or an oil finish. Scratches and chips in the lacquer are easy to repair. (See "Repairing a Chipped Finish" page 32 and "Repairing Scratches in the Finish" pages 34-36.) To repair an oil finish see page 28.

Rawhide is occasionally used to tie pieces of wood together on some styles of furniture, or as a decoration on others. If the leather should dry-out or break it should be removed and replaced. Carefully study how the rawhide is wrapped before removing it, or take Polaroid pictures, so you can duplicate the wrapping pattern. Replacement rawhide is available from many woodworking supply stores and some seating supply stores. See the Appendix for a list of sources.

To clean, or remove stains from leather chair seats, see page 72. To clean or condition leather tops, see pages 95-98. To remove stains or indentions from leather see pages 99-100.

Furniture made with tanned skins or animal hides should not be cleaned by an amateur. Improper cleaning will remove the tanning chemicals and can stiffen and discolor skins and cause the fur to fall out. If these items become stained or need to be cleaned, contact a local taxidermist. For general maintenance, carefully vacuum the piece using the hose and brush attachment or lightly brush with a suede brush to remove dust and surface dirt. Always use gentle pressure and brush with the grain of the hide *not* against it.

Repairing Antler and Horn Furniture

Antler furniture often has a delicate, abstract appearance but its looks are deceiving. The antlers are held together with screws and very strong resin - based glues and the furniture is very durable. Contemporary antler furniture is often finished with a honey or tan colored stain to give a more even color tone to the furniture. The stain is then sealed under a thin coating of lacquer. If the color should wear thin, it can be touched-up in the same manner as wood. See page 36 "Repairing Worn Edges and Worn Spots".

Antler furniture needs no special care to maintain its unique appearance. Dust regularly with a soft cloth, as you would wood furniture. A light coat of paste wax can be applied if you wish to provide an extra layer of protection or if you desire a little more of a sheen.

Care should be taken when cleaning horn trimmed furniture. Wipe with a soft cloth that has been slightly dampened, and then wrung out until almost dry. To remove stubborn dirt, use a very fine abrasive such as jeweler's rouge.

Horns are a gelatinous substance and can become dry and brittle with age. Rough edges that may develop can be smoothed by lightly buffing with very fine sandpaper. Broken decorative pieces of horn can be reattached using an epoxy resin glue. If the broken horn is part of the structural frame, it is unlikely the furniture can be successfully repaired or will be durable enough to withstand use after the repair. Consult a professional furniture restorer for major breaks or larger repairs.

Chapter 12

Repairing Mirrors and Frames

Mirrors are commonplace in homes today, and are often taken for granted, but this was not always the case. Early mirrors were handmade, using a long difficult process. This resulted in high prices that could only be afforded by the very wealthy. At one time mirrors were one of the most sought after luxury items in Europe. The original process for creating looking glasses (as mirrors were originally called, and remained named until about 1875) was discovered around 1480 in Venice. The process used to create the looking glass was such a guarded secret that divulging the information was a crime punishable by death, and glassmakers were forbidden to travel beyond their local area. The knowledge of the process eventually made it's way across Europe and beyond, but it remained an expensive and exclusive process. During the 1680s, a 3 foot by 4 foot mirror may have been worth as much as $40,000 in today's currency.

The mirror production process became more technologically advanced in the early part of the 1800s. Because of this, mirrors became more affordable and commonplace and by 1820, could be found in most working class homes. By the 1870s, working class families may have had 12 or more mirrors of various sizes in their home. Large mirrors were manufactured to be placed between doors or windows, and small mirrors were available in almost every shape and size. Almost every type of cabinet wood was used as a mirror frame, but, by the end of the 19th century, oak framed mirrors were the most popular style. The oak was not usually used in its natural light color, but was often fumed or artificially darkened or painted white, green or black. Mirrors representative of the 20th century are most frequently framed with plastic, ceramics, chrome or steel, and a variety of other "industrial" materials.

 Pro Tip:
Manufacturer's labels were often glued on the outside of the backboard, but can also be found on the inside of the backboard or on the back of the glass itself. The presence of a label or stamp can increase the value of the mirror and care should be taken to preserve them.

It is easy to determine whether a mirror is made from old glass or more modern glass. A little detective work will easily uncover the differences. Tap a coin on old glass and you will hear a definite, sharp tinny ringing sound. Tap a coin on a modern glass mirror and you will hear a more muted, dull sound. Old mirror glass seldom exceeded 3/16" and is considerably thinner than the glass used today. Very old glass is always thicker at the bottom than it is at the top. Modern glass is nearly double the thickness of old glass – averaging between 1/4" to 3/8" thick. You can check the thickness of the glass by placing a business card or the edge of a coin against the surface of the mirror. The distance between the reflection and the card will equal the thickness of the plate.

Many older mirrors had beveled edges. The beveling process on pre-Victorian mirrors was done by hand with a pumice stone and the beveling often appears irregular, uneven and soft-edged. Modern beveling is achieved by using a machine with a sandstone wheel. This results in a hard, sharply defined edge. If the beveled mirror edge produces prismatic colors when viewed from an angle this is usually an indication the mirror has been made from new glass.

Old glass will have a yellowish or greyish reflective color. New glass has a colorless, very clear reflective quality. To check for the color, hold a plain white card against the mirror surface. If the reflection is a close match to the original it is Victorian glass or modern glass. If the reflection has a yellow, blue or grey tone to it, the glass is old. This dark tone is caused by the high tin content of the glass itself, not from the silvering on the backing. The backing on an old mirror was silvered with a combination of mercury and tin. Modern glass is coated with a thin layer of silver or aluminum and then finished with an application of lacquer.

Regardless of whether the backing is lacquered or a combination of mercury and tin, mirrors exposed to moisture or humidity, and sometimes just time itself, will eventually develop age spots which will appear as non-reflective grey spots on the mirror's face. On old glass, these spots will often appear to be large swipes or blobs. These are a result of the uneven application of the original mercury and tin during the silvering process. The mercury and tin mixture was poured on to the back of the mirror and then spread toward the edges. When all of the backing was coated, the mirror was tipped so the excess could run off of the edges. This uneven application of the original coating is what causes the deteriorating uneven look we see today.

Silvering on old mirrors will break down and deteriorate from the center of the mirror to the outer edges and eventually from one end to the other. These defects can be removed by having the mirror professionally re-silvered, but be forewarned, re-silvering can be expensive. Ask around your local antique stores for the name of a professional who specializes in re-silvering, and ask to see samples of their work.

If your mirror is a true antique, the mirror should not be re-silvered. A perfect antique mirror is usually concealing a previous repair or could possibly be a fake. Very few perfect antique mirrors exist, and most of them are in museums. Imperfections add to the authenticity, and may actually add to the value. In some cases, original glass in a mirror may increase the value by as much as 25-50%. If the silvering has completely deteriorated, remove the mirror, store the original, and fill the mirror frame with a good quality replacement. In most cases, replacement glass will not significantly detract from the value of an antique mirror. If only a small section of the silvering has worn away it can be repaired using the technique below.

Patching the Silvering on a Mirror Backing
Carefully remove the wooden backing from the mirror. Measure the size of the damaged area on the silvered backing. Cut a piece of reflecting foil (available at craft supply stores and some woodworking supply stores) so that it is the size of the patch plus 1/2" on all side. Carefully place the foil over the damaged area, and use your fingers to smooth the foil over the backing. Use tape to hold the foil in place. Replace the wooden backing.

Cleaning Mirrors
Carefully rub the surface of the mirror with a ball of newspaper or paper towels dampened with denatured alcohol, or rubbing alcohol diluted with water. Rub and buff until dry. To avoid damage to the mirror backing, always apply the moisture to the paper towel or paper and not the mirror. Never allow the cleaner to run around the edges.

Commercial window cleaners are not recommended for use on new or old glass mirrors because they can cause the silver backing to oxidize almost immediately upon contact. Virtually any cleaner including vinegar, ammonia or alcohol can potentially damage the silver backing, but the high alkaline content in commercial spray cleaners makes them the harshest and most dangerous.

Many newer mirrors are made with a sealer over the silvering to help prevent damage to the mirror backing. A light coat of clear spray varnish can be applied to the back of an older mirror to help protect the silvering and prevent potential moisture damage.

Replacing Backboards on Mirrors

The wooden backing on a mirror is usually unfinished wood similar to that used for backboards on dressers, chests and desks. The backboard protects the delicate silvered mirror back and provides support to keep the mirror frame square and rigid. Old mirror frames often have a scattering of screwholes in the wood from attachments used to secure the mirror to walls or furniture over the course of its lifetime. If the holes have begun to join together and break the wood, or the wood dries out and begins to crack, the backboard will need to be replaced. If you believe your mirror is a true antique, consult a professional for this job to prevent damage to the old glass.

To replace the backboard: lay the mirror on a blanket or other padding on a firm surface such as a large table or on the floor. Use a tack puller and needle-nosed pliers to remove the tacks or staples. Be careful not to damage the mirror frame. Use the old back as a pattern and trace the shape on to a piece of plywood the same thickness as the original piece. Cut the board along the traced lines. Carefully align the replacement back piece on the back of the furniture. Fasten the new back to the mirror with tacks or small nails. Be careful the nails are not driven in too close to the mirror's edge as this can chip or crack the glass.

Reconstructing Missing Decorative Pieces on Frames

Mirror frames can be made from a variety of materials – metal, plastic, ceramic, and wood to name a few. Older mirrors (especially those produced before the 19th century) were almost always framed with wood. These wooden frames often appear to have elaborate decorative carving, but this "carving" is actually gesso (a hard, plaster-like substance) or plaster imposed on to the wood rather than carved into it. Gesso and plaster decorations are easily dented and chipped and can develop hairline cracks as the material ages.

During the 19th century, "carved" frames were often made by applying layers of stucco over a wire frame. These stucco frames are easy to detect with a simple test. Take a sewing needle, and attempt to stick the needle into the reverse side of the frame. The needle will penetrate wood but will not penetrate stucco.

Missing pieces of carved wood or gesso can be easy to repair or replace if the area is small. Larger areas are usually difficult to repair, and the repaired area is usually very obvious once the repairs are done. Broken or missing wood and gesso decorations can be repaired using the same techniques. If the mirror frame is a true antique, this repair job should be left to a professional restoration service.

Remove any dust or flaking finish from the frame by lightly brushing with a soft, clean paint brush. Apply a thin layer of undiluted all-purpose white glue to the damaged area on the frame. Allow the glue to dry while you mix up the gesso. This glue layer will act as a foundation for the repair.

Gesso is made by mixing together plaster of Paris, water and water-soluble white glue. A small glass dish or shot glass is usually the perfect size for mixing the ingredients. The mixture will begin to set quickly, usually within about 3 minutes, so you want to make sure to mix small amounts at a time. If the mixture dries to the point where it begins to crumble it will not adhere properly to the frame and you will need to discard it and mix another batch.

Use a measuring spoon and measure 1/2 teaspoon of plaster of Paris into your mixing container. Add a little bit of water (use an eyedropper if you have one) and a little bit of water-soluble white glue. Stir the mixture with a popscicle stick or another small piece of wood to combine the mixture. Mixing gesso is one of those "learn from experience kind of things". Too much water will make the gesso too runny, too much glue will make the gesso too glossy or shiny (and will make it brittle and difficult to sand when it dries). Add a little more plaster of Paris to correct a runny mixture, or a little more water to help correct the addition of too much glue. If all else fails, throw away the batch and make a new one.

When the gesso is properly mixed, remove it from the dish and roll it between your fingers like putty. Form it into a ball and quickly apply it to the damaged area on the frame. Use your fingers to shape the gesso to match the surrounding design. Tools used for creating pottery, popscicle sticks or other small pieces of wood, toothpicks, and a variety of other household items can also be used to shape the gesso into the approximate shapes of the missing decorations.

Allow the gesso to dry overnight. When completely dry, it will have a chalky consistency. Sand any rough areas very gently, with super-fine sandpaper. Use a small chisel, file or emery board to help define the design if necessary. Brush any sanding dust from the surface with a soft, clean paint brush. Carefully wipe the frame with a tack rag to remove any traces of dust, then seal the repair with a coat of shellac to protect it from moisture.

If the damaged area is large, repeat the process, mixing new small batches of gesso until all of the repairs have been made.

Blend the repair to the rest of the frame by following the techniques described in "Repairing the Finish of the Frame", pages 222-224.

Repairing the Finish of the Frame

This can be a broad topic, because the techniques used to repair the finish will obviously depend on the type of finish on the frame.

Frames with a painted finish- If the frame has a painted finish, and the repaired area is small, you can use the techniques described for *stretching paint* ("Repairing a Chipped Painted Surface" page 32). Otherwise the frame will need to be repainted.

Stained wooden and clear finished frames- If the frame is made of stained wood, you can use oil paints or wood stain to stain the gesso to match the existing color of the frame. For general instructions see "Repairing Scratches in the Finish" page 34. Apply the colorant with a cotton swab, a small artist's brush or use your fingertip. Allow to dry completely. Seal the color under a light coat of shellac. Felt tip markers, (used to conceal scratches on furniture) can also be use to add color to the gesso.

Scratches in the clear finish of a frame can be repaired using the instructions for "Repairing a Chipped Finish" page 32-33 or "Repairing Scratches in the Finish" pages 34-36.

Less expensive wooden frames were often "grain-painted" or "false-grained" to imitate expensive figured wood. These grain-painted pieces were less expensive than their veneered counterparts during the 19th century, but are rare today. They can now be worth considerably more than veneered or solid wood pieces if the paint on the frame is original and in good condition. Make sure any figured wood on your frame is really wood and not paint before attempting to repair it. Once damaged it can be difficult if not impossible to repair and the damage can significantly reduce the value of the piece.

Damaged "false-grained" wood.

Repaired "false-grained" wood.

Frames with a gilt finish- If the frame has a gilt finish, and the damaged area is small, the gilt can be successfully repaired and blended to the undamaged area. Regilding small repairs on an antique mirror frame does not usually detract from its value *if* the gilt and the workmanship are of good quality, and the frame does not now appear to be "new" or over-gilded. Old gilt will have a patina or rubbed sheen to it, and can add as much as 30- 50 % to the value of the frame if left intact.

Prepare the surface before applying the gilt. A light coat of shellac applied over the gesso or the frame itself will provide a good base coat. Next, use a small artist's brush to apply a thin coat of liquid gold leaf paint. Work on a small area a time, but work fast – the solvent in the paint evaporates quickly and it will dry sooner than you expect. Gold leaf paint should not be used on large flat areas as this will accentuate the brush marks in the paint and make the repaired area obvious. Allow the paint to dry completely before proceeding with the repair.

Pro Tip:
Do not use "gilt paint" or gold metallic paint in place of the liquid gold leaf paint. Paint is very runny, difficult to work with, and most brands usually contain no real gold. Gold leaf paint will also help blend the repaired area with the original finish on the rest of the frame and draw less attention to the repair.

To complete the repair, wax gilt should be applied over the gold leaf paint to highlight the frame and help duplicate the original finish. Wax gilt is made from real gold that is suspended in a wax and turpentine base. It is available in yellow gold and many other colors including brass, silver, rose gold, and white gold. Choose the color or combination of colors you will need to duplicate the original finish.

To apply wax gilt, dip a soft cloth in a little turpentine to moisten the cloth, then into the jar of wax gilt. A little wax gilt goes a long way so don't attempt to load-up the cloth with wax or apply it too heavily to the frame. Spread the gilt over the gold leaf paint and blend the edges of the repair to the undamaged area with light feathering strokes. Use light pressure during the application to help bring out the full color of the gilt. Work on a small area at a time, and brush back and forth to help bring up the sheen of the gilt. When all of the gilt has been applied, use a clean soft cloth to buff the finish to a sheen to match the original finish.

Check your local arts and crafts store or woodworking supply store for wax gilt and gold leaf paint, or check the Appendix for sources.

Genuine gold leaf is made from 22 to 23-1/2 carat gold that has been beaten into very thin sheets – often less than 1/1000th of an inch thick. It is very expensive, and prices can change as the gold market fluctuates. The application of real gold leaf is a multi-step process requiring skill and special tools, and is not recommended for the amateur refinisher.

Repairing Cracks or Dents in Frames

Small cracks and dents in the frame can be filled by following the instructions for "Removing Dents" on pages 49 to 52. Splinters in a wooden frame can be repaired using the instructions on page 56 for "Repairing Furniture Splinters".

Repairing Separating Corner Seams on Wooden Frames

Old or antique wooden frames will, more often than not, show evidence of separating seams on the inside edges of the corners. This is a natural occurrence caused by the shrinking of the wood across the grain due to a combination of time, and changes in temperature and humidity. Newer wooden frames should have tight seams because, theoretically, the newer wood should not have been exposed to enough elements or had enough time to shrink. If the corner seam is loose on a newer frame, it has probably been severely mistreated or was poorly made in the first place.

Separated corner seams can often be successfully filled with either shellac or lacquer sticks or wax touch-up sticks. (See "Removing Dents" pages 49 to 52. If the frame is a gesso covered frame, a small batch of gesso can be mixed up and used to fill the cracks. For instructions for mixing and applying gesso, see "Reconstructing Missing Decorative Pieces on Frames" pages 220-221. Touch up the finish on the gesso frame using the instructions on pages 222-224.

Chapter 13

Furniture Maintenance

Furniture needs to be kept clean to protect the wood and the finish. However, excessive cleaning and polishing can leave residues that dull the finish, darken the color of the furniture, or in extreme cases, damage or remove the finish coat. Colored polishes formulated to cover scratches contain dyes that can darken furniture with every application. Cleaners containing water or harsh chemicals can dissolve or break down a finish coat. Even routine dusting can damage the finish if done improperly.

Furniture that is properly cleaned and polished is not only exposed to less potential damage but has the added bonus of requiring less cleaning and polishing.

The Five Basic Maintenance Steps

You can get more years of enjoyment from your furniture and avoid unnecessary repairs by following these five basic maintenance steps:

- **Keep your furniture dusted.**
Accumulated dust can scratch the finish, and trap moisture and pollutants from the air that will damage the finish or the wood.

- **Keep your furniture clean.**
Trapped oils, dirt and acids will deteriorate the finish if they are not removed.

- **Apply polish or wax as needed, to preserve the moisture level of the wood and protect the furniture finish.**
Almost all finishes benefit from the added protection of a coat of wax or polish. If you use wax, keep the furniture free of wax buildup. Trapped layers of old wax will not offer additional protection but will actually increase the deterioration of the finish.

• Do not expose furniture to radical changes in temperature or humidity levels.

Temperature changes cause wood to expand and contract. This can result in loose veneers, weak joints, and cracking finishes. Keep furniture away from direct heat sources (i.e.: radiators, wood stoves, fireplaces, etc.) and drafts. Set the thermostat in your home to between 68° and 70°. The optimal humidity level for most furniture is around 50%. If you live in a dry climate, consider investing in a humidifier to raise the humidity level in your home.

• Protect your furniture from potential damage by using coasters or pads under flower pots, drinks, and other containers holding liquids, and use trivets or pads under hot bowls, platters, or cups.

Don't use rubber mats or coasters unless they have felt beneath them. Some vinyl films and rubber compounds may stain or soften furniture finishes.

Dusting

Regular dusting is one of the easiest ways to maintain the beauty of your furniture. Dust can make even the shiniest finish look dull and lifeless. Layers of dust can darken the finish, obscure the wood grain, clog the wood pores and prevent the wood from breathing. Regular dusting prevents built-up dirt and grime and, under normal conditions, should be all that's needed to keep furniture clean.

Use a lambs's wool duster to gently dust the furniture from top to bottom, moving in the direction of the grain whenever possible. Or, dampen a soft cotton cloth and wring out all of the excess moisture. Use the cloth to gently go over your furniture, in the direction of the grain, from top to bottom. A few drops of lemon oil on the cloth will help cut through any grime or dirt. While dusting, check for loose areas that could be lifted by the duster. Never dust with a dry cloth. Dry dusting will scratch the finish or simply scatter the dust so it settles somewhere else. Remember to lift ashtrays, lamps and other objects off of the furniture when dusting to prevent dust from building-up underneath and to allow accurate assessment of the finish.

Pro Tip:
The use of feather dusters is not recommended. Feathers may break, leaving rough ends that can scratch delicate finishes and catch on carving or loose veneer. Intricate carving or detail can be gently cleaned with a make-up brush or other small, soft brush. Use the brush to draw the dust out of the crevices, do not push it further in.

Cleaning

Well maintained furniture that receives regular care, should only require a mild cleaning once a year, and major cleaning should become unnecessary. Furniture that has been abused or neglected will usually require some serious cleaning. All furniture should be thoroughly inspected before cleaning. Check for loose veneer or decorations and evaluate the condition of the finish. If the furniture appears to be in stable condition, remove the surface dirt with a lamb's wool duster or a vacuum. Then carefully dust with a soft cloth.

If dirt remains, mix a small amount of mild soap and room temperature water to make a very weak cleaning solution. Test to see if the finish will be affected by the solution by dampening a cotton swab with the mixture and applying it to an inconspicuous area. Rinse with another barely damp cotton swab until all of the solution is gone. Blot off excess moisture with soft towels. Then check the finish for damage before you continue.

If the solution did not damage the finish, take a soft cotton cloth, dip it in the cleaning solution, then wring it out as much as possible. The idea is not to get the furniture overly wet. Wipe the furniture carefully and work on a small area at a time. Rinse the cloth frequently, remove excess water, and continue to clean until no more dirt is removed. *Take your time and use gentle pressure.* To rinse, use room temperature water and a clean soft cotton cloth. Dip the cloth in the rinse water and wring it out as much as possible. Carefully wipe the furniture. Dry the furniture immediately with a clean soft cloth. Be careful not to wet any of the glued joints on the furniture.

Use extra care when cleaning painted furniture or pieces decorated with mother of pearl, brass, or other materials. When cleaning painted furniture, check the cleaning cloths frequently for any transferred coloration and stop the cleaning process immediately if any is noticed. Do not use metal polish or other specialized cleaners to clean inlayed brass or other decorative metal.

The chemicals in the cleaner may discolor or damage the surrounding wood or the wood finish.

Removing Mold

A fine coating of dust-like material that can not be wiped off the furniture may not be dust after all – it may be mold. To kill the mold, mix a solution of 1/2 cup of white vinegar and 1 gallon of room temperature water. Dip a soft cotton cloth into the solution, then wring out until almost dry. Work on a small area at a time and gently rub the mold. Rinse by wiping with a cloth dipped in clean water, that has been wrung out until almost dry. When all of the moldy areas have been cleaned, follow with the cleaning process as described above.

Polishing vs. Waxing

The debate between whether wax or polish is better for your furniture has probably been around as long as the products themselves. Most professionals who work with furniture have a definite preference for one or the other and can not be swayed to change their mind. The purpose of applying either wax or polish over the finish coat is not to make the wood shiny but rather to give the finish additional protection against heat, moisture, hard use and other potential damage and to make it easier to dust. Some "old-timers" recommend using self-polishing floor wax on furniture to provide a high gloss shine and protection. *These products are not recommended for use on furniture* (as the labels on these products will tell you) *and can destroy the finish.*

Contrary to popular opinion, wax, polish, and homemade concoctions passed along by furniture professionals will not "feed" the finish or the wood. Once a tree is cut down the wood is dead and "feeding" is rather unnecessary. One popular "feeding" formula, that has even been highly recommended by a well known woodworking magazine, contains turpentine, vinegar and linseed oil. In the worst case these homemade formulas may damage the finish, in the best case they will tend to make fingerprints more noticeable than commercial formulas. Homemade formulas should be used with great care if they are to be used at all. Ralph and Terry Kovel, authors of more than 70 books on antiques, specifically mention homemade linseed oil formulas in their book "Kovels' Guide to Selling, Buying, and Fixing Your Antiques and Collectibles" and recommend that you "Do not use it.". (page 87 "Kovels' Guide to Selling, Buying, and Fixing Your Antiques and Collectibles" Ralph and Terry Kovel, Crown Trade Paperbacks)

Linseed oil is not compatible with all types of finishes and may damage or remove them. It tends to darken with age and become quite hard, and is difficult, if not impossible to remove. The vinegar in the formula is intended to remove dirt and grime from the finish, but may, in some cases, damage or remove the finish along with the dirt. Quite often, one or two applications of this formulas will give satisfactory results, after which all subsequent coats will make the finish gummy or sticky and the polish will not dry properly.

From an objective point of view, both wax and mineral oil based polish have advantages and disadvantages. A lot of the success or failure of either one can be based upon how the product is applied, what type of finish it is applied on, and how the protective coat of oil or wax is maintained.

Wax can be successfully applied over varnish, shellac, lacquer, or synthetic varnish finishes. It should not be applied over penetrating finishes or oil finishes. Polish can successfully be applied over varnish, shellac, lacquer, or oil finishes, but should not be applied over synthetic varnish or penetrating finishes as the oil will not be absorbed by the "plastic" finish.

Furniture Wax

Wax was probably the first protective coating to be used on furniture. In Colonial days, tallow candles would drip wax on the unfinished wood furniture. When the furniture was scrubbed during cleaning, the wax would soften and become forced into the wood pores. As the furniture was buffed dry, the wax would take on a nice sheen. In between washings, the wax would keep moisture from penetrating the wood and prevent cracking and discoloring.

There are many types of wax but beeswax is most commonly used for furniture. Beeswax, as its name implies, is an insect product. It is excreted by the honeybee to construct the honeycomb. Beeswax can be found on all of the continents of the globe.

To extract the beeswax for use, the honeycomb is melted or boiled with water and the crude wax is skimmed off the top. The color of the crude material is dependent upon the type of flower which gave the pollen, the age of the hive and its care. Once the processing and packaging are done, beeswax is available commercially in yellowish brown (its natural color) or white (bleached of its natural color by additional processing involving remelting the crude wax and filtering it). Bleached beeswax can be more brittle than unbleached beeswax, especially when cold and the white color may be noticeable if left in carving or crevices.

The hardest natural wax is carnauba wax. It's produced by the Carnuba palm tree to conserve the moisture within the tree and leaves and prevent dehydration. The Carnuba palm grows in several parts of Brazil and adjacent countries in South America, Ceylon, and Equitorial Africa but because of the irregular rainy seasons of these places, the trees only produce wax in Northern Brazil.

The fronds containing the wax are cut off the tree between September and March and laid out to dry. As the fronds dry, they shrink and the wax coating begins to flake. The fronds are then threshed with sticks to make the wax fall off.

The color and quality of the wax are determined by the age of the leaves and the care used in processing the wax. The collected wax is melted and then formed into blocks. The resulting wax has a pale yellow color and is quite brittle when it is used alone. It is usually combined with beeswax or other waxes to make it more durable.

Wax polishes are usually used in their natural color, as any matter used to add color to the wax could affect the polishing qualities of the wax. The pale color of most natural waxes will not affect the appearance of all but the lightest shades of wood or stain.

Applying a Coat of Wax

Start the wax application by putting a small amount of wax on a soft cloth, then fold the cloth over the wax so it is covered by several layers of fabric. If you are using a quality wax, you should be able to cover an area of about two or three square feet with a dab of wax about the size of a pea. Cover a small area of the wood with wax and allow it to sit for about 10 minutes. Test to see if it's ready to buff-out by lightly rubbing the wax with the tip of your finger. If it starts to shine, it's ready. If you buff the wax too soon you will wipe off most of the wax and will have to reapply another coat. If you wait too long, the wax will be very difficult to rub out and it will need to be removed with turpentine before you can start all over again.

To buff-out the wax, rub it briskly with a lint-free cloth, first in all directions, then finish by rubbing along the grain. Remember, buffing is what brings up the shine. Wax should be applied to a small area at a time and then buffed-out thoroughly before moving on to the next area.

Thin coats of wax will dry harder and faster than thick ones, however, each coat must be completely dry before the next coat is applied. Wipe a dry, soft cloth across the wax finish prior to recoating. If the cloth moves smoothly across the finish it is dry enough to recoat. If it drags or sticks, give the finish more time to dry.

Most wax polishes have a very long shelf life. If the wax hardens, it can be resoftened by placing the container in warm water and mixing a small amount of turpentine into the wax.

Furniture Polish

The best furniture polish is mineral oil, or lemon oil. Read the labels carefully and **do not buy polish with linseed oil or silicone added**. Silicone is great for cars or plastic surfaces but it can be very difficult to remove and has little to offer most furniture. The problems with linseed oil have already been discussed. Mineral oil or lemon oil will clean dust and dirt from furniture while filling between the wood fibers to protect them from absorbing moisture.

Applying Furniture Polish

Oil polish will not leave furniture looking oily or feeling greasy if it is properly applied. Moisten a soft cloth with water then wring out as much water as possible. Sprinkle some polish on the cloth and wipe on the furniture. Buff off the excess polish with a clean rag. Do not leave excess polish on the furniture. It will not evaporate, and will probably not be absorbed by the wood. The remaining residue will stain anything that touches it and will attract dust and dirt.

The temperature of your house and the degree of humidity will usually dictate how frequently furniture should be polished. Some people find that weekly applications are necessary while others apply polish only once a month. At least once a year, polish should be applied to the back, undersides, and other unfinished portions of the furniture to protect the wood. Like human skin, all wood needs moisturizing and attention to keep it beautiful.

Commercial spray polishes consist of compressed gas, water, fragrance, inexpensive hard waxes, and, quite often, silicones to give the finish added shine. Silicones produce a high gloss, but often leave the surface dangerously slippery. These polishes also seldom contain the necessary oils to replenish wood or cover fine scratches and are not formulated with ingredients capable of cleaning the wood. Add to all of this, the fact that silicones can build up on or penetrate into the finish and eventually interfere with any necessary repairs or finish removal, and spray polishes quickly lose their appeal.

Polish	**Wax**
Relatively inexpensive.	Good quality waxes can be quite expensive.
Does not buildup on the finish.	Multiple coats of wax will buildup on the finish if they are not periodically removed.
Reduces the chances of cracking, crazing, crumbling and other related finish problems.	Provides maximum protection in high wear areas, and against alcohol and water damage.
Dust can be attracted to and cling to some polishes.	Dust will slip off a properly applied and maintained wax coat.
Polish may need to be applied weekly.	A good wax coat should only need to be applied once a year.
Polish will wear off or penetrate into the wood and requires no removal.	Wax coating should be removed prior to recoating.

Cleaning Glass and Plexiglass Tabletops

Obviously, commercial glass cleaner can be used to clean these surfaces. Take care to spray the cleaner on cloths or paper towels and not on the furniture to avoid potential damage to the surrounding wood or metal finish. Wipe dry with dry cloths or towels.

For a great, lint-free cleaner mix a capful of liquid fabric softener in a quart of water. Use a soft lint-free cloth to wipe the mixture on the glass or plexiglass surface, then buff dry with a clean lint free cloth.

Special Care for Laminated Composition-wood Modular Furniture

Composition-wood modular furniture is readily available at most home improvement stores and discount stores. It is inexpensive, easy to assemble, and requires little maintenance, but can not be treated like wood furniture. Composition-wood furniture warps easily when exposed to water or moisture and should not be placed in a damp environment. Do not clean with water – use only soft dry cloths. Do not use wax or furniture polish on composition-wood furniture. To remove grease, ink or stubborn stains, rub the area with a soft cloth dampened with a small amount of paint thinner. Small scratches on the finish can often be removed by using a vinyl protectant such as "ARMOR ALL" applied with a soft cloth. (Apply a small amount in an inconspicuous area before application as this may give the surface a glossier look.)

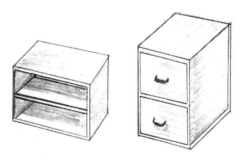

Special Care for Pianos

Pianos should *not* be cleaned and maintained with the same techniques as other finished wood. The high gloss finish is easily damaged and is difficult if not impossible for a nonprofessional to repair. Marks left in the finish from picture frames, vases, etc. will not rub out with home remedies or polishes, and any attempt to do so may permanently damage the finish. **Do not use furniture polish on a piano case.** Contact a professional if you have questions about how to treat the finish on your piano.

Remove fingerprints and dust with a soft, clean, lint-free cloth, very lightly dampened with water. (Cheesecloth works particularly well for this.) Wring the cloth out well and shake it to remove excess moisture. Fold the cloth to make a pad and rub the finish in the same direction as the grain of the wood. Rub lightly, and use long, straight strokes. Do not allow moisture droplets to remain on the finish. Wipe them off with a dry cloth.

The piano keys may be cleaned with a soft, clean cloth dipped in a mild white soap solution. Wring the cloth to remove excess moisture, then wipe the keys, lengthwise, one by one. Dry immediately with a dry cloth. Do not allow moisture to run down the sides of the keys. Use a separate cloth and soap solution to do the black keys to avoid possible transference of color. Do not use cleaning fluids, lacquer thinner, alcohol, or any other solvent on piano keys.

Preserving and Protecting Furniture Labels

Older furniture will often have a paper label on the underside of a drawer, under the table top, or on the back of the piece, identifying the manufacturer, or the retailer. These labels can add to the value of the piece of furniture and should be protected to help preserve them.

Professional restorers often protect furniture labels by covering them with small pieces of acrylic, cut to size. Acrylic sheeting is sold at glass and mirror shops and remnant pieces are often available. Do not attempt to preserve a paper label with transparent tape or plastic wrap. Transparent tape yellows with age and will deteriorate the label and plastic wrap will not remain attached to the label without the addition of some form of adhesive which will, over time, discolor the paper.

Carefully glue down any loose pieces of label by applying as little glue as possible to the loose edges. Press down carefully, and allow to dry.

Before attempting the following, be sure the results will not interfere with the operation of drawers, table extensions, etc. Measure the label. Add 3/4" to the measurements for both the length and width. This extra margin will allow 3/8" in each corner for the screws which will hold the acrylic in place and will keep the screws away from the label. Use a hacksaw blade to cut a piece of 1/8" – thick acrylic sheeting according to your measurements. Lightly buff the edges of the acrylic with 220 sandpaper to smooth rough edges.

Hold the piece of acrylic in place over the label and drill and countersink holes for small brass screws so the screwheads fit flush near the corners. Small washers can be placed on the screws between the label and the acrylic to hold the acrylic off of the label's surface.

Furniture labels identifying the manufacturer and the retailer.

Some furniture manufacturers branded their labels on the back or underside of the furniture. The label on the right is a Heyood-Wakefield.

Glossary

acetone   A colorless, inflammable liquid used as a solvent for varnish.

acrylic   A man-made resin.

alligatored finish   A pattern of cracks in a finish resembling an alligator's skin, caused by inflexibility of the finish, or improper surface preparation.

analine dyes   A permanent, transparent, man-made tint that can be formulated to dissolve in oil, water, or alcohol, and is used to change the color of wood.

animal glue   A traditional adhesive made from the natural gelatine of skins, bones, hooves, etc.

antique   Any piece of furniture from an older style or period. Traditionally, furniture which is 100 years old.

antiquing   The process of treating wood or the finish on furniture to make it look old.

Antler and Horn   The name of a style of Rustic furniture constructed of animal antlers and horns.

band clamp   A canvas band that encircles irregular shaped furniture frames, etc. used to apply pressure on glued joints. The band is tightened by screw action. Self-locking cams hold the band securely in place so that it cannot slip. Band clamps can provide pressure up to the strength of the band itself (approximately 2,800 pounds for a 2" wide band.).

bar clamp   A length of pipe or bar with an adjustable stop and screw mechanism for tightening, used to apply pressure on glued joints.

beeswax   A natural substance obtained from honeycombs. It is usually combined with other waxes for use on furniture.

bentwood   Wood that has been moistened and bent into various furniture parts (i.e. : legs, arms, etc.)

benzene   An inflammable liquid made from petroleum used as a spot remover for clothing, etc. Also called *naptha*.

bloom   A cloudy, whitish, translucent discoloration in a finish, usually caused by moisture or a defect in the finish material while it is still wet.

blushing   A term used to describe a white, cloudy-look generally found on old clear finishes that have been exposed to high humidity or low temperatures.

boiled linseed oil   Oil from the seed of the flax plant which has been heated and cooled and had special drying agents added, or had chemical driers added in lieu of applying heat. It is not produced by boiling raw linseed oil.

burn-in knife   An electric tool used to melt shellac sticks into wood blemishes to repair dents, scratches, burn marks, and gouges.

cane   Flexible pieces of rattan bark woven in an open pattern for chair seats, backs, etc.

casein glue   A powdered glue made from skim milk, hydrated lime, and other chemicals. It is mixed with water and cured for approximately 8 hours before use.

checking   A term for wood that has been roughened by moisture. Checking can occur under finishes that are waterproof if moisture can gain access from behind the finish. The term can also be applied to cracks in the finish which may not occur in the wood.

China oil   (See *tung oil*.)

corner blocks   Triangular blocks of wood cut to fit into the corner of a chair frame, and used to stabilize the chair frame.

crazing   A fine network of cracking in a finish that sometimes gives the finish an opaque appearance.

cupping   The correct term for warped wooden furniture tops.

Danish oil   A penetrating oil finish made from a mixture of synthetic oils, driers, resins, and solvents.

denatured alcohol   Ethyl alcohol (wood alcohol) with additives. The solvent for shellac.

dent   A concave depression caused by pressure or a blow to the wood.

distressing   Intentionally inflicting damage to a finish or the wood itself to simulate wear and age.

dry rot   Damage to the wood caused by either insects or fungi.

dust panels   Thin pieces of wood between the drawers in better furniture, that keep dust and dirt from falling from one drawer to the next.

epoxy glue (epoxy resin adhesive)   An extremely durable synthetic adhesive. It usually comes in two tubes and needs to be mixed prior to application.

escutcheon   A metal, wooden, or occasionally porcelain covering on the front of a key-hole.

false-graining   A technique used on lesser quality wood or plain woods to imitate expensive figured wood. Also called *grain-painted*.

feathering   A technique of blending the edges of a finished area by lifting the brush at the end of the stroke so that the edges become indefinite.

fish glue   A liquid animal glue made from heads, skins, bones, and swimming bladders of fish. It is more expensive than other glues, and only available through a limited number of woodworking stores.

frass   A fine sawdust-like residue consisting of wood particles and deposits from wood-boring insects.

French polish   A mixture of shellac and denatured alcohol used to give a traditional finish to wood furniture.

fuming   A method used to darken and change the color of woods that contain tannin by exposing them to ammonia fumes.

gesso   A hard, plaster-like substance used to create three dimensional decorations on furniture, mirror frames, etc.. Traditionally, gesso was made from a mixture of rabbitskin glue and chalk powder. Today it is more commonly made from plaster of Paris mixed with water soluble white glue and water.

gilt paint   A thin, runny metallic paint that usually contains no real gold.

glue block   A piece of wood glued across a joint to reinforce and strengthen it.

glue injector   A specialized syringe used to apply glue to hard to reach areas.

gold leaf   Genuine gold leaf is made from thin sheets of 22 to 23-1/2 carat gold. It is applied over a special base coat and adhesive size with special tools.

gold leaf paint   A gold metallic paint used to repair gilded frames and furniture. Most brands contain real gold.

grain   The pattern produced in a wood surface by the fiber structure of the wood.

grain-painted   (See *false-grained*.)

hardwood   A wood from any tree that bears flowers during each growing season, and has broad leaves that it loses each year. In furnituremaking the usual hardwoods are: ash, beech, birch, cherry, elm, hickory, mahogany, maple, oak, poplar, rosewood, sugar maple, tigerwood, walnut, and zebrawood.

hazing   The same as *blushing*. It is the result of moisture damaging a finish.

hide glue   A water-soluble adhesive made from skin, bones, and intestines of animals. Also known as *Scotch glue.*

hip rests   A curved piece of wood, attached to the seat with screws, which joins the back of a chair with the seat at each side.

hydrogen peroxide   A colorless liquid used as a bleaching agent.

Indiana Hickory   The name of a style of Rustic furniture constructed primarily of branches of young hickory trees.

inlay   A decorative pattern of veneer wood, metal, mother of pearl, etc. set into the surface of the wood so that it appears flush with the finish.

lacquer   A tough, fast-drying clear finish that dries to a hard, glossy finish. Usually sprayed on, but some special "Brushing Lacquers" are available.

lacquer sticks   (also known as *shellac sticks*) A shellac and resin based product which is melted with heat and then used to repair dents, gouges, burns, and scratches in wood.

lacquer thinner   A colorless liquid used as a solvent for lacquer.

lemon oil   Mineral oil with lemon oil added. Used as a furniture polish.

linseed oil   Oil processed from flax seed. Without the addition of dryers, it will not dry properly.

milk paint   Originally an old homemade paint concoction made from rancid milk or buttermilk with natural ingredients added for coloring. Now milk paint is available in a powdered form. It is mixed with water before use.

mineral oil   A lightweight natural oil obtained from petroleum.

mineral spirits   A petroleum-based solvent used in oil-based paints and varnishes. Also known as *paint thinner.*

mortise-and -tenon joint   A hole or slot in the wood into which the tenon or tongue fits to join two pieces of wood together, creating one of the most important joints in woodworking.

naptha   An inflammable liquid made from petroleum used as a spot remover for clothing, etc. Also called *benzene.*

natural oil   Oils that are from natural ingredients, not man-made (i.e.: linseed oil, tung oil, teak oil, etc.)

Northwoods   The name of a style of Rustic furniture that is very geometric in appearance. Often mistakenly called "Adirondacks".

oil finish   A clear finish produced by rubbing an oil into bare or stained wood.

oxalic acid   A poisonous organic acid used for bleaching and removing stains.

paint thinner   A petroleum-based solvent used in oil-based paints and varnishes. Also known as *mineral spirits*.

paraffin oil   A mineral oil used for rubbing out a finish. Also called *rubbing oil*.

paste wax   A non-liquid form of wax consisting of wax and mineral spirits. It is used to polish and protect a finish, or it can be used as a finish coat.

patina   An aged appearance caused by environmental factors.

penetrating finish   A finish coat that is absorbed into the wood pores instead of drying as a film on the wood surface.

pipe clamp   A clamping device consisting of varying lengths of pipe and a set of clamp fixtures (a clamp head which screws on to the end of the pipe and the fixture feet which slide along the pipe to the adjustment point). Used to apply pressure while bonding glued surfaces.

polyurethane   A modern synthetic resin used in paints and finishes.

pumice   Solidified lava foam. A fine-powdered abrasive, used with water or oil to rub-out finishes.

rack   To become "un-square".

rail   Horizontal members of a chair, table, or other furniture frame.

reamalgamation   The process of softening the existing finish with the solvent for that particular finish, then spreading the newly liquefied finish over the surface of the wood.

reed   A tall grass with a hollow stalk. Also the core of a stripped rattan vine.

refinisher   A chemical product developed in the 1800s that allows a finish to be revived without stripping the finish or destroying the patina in the wood. Usually consists of a basic formula of 50% denatured alcohol and 50% lacquer thinner.

resin   A natural or man-made chemical that, when dry, results in the film of the finish.

restoring furniture   A touch-up operation involving minor repairs of either the finish, the wood portions, or both, while retaining as much of the old finish and structure as possible.

rheostat   An instrument used to regulate electric current.

rottenstone   A fine-powdered limestone (finer than pumice) used as a polishing agent.

rubbed finish   A finish of varnish or lacquer which is given a smoothness and low lustre by careful rubbing with pumice, rottenstone, or extremely fine waterproof abrasive.

rush   The stems of cattails and other swamp grasses used to weave chair seats.

rushing   The process of weaving natural rush or a substitute around the outer edges of a furniture frame to provide a decorative surface or a seating surface.

Scotch glue   (see *hide glue*)

set   The initial hardening of a finishing material, sometimes called "dust-free", after which settling dust will not cling to the finish

shellac   A clear finishing material made from lac (the natural resin product produced by insects) dissolved in denatured alcohol.

shellac thinner   (see *denatured alcohol*)

shellac sticks   (see *lacquer sticks*)

silicone wax   A chemically manufactured substance similar to natural wax. Silicones penetrate into a finish and can cause the finish to resist additional finish coats.

silvering   The backing on a mirror which produces the characteristic reflective quality.

slip seats   Easily removable drop-in seats, held on to the chair frame with screws and usually *corner blocks*,

softwood   A wood from trees in the evergreen family (i.e.: cedar, chestnut, fir, gumwood, hemlock, larch, pine, redwood, and spruce). These trees are all cone-bearing and retain their greenery throughout the year. Softwood is usually less expensive than hardwood because softwood bearing trees grow faster. Softwoods often have very pronounced grain patterns and can be difficult to stain because of the porosity of the wood..

solvent   A liquid used to dissolve other substances.

Southern Root and Twig   The name of a style of Rustic furniture most commonly constructed from branches of rhododendron bushes, or willows.

splat   The vertical center piece of wood in a chair back.

spontaneous combustion   A fire caused by built up heat produced by oxidizing oils in rags or clothing worn during chemical use.

spline   A strip of wood or rattan, wider at the top than at the bottom, used as a wedge to hold prewoven cane into retaining grooves in slat rails.

stretcher   Crosspieces or rungs that run horizontally from side to side under a chair seat or table to hold the legs apart.

stretching   A process similar to *reamalgamation*, in which a damaged painted surface is repaired by softening the paint with a solvent which is then rebrushed over the chips or cracks in the surface.

stripping   The process of removing an old finish down to the bare undersurface.

synthetic oil   A man-made product substituted for natural oil.

synthetic varnish   A varnish that uses man-made resins in place of natural resins.

tannin   An acid found in certain types of woods (i.e.: mahogany, oak, hickory) used in tanning, dyeing, and to make ink.

T.S.P. (trisodium phosphate)   A cleaning preparation used to remove grease, wax or dirt before applying a finish.

tack cloth   A piece of cheesecloth or other lint-free cloth that has been made sticky by the application of varnish, used to wipe dust particles from a surface before finishing.

tack rag   Another name for *tack cloth*.

tambour   A flexible shutter or door, operating either vertically or horizontally in a groove, made of thin strips of wood glued to a linen backing.

tenon   A tongue or projecting part of wood that is fitted into a corresponding hole.

testers   The framework of boards attached to the four bed posts on a four-poster or canopy bed.

thinner   Any material used to reduce a finishing material.

tongue and groove   A wood joint in which a continuous projecting member fits into a similar rabbet or groove.

tough shellac   An early 20th century shellac finish made more durable by the addition of lacquer.

tung oil   The oil processed from the seed of the tung tree. It is used by itself or mixed with other oils to make penetrating oil finishes. Also known as *China Oil*. It is *not* the same product as tung oil varnish.

tung oil varnish   A clear varnish finish with tung oil added for extra durability. This product is thinner than traditional varnishes and is not brushed on the wood. It is rubbed on with a padded cloth or the palm of a bare hand.

turpentine   A liquid solvent used in oil-based finishes; distilled from the gum of pine trees.

twist   Wood warpage with the unevenness running lengthwise of the grain.

universal tinting colors (universal colorants)   Liquid tints that are compatible with either water-based or oil-based products and can be added to wood stains and finishes to change the color of the wood. They may not be compatible with some lacquers, epoxies or catalyzed finishes. It is always a good idea to confirm the compatibility before using these products.

varnish   A generic, catch-all term for a variety of finishes of various chemical composition. A transparent finish made with natural or synthetic resins or oils.

veneer   A thin sheet of wood, usually chosen for its attractive or unique color or grain, applied to another piece of wood as a decorative surface.

warp   A concave or convex distortion in the wood. The unevenness is *only* across the grain.

wax   A fatty substance that may be animal, vegetable, or mineral in origin. Wax is used to polish and protect a finish, or can be used as a finish coat.

wax gilt   A product made for repairing gilded frames and furniture consisting of real gold suspended in a wax and turpentine base.

wax touch-up sticks   A nonpermanent, colored wax product used to repair cracks, scars, and holes in wood.

Western and Cowboy   The name of a style of Rustic furniture most commonly constructed of lodgepole pine or juniper trees, often decorated with rawhide, skins, or animal hides.

white glue   A nontoxic, water-soluble, commonly available all-purpose glue, that is white in color but dries clear. It can be used to repair wood, leather, cloth and most porous materials.

wicker   A generic term for furniture woven of various natural or synthetic materials.

willow   A flexible, versatile natural weaving material obtained from the willow tree. Resembles blonde-colored twigs.

wood dough   A synthetic wood patching product, available in various shades to blend with the wood tone.

wood filler   A product which is used to fill open pores (grain) in the wood to provide a smoother finish.

wood putty   A soft patching material available in a variety of colors. It does not harden, and is used for shallow repairs in areas not subjected to body heat or excessive wear.

wood rot   Damage to the wood caused by water or humidity.

wood glue (woodworker's glue)   A commonly available, nontoxic glue specially formulated for wood repairs.

wood worm   Incorrect term applied to a variety of wood-boring beetles.

wormholes   The resulting damage caused by wood-boring beetles, or artificially created holes intended to simulate the damage of wood-boring beetles.

Appendix

Adirondack Museum
P.O. Box 99, Route 30
Blue Mountain Lake, New York   12812
(518) 352-7311

Albert Constantine & Son, Inc.
2050 Eastchester Road
Bronx, New York   10461
(800) 223-8087
FAX (800) 953-WOOD
website address www.constantines.com

American Home Supply
P.O. Box 697
Campbell, California   95009
(408) 246-1962

Antique Hardware and Home
19 Buckingham Pltn. Dr.
Bluffton, SC   29910
(800) 422-9982 ext. 1303

Antique Trunk Company
360 Kenilworth Rd.
Bay Village, Ohio   44140
(440) 808-8085

Ball & Ball
463 W. Lincoln Highway
Exton, Pennsylvania   19341
(610) 363-7330
orders (800) 257-3711
FAX (610) 363-7639
website www.ballandball.us.com

Bristol Valley Hardwoods
4054 Bristol Valley Road
Bristol, New York   14424
(800) 724-0132

Cane and Basket Supply Company
1283 S. Cochran Avenue
Los Angeles, California   90019
(213) 939-9644

Charlotte Ford Trunks
Box 536
Spearman, Texas   79081
(806) 659-3027

Connecticut Cane and Reed Company
P.O. Box 762
Manchester, Connecticut   06045
(860) 646-6586

Crown City Hardware Company
1047 N. Allen Avenue
Pasadena, California   91104-3298
store: (626) 794-1188
catalog direct: (626) 794-0234

Eugenia's Antique Hardware
5370 Peachtree Road
Chamblee, Georgia   30341
(800) 337-1677

Frank's Cane and Rush Supply
7252 Heil Avenue
Huntington Beach, California   92647
(714) 847-0707

Hodge's Fabrics and Upholsterers
510 S. Mountain
Ontario, California   91762
(909) 984-0165

Horton Brasses
Nooks Hill Road
P.O. Box 95
Cromwell, Connecticut   06416
(860) 635-4400

Klingspor's Sanding Catalogue
P.O. Box 3737
Hickory, North Carolina   28603

Kraft Hardware
306 E. 61st Street
New York, New York   10021
(210) 838-2214

McFeely's Square Drive Screws
P.O. Box 11169
Lynchburg, Virginia   24506
(800) 443-7937

Muff's Antiques/ Restoration Hardware
135 S. Glassell Street
Orange, California   92866
(714) 997- 0243

Museum Shop
Hancock Shaker Village
P.O. Box 927
Pittsfield, MA   01202
(413) 443-0188

Old Fashioned Milk Paint Company
P.O. Box 222
Groton, Massachusetts   01450
(978) 448-6336

Old Hickory Furniture Company
403 S. Noble Street
Shelbyville, Indiana   46176
(800) 232-2275

Phyllis Kennedy Hardware
10655 Andrade Drive
Zionsville, Indiana   46077
(317) 873-1316

Shaker Workshops
P.O. Box 8001
Ashburnham, Massachusetts   01430
(800) 840-9121

Tri Star Environmental
Tri Star Plus Cleaner and Degreaser
(909) 886-9479

University Products
517 Main Street
P.O. Box 101
Holyoke, Massachusetts, 01041
(800) 628-1912

Woodcraft
210 Wood County Industrial Park
P.O. Box 1686
Parkersburg, West Virginia   26102
(800) 225-1153

The Woodworkers' Store
Rockler Companies, Inc.
4365 Willow Drive
Medina, Minnesota   55340
(800) 279-4441
FAX (612) 478-8393
website www.woodworkerstore.com

Woodworks
4521 Anderson Blvd.
Fort Worth, Texas   76117
(817) 581-5230
(800) 722-0311
FAX (817) 581-5235

Antique Furniture Keys and Lock Repair
Muff's Antiques/ Restoration Hardware

Antique Hardware:
Eugenia's Antique Hardware
Muff's Antiques/ Restoration Hardware

Biodegradable Cleaners:
Tri Star Environmental

Chair Loc:
Cane and Basket Supply Company
The Woodworkers' Store

Hoosier Cabinet and Ice Box Supplies:
Albert Constantine & Son, Inc.
Charlotte Ford Trunks
Muff's Antiques/ Restoration Hardware
Phyllis Kennedy Hardware, Inc.
The Woodworkers' Store

Leather Cleaners:
University Products

Leather Seats:
Albert Constantine & Son, Inc.
Cane and Basket Supply Company
The Woodworkers' Store

Metal Cleaners:
Albert Constantine & Son, Inc.
University Products
The Woodworkers' Store

Milk Paint:
Albert Constantine & Son, Inc.
Old Fashioned Milk Paint Company

Mirror Hardware:
Albert Constantine & Son, Inc.
Muff's Antiques/ Restoration Hardware

The Woodworkers' Store

Rawhide:
Frank's Cane and Rush Supply
Cane and Basket Supply Company

Reproduction Hardware:
Albert Constantine & Son, Inc.
American Home Supply
Antique Hardware and Home
Ball & Ball
Charlotte Ford Trunks
Crown City Hardware Company
Frank's Cane and Rush Supply
Kraft Hardware
Horton Brasses
Muff's Antiques/ Restoration Hardware
Phyllis Kennedy Hardware, Inc.
Woodcraft
The Woodworkers' Store

Rolltops (tambours):
The Woodworkers' Store

Rustic Furniture:
Adirondack Museum
Old Hickory Furniture Company

Trunk Repair Supplies:
Albert Constantine & Son, Inc.
Antique Trunk Company
Charlotte Ford Trunks
Muff's Antiques/ Restoration Hardware
Phyllis Kennedy Hardware, Inc.
Woodcraft
The Woodworkers' Store

Upholstery Supplies:
Albert Constantine & Son, Inc.
Frank's Cane and Rush Supply
Hodge's Fabrics and Upholsterers
The Woodworkers' Store

Veneer:

> Albert Constantine & Son, Inc.
> Bristol Valley Hardwoods
> Woodcraft
> The Woodworkers' Store

Wickerwork and Seating Supplies:

> Albert Constantine & Son, Inc.
> Cane and Basket Supply Company
> Connecticut Cane and Reed Company
> Frank's Cane and Rush Supply
> Hodge's Fabrics and Upholsterers
> Museum Shop, Hancock Shaker Village
> Shaker Workshops
> Woodcraft
> The Woodworkers' Store

Wooden Handles and Wheels:

> Albert Constantine & Son, Inc.
> Frank's Cane and Rush Supply
> Woodcraft
> The Woodworkers' Store
> Woodworks

Woodworking and Woodfinishing Supplies:

> Albert Constantine & Son, Inc.
> Bristol Valley Hardwoods
> Klingspor's Sanding Catalogue
> McFeely's
> Woodcraft
> The Woodworkers' Store

Personal Appendix

 Use the following pages to create your own Personal Appendix. Record the names, addresses and phone numbers of local sources for the supplies and services you will use, or attach business cards to the pages for easy reference.

Personal Appendix – Page Two

Personal Appendix – Page Three

Personal Appendix – Page Four

Index

G

Notes

Notes

Notes

Notes